Not About us Without us

Client Involvement in Supported Housing

Mike Seal

Russell House Publishing

First published in 2008 by:
Russell House Publishing Ltd.
4 St. George's House
Uplyme Road
Lyme Regis
Dorset DT7 3LS

Tel: 01297-443948
Fax: 01297-442722
e-mail: help@russellhouse.co.uk
www.russellhouse.co.uk

British Library Cataloguing-in-publication Data:

A catalogue record for this book is available from the British Library.

ISBN: 978-1-905541-25-6

Typeset by TW Typesetting, Plymouth, Devon
Printed by Biddles Ltd

About Russell House Publishing

Russell House Publishing aims to publish innovative and valuable materials to help managers,
practitioners, trainers, educators and students.

Our full catalogue covers: social policy, working with young people, helping children and
families, care of older people, social care, combating social exclusion, revitalising communities
and working with offenders.

Full details can be found at www.russellhouse.co.uk and we are pleased to send out
information to you by post. Our contact details are on this page.

We are always keen to receive feedback on publications and new ideas for future projects.

Contents

Special photocopying permission
to support client involvement

To encourage and support the active involvement of clients in supported housing, the author and publisher are extending the normal permissions for copying under copyright law. We are giving special permission to photocopy and distribute the following chapters only, for the sole and express purpose of making them accessible to clients:

Barriers to Client Involvement in Supported Housing
Principles Behind Effective Involvement in Supported Housing
Making Sense of Structures: Power, Influence and Managing Stakeholder Interests
The Process of Involvement: Organisational Change and Initiative Development
Levels of Involvement: The Breadth and Depth
Methods and Techniques for Involvement
Appendix: Resources on Client Involvement

Restrictions on this special permission

1. Permission is given to copy these chapters for the sole and express purpose of making them accessible to clients who are involved in supported housing.
2. Permission is only given to organisations who have bought a copy of the book and then only for distribution at the local level within their organisation. The price of this book has deliberately been kept affordable to smaller organisations. It is therefore expected that, as a matter of honour, larger organisations – for example national or county-wide statutory or voluntary organisations – who might want to use the photocopiable material, will buy a copy of the book for use in each locality where they are using the material.
3. If a trainer or an educational organisation wants to copy and distribute these chapters to assist their work with clients in organisations where they are training, they must buy a copy of the book for each organisation where they undertake such training, and one for each locality when they are training in a large organisation such as set out immediately above.
4. Under no circumstances should anyone sell photocopied material from this book without the express permission of the publisher.

If in doubt, anyone wanting to make photocopies should contact the publisher, via email at *help@russellhouse.co.uk*.

Other photocopying permission

Anyone wishing to copy all or part of the chapters that are specified here **in any context other than the one that is expressly described here** should first seek permission in the usual way:

- either via Russell House Publishing
- or via the Copyright Licensing Agency.

Anyone wishing to copy **any other part of this book in any context**, should first seek permission in the usual way:

- either via Russell House Publishing
- or via the Copyright Licensing Agency.

Preface

There is growing recognition across providers, commissioners and government departments, of the need to effectively involve clients of supported housing services in the management, planning and day-to-day running of the organisations that provide services to them. Client involvement is one of the main drivers behind the Quality Assessment Framework for Supporting People, which is the main funding stream for most projects in supported housing. There are specific standards relating to client involvement and its theme threads through all the other standards, often making the difference between an organisation getting a 'C' and an 'A' grade. Client involvement is also a theme that runs through the Housing Corporations charter mark, tenant participation compacts for registered social landlords and Best Value for local authorities.

Legacies to overcome

However, as I will expand upon in the book, the supported housing sector does not have a good history of client involvement, and there are legacies of ingrained cynicism, a lack of participatory cultures and a lack of confidence in the area, to overcome. Client involvement is very easy to pay lip service to, with token clients on management boards, or clients simply reading out questions in interview panels. It is also something workers, and those trying to undertake it, want quick solutions to. 'Just tell me what works' is a cry often heard from practitioners. However, 'what works' will depend very much on what they are trying to achieve, and the context in which they are trying to achieve it. 'What works' is also something that will, and should, evolve and develop over time. Effective client involvement needs to be thought through, and planned for, in a considered way.

The context of this book

The aim of the book is to aid agencies and those developing client involvement initiatives to do this effectively. While client involvement is covered in a range of disciplines, in the context of supported housing it has still to be developed systematically. The texts that do exist tend to be from a practice basis with little grounding in theory. As such, this book is intended to develop the theoretical basis of current guides, particularly Supporting People's *A Guide for Client Involvement*, to which it is an invaluable companion, and to enrich practical examples with a deeper context, exploring issues particular to the supported housing sector.

Fight it, fix it, escape it, replace it

In addition, the book will argue that we need to go beyond having the aforementioned token client on management committees, and to these ends a more radical vision of client involvement will be given from a client perspective: 'We should fight it, fix it, escape it and replace it' as one client remarked with regard to the system of services that was meant to serve him. Clients need to be involved in campaigning for changes in services (fighting it); advising them on remedying what they are doing wrong (fixing it); creating alternative spaces for clients to recover and discuss ideas (escaping it); and setting up their own initiatives (replacing it). The book will show how client involvement, when it works, is often the best way of intervening with clients and fulfilling the strategic aims of the organisation. However, it will show how to take client involvement seriously will necessitate a thorough re-evaluation of the way organisations relate to clients and deliver services to them.

The aims of this book

The book will have several underlying themes: working with the aforementioned cynicism resulting from a bad history of client involvement; taking account of the likelihood that client involvement will develop unpredictably and even negatively initially; managing the presence of different, and sometimes conflicting, motivations from different stakeholders; and acknowledging the sometimes unacknowledged ideologies that underpin how agencies often negatively view their clients.

Powerfully in support of client involvement, and hopefully about how to make progress, this book shows: how agencies can work towards redressing the balance of power in favour of the clients; how workers and clients can come to see each other as allies; that effective client involvement takes time, commitment and resources . . . and acceptance that fundamental changes will ensue in how agencies function and relate to clients.

Who this book is for

It is aimed at anyone trying to develop a strategy for client involvement in their organisation and the more general reader, including activists, interested in issues of client involvement in supported housing. While not wishing to fall into the trap of outlining prescriptive formulas for 'what works', it will emphasise the need to have champions of client involvement at all levels of an organisation, a demonstrable commitment from senior management, independent advocacy for clients, and for organisations to be open to ideas about changing their structures.

Clients are not the problem

The ideas in this book have been developed out of the working practice, experience and knowledge of the author and the workers, researchers and activist clients he has worked with over the years. The bulk of this activity has been through Groundswell, the leading client involvement and self-help organisation for supported housing clients in the UK, of which the author was a founding member and trustee. Groundswell believes clients are not the problem, and must be part of the solution.

Introduction

In this introduction I will firstly define and delineate what we mean by client involvement in a supported housing context; secondly, I will present the approach, and themes, of the book, outlining two pertinent debates; thirdly, I will contextualise the book within the existing literature on the subject; and finally, as a navigation tool, I will give a brief overview of each chapter.

A note on the focus of the book and its intended audience

Before all that, however, I need to identify the aim of the book and its intended audiences. The book's primary concern will be in looking at how clients can be involved within organisations and agencies and the services that are provided to them. I have assumed that the client involvement 'initiative' or 'project' is being developed by the agency and its workers, hence the title of the book. I will concentrate on the issues they will need to consider. This is not to say that the initial push will not come from clients: often, it will. I will therefore frequently look at the issues from the client's perspective. As such, I hope this book is also of use to clients in supported housing, or activists in their communities.

To these ends, Part One and the first three chapters are aimed firmly at agencies, particularly Chapter 3 on strategic policy. Activists and front line workers may want to start with Chapter 4 (Part Two). However, I hope that some may read the first two chapters, particularly the second, as it is all too easy for an activist to re-invent the wheel and not take on board the lessons of earlier activists.

What is client involvement in supported housing?

What is supported housing?

> *Due to illness or disability, many people are unable to live independently in their own homes without the care and support of others. For some, the need for high levels of care and support means that they may have to move to some form of supported accommodation or residential care.*
>
> (Mind, 2007: 1)

What do we mean by supported housing? On a basic level it would be where people are in housing where they also receive some form of support. More specifically, I would define that as some kind of institutional support, where an agency is paid to provide it to an individual. That is to distinguish such support from, say, a community project that broadly serves a council estate. As the Mind quote above indicates, it is where the individual is perceived to be vulnerable in some way, so that, without support, the person could not sustain their accommodation.

   While this book is aimed at a wide audience, it should prove of particular use to those funded through the *Supporting People* Initiative. The *Supporting People* programme is a government initiative launched on 1 April 2003. The programme provides 'housing related support to prevent problems that can often lead to hospitalisation, institutional care or homelessness and can help the smooth transition to independent living for those leaving an institutionalised environment'. It provides housing related support services to over 1.2 million vulnerable people. The programme is delivered locally by 150 Administering Authorities, over 6,000 providers of housing related support, and an estimated 37,000 individual contracts. It is a commissioning model, whereby local authorities contract with providers and partner organisations for the provision of *Supporting People* services. Local teams then have a monitoring role. There is a Quality Assessment Framework, something I will return to, that agencies are measured against to ensure standards within provision (ODPM, 2004).

> *The primary purpose of housing related support is to develop and sustain an individual's capacity to live independently in their accommodation.*
>
> (ODPM, 2004: 2)

The *Supporting People* definition of supported housing above differs from MIND's in that it emphasises the purpose of support being to develop the capacity for independence in the individual. This is not to say that it does not accept that some will always need care, because it does. Rather that these capacities should be developed to the fullest, which for *some* will mean independent living. The programme has defined client groups that include:

- People who have been homeless.
- Rough sleepers.
- Ex-offenders.
- People at risk of offending and imprisonment.
- People with a physical or sensory disability.
- People at risk of domestic violence.
- People with alcohol and drug problems.
- Teenage parents.
- Elderly people.
- Young people at risk.
- People with HIV and AIDS.
- People with learning difficulties.
- Travellers.
- Homeless families with support needs.

Why client involvement, rather than user participation?

We need to define client involvement and why I prefer it as a term. To do this three concepts need breaking down:

- Why the term 'clients', as opposed to other terms such as 'service users'?
- Why 'involvement', as opposed to other terms such as participation?
- What the term means in practice i.e. involvement in what?

On the first point, I always use the term clients. I have covered the reasons for my choice of this term in a previous book and will repeat my rationale:

The name we give to clients is not neutral. Clients are often called service users, or members or even customers. All these terms have implications of the clients' having chosen the service, at least in terms of consumer choice, when often the choice people have is minimal or none at all . . . I have (therefore) used the term clients – while it is a medicalised term, it expresses to me a more accurate portrayal of the power dynamic between worker and client, with a resulting implication of the professional responsibility of the worker for his or her actions.

(Seal, 2005: 128)

At a training event recently, a participant said we should use the term customers because it is what we should aspire to. While I take that point, I would prefer to use a term that reflects what the situation is, rather than what it could be, as I think terms like 'customer' can all too easily allow us to evade issues of power.

The choice of terms remains a debate. *Supporting People*, for instance, favours the term 'service users' (Godfrey et al., 2003), and I have respected their use of those terms. What all those terms have in common is 'those who live in the supported housing we provide'. This is as opposed to those who may also use or be affected by our service, such as the local community, other agencies, etc. which I have called stakeholders. Their perspectives are nevertheless important and we shall return to how to manage them subsequently in Chapter 6.

I have used the term involvement because the book focuses on how clients can be involved in agencies or organisations, terms I have used interchangeably. The ideas and models we will examine will acknowledge the fact that clients will be involved in activities beyond our agency, and that we have a place in moving them towards such endeavours.

Involvement in what?

We aim to enable homeless people to set up and run their own projects, increase homeless people's influence in policy and decision making and increase homeless people's meaningful involvement in the services they use.

(Groundswell aims, 2007)

The Groundswell aims serve as a starting point for exploring the third concern with the term client involvement, i.e. involvement in what? However, it is not the concern of this book to look at helping clients set up and run their own projects, unless it is in the context of an agency or organisation. Groundswell has also done a lot of work in the past brokering dialogue between government and policy makers on client issues. Again, this is not the focus of this book, apart from in the context of examining processes of decision making within an organisation. Groundswell has produced two excellent publications that cover these areas; they are respectively the *Toolkit for Change: The Groundswell Self Help Manual* and *The Speakout Recipe Book*. Instead, this book will concentrate on increasing the meaningful involvement of supported housing's clients in the services they use.

There are four levels at which service clients can and should be making contributions: dialogue/information, day-to-day running of the organisation, planning and policy in the organisation and service management.

(ODPM, 2002: 9)

The ODPM quote from *Supporting People* outlines their interpretation of what areas this meaningful involvement may include. Many agencies often only think of client involvement in terms of governance, often in the form of a token client on the management committee. The other areas the ODPM mention are equally important; the point being that different areas will appeal to different clients, as we will see throughout the book. My main issue with the ODPM statement is that it feels a little staid; it comes from an agency perspective and is definitely couched in organisational language. I am not sure if, put like this, client involvement would have much appeal for clients. The quote below illustrates a more radical vision of what the client should be involved in within supported housing, although it is actually conveying similar ideas, just from a client perspective:

> *We should fight it, fix it, escape it and replace it*
>
> (Peck and Barker, 1997: 45)

Clients need to be involved in campaigning for changes in services (fighting it), giving advice to the services on what they are doing wrong, and how to remedy it (fixing it), creating alternative spaces for clients to recover and discuss ideas (escaping it) and, where necessary, setting up their own initiatives (replacing it). With the possible exception of the last dimension, agencies have a part to play in facilitating all of these, to different degrees.

The approach and themes of the book

Two debates and two positions

Before I move onto the themes of the book I think two debates are worth mentioning as they frame the approach of this book. I think they are particularly important for any activists reading the book who think that the other areas of concern Groundswell and Peck and Barker mention have more merit. Within Groundswell and its network, there have always been two main points of contention and discussion:

- Firstly, what should be the relative priority of the areas of activity outlined in the quote for the client movement?
- Secondly, what role, if any, do workers and organisations have in enabling clients to fulfil them?

On both of these points I cannot claim to give an answer but only a perspective. On the first question I think they are all important and we should work on all these levels. The real question is which areas agencies should concentrate on at what particular time and to what end. In my view, we should work on that area that has the highest chance of creating momentum, balanced with what will give the greatest leverage towards developing the potential of the other areas. Recently an activist said to me that unless we changed the whole system there was no point to the work, it was only tinkering. I understood his sentiment but for me, to say an area is wrong in principle seemed dangerous. As Alinsky (1968) says, only those of us who want to gloriously lose, or those who are in power, can afford to stand on principle on what we do or do not do or even, to a degree, how we do it. The true radical has to be prepared to get their hands dirty. We should work on what we can, when we can and build towards working on the other areas. Momentum is particularly important here as two of Alinsky's 'rules for radicals' are never to go outside the experience of your community; and the best tactics are ones that your community enjoys.

Groundswell has moved between all four areas depending on the prevailing circumstances. Importantly, there have been discussions about these changes, with the criteria for decisions being what has the greatest chance of succeeding, balanced with a consideration of ethics and of our overall aims, rather than mere opportunism. Presently, Groundswell is spending a lot of time working with agencies in developing client involvement and creating enterprise opportunities for clients. In the past, the emphasis was more on campaigning and creating alternative spaces for clients to make sense of their experiences.

Alinsky is also useful in bridging us between the first debate about priorities and the second about the role for organisations and workers. For Alinsky, it is important that the radical, at least in the first instance, works within the system. His position on this, in the late 1960s, was a challenge to many radical groups who were quite separatist at the time, advocating that communities, or even just the active militants in a community, should withdraw and organise internally. He likened this approach to being a rhetorical radical rather than a realistic one:

> *As an organiser I start from where the world is, as it is, not as I would like it to be. That we accept the world as it is does not in any sense weaken our desire to change it into what we believe it should be – it is necessary to begin where the world is if we are going to change it to what we think it should be. That means working in the system.*

My perspective on the second question (what role, if any, do workers and organisations have in enabling clients), stems from this. While I would agree with some authors' comments that any oppressed group needs to spend time on their own to get a sense of themselves (Garvey, 2005; Cross, 2004), I am not convinced that workers and agencies have no part to play. Neither would I want to espouse a form of orientalism (Said, 1979), saying that only clients and ex-clients can understand what it is like to go through the housing system. Even if that experience gives them a certain insight, which I think it does, I would challenge that this is always the most fundamental thing. It would be too easy and unfair in supported housing to label all workers as only being there for the money or getting off on the power they have over clients, and organisations as just money makers off the poor and agents of the state. I use these phrases because they are all ones I have heard from clients either through training or being involved in the self-help movement. As I explored in my last book, many workers come into the sector with positive motivations (Seal, 2006) or because of their own experiences (16 per cent are themselves ex-clients), and with democratic and radical sensibilities. I do not think those who just want to make money, exercise power or be voyeuristic last that long. Sadly, I also related in that book how I, and I suspect other workers, may have lost sight of these starting-points through being exposed to a more oppositional working culture where clients are seen as the enemy, and not to be trusted (Seal, 2005). Ruth Wyner clearly made this link with regard to workers in the homelessness field in the late 1990s:

> *The vast majority of people working in homelessness openly support client involvement, in principle. It's seen as a good thing, something to work towards, and to the benefit of the client group. But it is also seen as difficult and challenging, and sometimes as a threat to staff, to their authority in the hostel.*
>
> (Wyner, 1999: 1)

I would also contend that most organisations were originally set up for altruistic reasons, even if they can be slightly patronising and misguided in their presumptions and lose their way. Positively, I think this gives us a lot of potential allies that the client movement in supported housing ignores at its peril. I will explore in later chapters why it may be understandable that clients hold these views, they do not get us anywhere in the end. As workers, we should work with whom we can and make a start where we can, but never forget that the power balance is in our favour and the impact this may have, and keep the goal of giving up power in our mind.

The themes of the book

Throughout the book certain themes recur. It is worth outlining them now because they encapsulate the perspective on client involvement I am seeking to promote and I want to identify them so that readers can evaluate them as they read the book.

The *first theme* in this book is an ideological one and stems from the above discussion. It is that workers and clients should work together in developing client involvement, seeing each other as natural allies rather than natural enemies, and in doing so will both benefit from it.

The *second theme* is that the supported housing sector does not have a good history of client involvement and this leaves legacies to be overcome in the form of ingrained cynicism, a lack of participatory cultures and a lack of confidence in the area.

A *third theme* is that we understand and therefore construct clients, and consequently the ways that they are allowed to participate in certain, often negative, ways that are underpinned by ideologies that we rarely acknowledge.

A *fourth related theme* is that behind an apparent consensus on client involvement, different stakeholders have different motivations for client involvement that come from different, and sometimes conflicting, ideological bases.

A *fifth theme* is that client involvement will take time, commitment and resources to be effective. Furthermore, the most important resources are human ones and the most important commitment is to an acceptance of the fundamental changes that will ensue in how the agency functions and relates to its clients.

A *sixth theme* is that client participation, particularly if it is working, may induce a negative reaction in clients initially and go in ways that we cannot predict and that organisations need to be able to incorporate this.

A *seventh theme* is that client involvement and participation should not be seen as an adjunct to workers' role in supported housing, but that it is often the most effective, or sometimes only, way of intervention.

My final *eighth theme* is that in developing client involvement workers should be practical and yet principled. We should work with whomever is willing to work with us, on what they want to work on. We should not, however, forget the underlying principles of client involvement.

The book generally takes the position that we should not be prescriptive about what agencies should put in place, and to try to do so is dangerous and an evasion of responsibility. However, there are four phenomena that recur throughout the book and across agencies that seem to help embed client involvement when they are present. They have become recommendations that Groundswell and I have consistently made to agencies. They are:

● *The importance of champions.* Client involvement needs champions, people with a passion for, knowledge of and, importantly, time to promote, client involvement. Crucially, they are needed at all levels of the organisation and preferably in all its projects. This way client involvement can achieve critical mass, rather than relying on a few committed individuals who inevitably burn out.

- *Commitment from senior management.* As we shall explore, commitment is needed from all areas as power and influence threads through organisations. However, we cannot deny that senior management has significant power and influence and without their active commitment client involvement will always be piecemeal and often token.
- *Independent advocacy.* We will see in the chapters on barriers that many clients have real fears about talking to managers, or anyone they perceive as having power over them. Independent advocacy is a good way of getting over this, at least in the first instance and often permanently. This should preferably by done by current clients, ex-clients or someone that the client feels they have a natural affinity with.
- *It is agencies that need to change their structures.* This stems from the eighth theme of the book, but is one that I point out early on when engaging with agencies. Many agencies concentrate on 'getting clients up to speed' to be able to engage in our structures through training, etc. It is we that need to come out of our comfort zones, both to be able to engage in any real sense with clients' perspectives, and also to prepare us for other changes we might need to undertake as a result of what they say.

The existing literature

The literature on client involvement tends to fall into several camps. Firstly, there are many practice guides, often produced by second tier organisations, such as *Have we got Views for You: Service Client Involvement in Supported Housing* by Novas Ouvertures, *Raising the Roof: Supported Housing Client Consultation* by the Housing Corporation and *People and Participation* by INVOLVE. These normally cover the basic principles that should underpin the work and barriers that may be encountered, and they then concentrate on detailing examples of client involvement in supporting housing. For details of specific techniques they are invaluable and I would refer the reader to these publications.

On the other hand, there are academic treatments of developing participation in care sectors, though not specifically housing, such as *User Involvement and Participation in Social Care: Research Informing Practice* (Kemshall et al., 2000), or *Developing User Involvement: Working Towards User-Centred Practice in Voluntary Organisations* (Robson et al., 2003). I have made particular reference to *Community Participation and Empowerment: Putting Theory into Practice* by Wilcox (1995). While theoretically rich they rarely address developing client initiatives in practice or the specific context of supported housing.

Lastly, there are a number of publications that consider client involvement in related sectors, specifically youth work, mental health and drugs work. Many of these will appear in the appendix as further reading. I have found Petty et al.'s *Participatory Learning and Action: A Trainer's Guide* and any of the work by Beresford and Croft to be of particular use; and they have been an influence on this book. I also found several Mind publications, particularly the work of Roberts (2006, 2007) and Campbell (1996, 1997) on client movements, give good historical background to the issues. They go some way to bridge the theoretical and practice divide, within specific contexts.

Potentially the closest works to this book are two publications; *Consulting with Hard to Reach Users of Housing Related Support Services* by Brafield, and *Supporting People: A Guide to User Involvement for Organisations Providing Housing Related Support Services* by Godfrey et al. The former is concerned with the development of client involvement at a strategic partnership level, and while that and this publication complement each other they have distinct audiences. The latter is the major resource for organisations funded by *Supporting People*, in developing client involvement. This book is intended to be a companion to that document, and seeks to take the ideas in the guide further and help people develop a strategy for client involvement in their organisation. In doing this, it will develop some of its ideas theoretically, provide a deeper context to the examples and occasionally give a counterpoint to some of its positions.

The structure of the book

In keeping with my first book (Seal, 2005), the many comments I have included from practitioners are largely drawn from training sessions I have facilitated, and the consultancy work on client involvement I have been involved in over the years. Some of these training sessions have been deliberately structured with an eye to research. Hopefully using participative methods has led to the generation of some grounded research (Strauss and Corbin, 1998). This has particularly been the case in the development of the set of principles for client involvement in Chapter 5, people's thoughts on the barriers to client involvement in Chapter 4 and people's reflections on power in Chapter 6.

The book is divided into three sections. As I stated in the opening comments I would not necessarily recommend that it is read sequentially, or, for some, in its entirety. However, there is a logic to the structure of the book and it would benefit readers to read it a section at a time.

Section One

The first section, aimed primarily at agencies and those looking at client involvement at strategic levels, consists of three chapters on the rationale for client involvement, the policy drivers for it and lessons we can learn from other sectors. Chapter 1 asks the initial question of why client involvement is important. It will outline four perspectives and the ideological traditions that underpin them: consumerist perspectives, linked to libertarian views on the importance of the market; rights perspectives, stemming from a liberal-democratic tradition; personal development perspectives, stemming from the humanist tradition and critical perspectives, coming from a more Marxist, radical tradition. The chapter will then examine the importance of organisational clarity on the different weights these perspectives are given and of explaining them to the client.

Chapter 2 will examine the lessons that can be learnt by the supported housing sector from client involvement in the social housing and mental health sectors. Within housing, it will examine the influence of the tenants 'movement' on the development of social housing. Within the care sector, it will examine the impact of client-led initiatives within mental health on service development. It will seek to establish the similarities and differences between these other sectors and supported housing both in context, philosophy and starting points. It will set up the context for the Chapter 4 examination of the particular barrier facing the supported housing sector.

Chapter 3 will examine the policy context for client involvement in the supported housing sector. This will include examining recent policy initiatives such as the Housing Corporation Charter, Tenant Participation Compacts, Best Value and, in particular, Supporting People. It will evaluate the perspective on client involvement that underpin these initiatives and the extent to which they have potential to achieve their goals. It will argue that as well as being specific standards within the quality assessment framework for *Supporting People*, along with working with other agencies, the theme of client involvement goes across the standards and is what makes the difference between attaining a 'C' and an 'A' grade for a service.

Section Two

This section looks at some of the barriers we face to developing client involvement in supported housing including how we manage power relations and structure involvement for clients. It will seek to develop a set of principles that should underpin the ethical development of client involvement. Chapter 4 will examine horizontal and vertical barriers to client involvement. It will examine vertical barriers that may be particular to clients, front line workers, managers, the whole organisation and the wider political context. It will also examine horizontal barriers that go across these stakeholders such as resources, cultural and attitudinal barriers. It will argue that all parties have vested interests in blaming other aspects of the service for not tackling the barriers when in fact it is a responsibility for all, whilst acknowledging power differentials. It will take the view that many barriers that are presented as resource led are actually attitudinal or cultural in nature. The biggest barriers are actually fear and lack of trust expressed through mis-communication.

Chapter 5 is based on the view that before we develop a strategy for client involvement it is important to establish certain principles that should inform the development of an initiative. These are taken from a number of sources and perspectives as outlined in the first chapter. They are:

- accessibility,
- educating people about participation,
- having a diversity of approaches,
- being comprehensive,
- starting at their point of interest,
- developing permission and protection,
- demonstrating potency and commitment,
- being conscious of space and establishing reciprocity.

The first section of Chapter 6 examines the dimensions of power within organisations in relation to client involvement. I will build on the critical perspective of client involvement outlined in the first chapter, arguing that abuses of power can operate on three levels, overtly, covertly and institutionally or structurally. I will seek to make a distinction between power and influence and show how they can be viewed as a circuit that flows. I will finish by developing a model, with examples of how power has operated within one organisation, which the reader could use to examine their own organisation. The second section examines managing the different priorities and interests of different stakeholders, including funders and the wider community. It takes the view that negotiating their relative levels of participation appropriately is an important dimension of the work, particularly if we are to go beyond tokenistic or symbolic client involvement and want them to have real power and influence.

Section Three

The third section of the book is concerned with putting these ideas into practice. It will examine the process of doing this, the depth of and breadth by which it can be implemented and the techniques and methodologies we could employ in operationalising it. Chapter 7 will look at processes from two perspectives. Firstly, the processes an organisation will need to go through to be able to hear the message of clients. It will build on literature about reflective and learning organisations (Senge, 1990; Cibulka et al., 2003), and will develop criteria by which we can judge an agency's ability to listen to clients' messages. Then the chapter will examine the process any client involvement initiative may go through. This section is based on, and will build upon, the work of Wilcox (1995) contrasted with the *Supporting People* model as outlined by Godfrey et al. (2003).

Chapter 8 will look at the levels of involvement for clients from both the perspective of the depth, and the breadth of involvement. Firstly, it will explore the breadth of activities that the client could be involved in, in the organisation, and beyond. Secondly, it will examine the depth of their involvement as to how far clients are allowed to influence these activities and their processes. It builds on Arnstein's, Wilcox's and Cameron et al.'s models of participation, and develops an integrated model. Three examples from practice will be discussed that seem relevant to supported housing: the recruitment of staff, the designing of a drugs policy and involving clients in the disciplining of other clients.

Chapter 9 will examine the range of involvement techniques. It is not intended to be comprehensive and will again point the reader to other resources that investigate methods in more detail. It will develop a model of methods on two axes, one about the numbers we involve, from individuals to group techniques, and the other about how incorporated the methods are, from being integrated into working practices to being an adjunct or 'event'. It will argue that while all of these can be appropriate we tend towards groups and events, but for the wrong reasons.

Conclusion

The conclusion will mainly be given over to a colleague, Jimmy Carlson, to reflect on where he thinks supported housing agencies are in terms of client involvement. Jimmy is a recovering drinker who went through the care system, including homeless and alcohol services, prisons and mental health institutions for over 20 years. He has been involved with developing client led provisions in drug, alcohol and homeless services since 1996 and I have conducted many training sessions on client involvement with him in this time.

About the Author/ Acknowledgements

Mike Seal is a senior lecturer in informal and community education and programme director for the Advanced Professional Certificate in Working with Homeless People at the YMCA George Williams College in East London. He has worked in the supported housing field for 18 years as a front line worker, trainer and development worker in a variety of settings. He is the author of *Resettling Homeless People: Theory and Practice* (RHP, 2005), *Working with Homeless People: A Training Manual* (RHP, 2006), and *Understanding and Responding to Homeless Experiences, Cultures and Identities* (RHP, 2007).

Dedication

To all at Groundswell, past present and future, and all the activists I have worked with over the years, you know who you are.

Acknowledgements

For all those who I have bounced these ideas off over the years especially Jimmy, Simone, Athol, Steve S, Steve J, Andy W, Tony D, Amarjit, Jerry H, Toby B, Ashlin, Janet, Spike, Andrew, Namdi, Donovan, Corrin, Mark F, Hussein, Sam and all the rest. For my Dad for proof reading the book and being so complimentary about it. Finally, for all at Russell House for knocking my ideas into an accessible shape.

Part One

Rationale for, History of and Policy Background for Client Involvement

1

Why Client Involvement: Developing a Rationale

The toughest problems in participation processes do not stem from apathy, ignorance or lack of skills among clients but because organisations promoting it aren't clear about what they want to achieve, are fearful of sharing control, and seldom speak with one voice.

(Wilcox, 1995: 4)

Wilcox illustrates the need for both clarity and unity as to why an organisation is undertaking client involvement. The following example illustrates the consequences of not doing this; I remember, as a day centre worker, discussing with one client why he had not attended the residents' meeting in his supported accommodation. (The meeting was broadly meant to ascertain clients' opinions about the service.) I was puzzled as in previous discussions he had seemed quite keen and had some coherent point he wanted to get across. His reply centred on his questioning of the workers prior to the meeting as to the organisation's motives for holding it and therefore why he should attend. One replied that it was his right and responsibility to be heard, given that public money was given to the service. Another said that it was the organisation's way of finding out whether it was giving a good service or not to clients. A third worker felt that it might be a good way for the client to meet new people and build self confidence, something he had expressed an interest in doing. The final worker was more cynical, saying that the organisation was doing it because the funders said they had to. His conclusion was that the organisation and its workers were not clear as to why it was undertaking client involvement and what it was trying to achieve, and it put him off investing time and emotions into such an initiative.

Positively, *Supporting People* recognise the dangers of not being clear in our aims for client involvement and that to not do so will have similar reactions to the ones described above.

Agencies need to be clear regarding the reasons for involving clients. Is it because their views are valued or is it simply to satisfy the conditions of funders or regulators? Involving clients simply so you can say you involve clients is a shortcut to disillusionment and resentment.

(Godfrey et al., 2003: 12)

Most current guides to client involvement (Braye, 2000; Godfrey et al., 2003; Involve, 2005; Robson et al., 2005) agree that we need to know why we want to involve clients in our services. The reason given is often clarity, or more simply that it is probably a good idea to be clear about why an organisation is undertaking any new endeavour or initiative. Typical of this approach is the guidance given by the Welsh Assembly:

It is helpful for you, as a service provider, to be clear about your own starting point, in order to avoid misunderstanding when talking about involvement and consultation.

(Welsh Assembly, 2004)

We need to be clear about our rationale, to ourselves and others, and give the development of a coherent rationale some attention, or we may lose both staff and clients at the first hurdle. Creating a coherent rationale is therefore the subject of this first chapter.

The apparent consensus that participation is a good thing masks major differences of ideology between different interest groups.

(Braye, 2000: 9)

Braye (2000) reminds us that there are many different reasons for client involvement and they relate to the many different, sometimes competing, aims we may have for client involvement and that these aims have ideological underpinnings. We therefore need to get behind the glib consensus that client involvement is a good thing, and get at why we are doing it and what we want it to achieve. In this chapter I will outline four common rationales for client involvement and explore the ideological positions that underpin them: a consumerist perspective, seeing feedback from the client as essential for efficiency, ensuring that services accurately reflect the needs of the client, linked to ideological perspectives that privilege the importance of the market; democratic perspectives, seeing that to be involved is a right stemming from a particular liberal-democratic view; a personal development perspective, whereby whether involvement leads to organisational changes or not it is of benefit to the individual, linked to humanism; and finally a critical perspective, seeing involvement as important to break the ongoing power dynamic which oppresses homeless people, of which agencies are a part, with links to more radical perspectives and post-modern concerns with power. To conclude, I will come back to some fundamental questions to ask ourselves in articulating our rationale: where do we stand in relation to these aims and rationales for client involvement, what balance do we want to strike between them, and why we are privileging certain perspectives?

Consumerist perspectives

In project management, the client's active involvement is an asset which increases the chances of success at each stage of the operation: at the time of design, in order to fit the objectives to the client's needs and expectations; during implementation, to assist the professionals work, possibly to ensure a better framework for evaluation, which cannot be complete, or perhaps significant, without the clients' own opinion.

(Bryant, 2001: 23)

'Would you tell me please, which way I ought to go from here?' said Alice. 'That depends a good deal on where you want to get to,' said the cat.

(Lewis Carol, *Alice in Wonderland*)

Generally, arguments from a consumerist perspective, as espoused by the first two quotes above, are that client involvement improves efficiency, it aids evaluation of our service and hence improves credibility with funders. Ultimately, clients have direct experience of what works and what doesn't; what they experience as positive as well as what is essentially demeaning or unhelpful. Beresford and Croft (1993) trace how notions of consumerism are embedded in social policy and practice guidelines in social care and we will see in Chapter 3 that supported housing is no exception. Several authors (Braye and Preston-Shoot, 1995; Braye, 2000; Peck and Barker, 1987), have traced how the idea of a client being a consumer is problematic, perhaps most succinctly, and extremely, put by Peck and Barker in the quote below.

> *Survivors of the mental health system are no more consumers of services than cockroaches are consumers of Rentokil.*

> (Peck and Barker, 1987: 1)

Critics such as Peck and Barker argue that consumerist models underestimate the power imbalance between clients and agencies, and professionals, something touched on in the introduction to this book. The over-riding lack of consumer choice in supported housing, and complicating factors like coercion and paternalism, whether implied or overt, underline this. In the next chapter we will examine the disabling effects on clients of having been through paternalistic models of care, something that I will also argue is common in supported housing.

Finally, the consumer model is restrictive in its scope. While services may become more responsive, flexible and relevant to clients' needs, ownership and control remain within the agency and the professionals who run it. In a market model such issues of control and ownership are non-questions. All these critiques are not to say that on a day-to-day practical level, client involvement is not about improving services, often it is. However, it is important to remind ourselves of the limitations of thinking in such a way, particularly when it is the only rationale we use. Practically, it potentially limits client involvement to a level of information-giving and consultation, something we will return to in Chapter 8. Even if more active forms of involvement can be negotiated, they will be judged on efficiency and cost effectiveness rather than on the basis of a democratic ideal.

Democratic rights perspectives

Generally, democratic perspectives run along the lines that people have a right to be involved, it is democratic to involve people and therefore is something that we should be doing. There are two aspects to such views, a human rights perspective and a citizenship perspective. A rights perspective is epitomised by acts such as the UN Convention on The Rights of the Child. Article 12 says we have the right to express views freely and for those views to be given due weight. Article 13 enshrines the right to freedom of expression, to seek, receive and impart information and ideas, and Article 23 gives us the right to active participation in the community. Unfortunately, its expression in other acts such as the Human Rights Act 1998 based on the European Convention on Human Rights, is not as clear and has yet to be effectively clarified by precedent (Homeless Link, 2000).

> *In some supported housing organisations, consultation is driven by organisational and individual values and ethics; the view is that clients have a right to be consulted.*

> (Welsh Assembly, 2004)

Rights perspectives are also the basis of many governmental policies, evidenced by the Welsh Assembly statement made above. The problem with rights based models is that there is little agreement on what people's precise rights are and what are their source. It is still debateable whether housing is a right, with such things as homeless legislation distinguishing between those who deserve housing and those who do not (Anderson and Thompson, 2005). While this may seem like a semantic debate, I think it has real relevance to people who have been subject to government policies that have denied them housing or been excluded by the eligibility criteria of agencies. It may well be an argument that does not wash with a client.

To illustrate, I recently ran a training course for clients and workers on client involvement. I remember one client's comments clearly. A worker on the course had said that the client had a right to be heard in the context of their accommodation. The client responded that workers had denied so many of his rights (to privacy, to freedom of movement, to the worker he had to work with, even who he socialised with), so why were we so keen to uphold his rights on this issue? And why should he believe us? As we shall explore in subsequent chapters people's willingness to become involved is often determined by whether they have faith in the system and whether it is presented to them with integrity.

> *Client involvement is important for reasons of dignity and citizenship: receiving help may be necessary, (but) . . . It also undermines one's sense of citizenship, i.e. the sense of belonging to a community based on mutual solidarity.*
>
> (Cameron et al., 2005)

For the citizenship perspective, as encapsulated by Cameron (2005) above, to involve clients is linked to a wider project of promoting democracy including encouraging them to become citizens and embrace liberal democratic values, such as responsibility, autonomy, mutuality and interdependence (Smith and Jeffs, 2001). This may be seen as particularly important when many clients who are in supported housing may be 'returning' to, or 'integrating' into, mainstream society from a culture or sub culture that may have a very different value base (Daly, 1996; Seal, 2006). However, there are many issues with such a project. Firstly, the notion of what is meant by liberal democratic values is hotly contested (Fraser, 1990; Keyssar, 2001), as is the notion of citizenship (Driver and Martell, 1998; Lister, 2003). Secondly, any notion of societal values is rarely pervasive or homogenous throughout a society's members (Schwartz and Sagie, 2000; Whalley, 2003). Whether these values are the ones clients will encounter once back in the community is therefore questionable; particularly so for many clients of supported housing. Their reception by their new 'host community' is not always what it could be (Stein, 1996; Oakley, 2002).

Certainly, clients are unlikely to have experienced consistent treatment from services (Seal, 2007; Ames, 2007; Butchinsky, 2007). I remember co-facilitating a session with a client on people's experiences in supported housing. He related how in growing up the hardest thing he found about his relationship with his father, which had been abusive, was not knowing how he would be treated when he walked into the room. It depended on his father's mood, which could switch in a moment. This was also the hardest thing he found about supported housing – he faced the same inconsistency in how the staff would treat him.

The lack of consistent values applies particularly to our sector. I have previously highlighted the lack of a common set of values for the supported housing sector, either in how we work with clients or how we treat them in our accommodation (Seal, 2005). This is also not just about consistency; Homeless Link in 2000 explored ways in which the homeless sector has been culpable in our treatment of clients under the Human Rights Act. The dignity and respect Cameron el al. (2005) mention in their quote is not something we have always afforded to our clients (Homeless Link, 2000). Is it any wonder that we face a certain cynicism on the part of clients about the values we wish to 'instil' in them.

A more positive spin on the idea of a democratic model of involvement is what Braye (2000) calls 'participatory rights' as opposed to welfare needs. It is linked to the model of welfare whereby the state or, in our case, the organisation or worker, has an explicit role in reducing social inequalities (Everitt et al., 1992) as well as looking after people. What appeals to me about this formulation is its explicit statement that involvement is about change and equality, perhaps acknowledging some of the part we as organisations have played in maintaining these inequalities.

> *If one accepts a fundamental premise that clients have a right to be involved, it is difficult to argue against the notion that applying boundaries to that involvement constitutes a dereliction of principle.*
>
> (Phillips, 2004)

As Phillips indicates, unless involvement is about change there is a danger that democratic models become consultative at best and manipulative at worst (Arnstein, 1969), giving an illusion of democracy (Foot, 2006). Foot says that unless there was some form of economic democracy, in our case the ability to change some of the fundamentals of an organisation such as access to resources, funding streams and personnel, political democracy will always be undermined and become meaningless.

Recently, I was talking to a client involvement worker (a phenomenon I will come back to several times) in a supported housing organisation. He was getting grief from the managers because the client group he had been involved in setting up had just circumvented the managerial process, because they had found it did not work. I reassured him that, to me, this was a sign, not that client involvement was not working but, that it was *really* working. The task now was to get the organisation to see this. It comes back to the sixth theme of this book; that if client involvement goes in unpredicted ways agencies may resist it (McGreggor, 1980). If we want to champion client involvement, overcoming such organisational resistance (Argyris, 1990) is a large part of our task.

Personal development perspectives

In 2001, Robert Putman undertook research for his seminal book *Bowling Alone*, starting the debate about the role of social capital, the positive effects of the interactions of individuals in bonding societies together (Smith, 2005). He had found that many Americans were not engaging in social group activities any more, they were literally 'bowling alone', and he wanted to assess the impacts of this. As part of this research he did a cost-benefit analysis in terms of the impact on health of being involved in group activities. He found that to become involved in such an activity had health benefits on a par with giving up smoking. To me this is powerful:

> *Contributing to a collective activity may bring major benefits . . . They are gaining on many fronts: a sense of enterprise, responsibility, experience, self-confidence and, often, real pride resulting from an original and shared achievement.*
>
> (Cameron, 2005: 5)

Cameron (2005) cast some light on why involvement can be so beneficial to clients. Other authors link being involved to being able to deal with conflict and learning negotiation skills

(Godfrey et al., 2003), to the skills of becoming independent (Edgar et al., 1999; Welsh Assembly, 2004), or more simply that care programme approaches have been found to be more effective if clients are involved in the planning and implementation of the programme (Bryant, 2001; Carpenter and Sbarani, 1997):

> *In many areas of professional practice the goals of intervention are enhanced by participation, or indeed that participation is essential to their achievement.*
>
> (Braye, 2000: 54)

The importance point of this personal development perspective is brought out by the above Braye quote. We are not just talking about client involvement in groups, we are talking about the importance of involvement at the base level of people's care plan. I mention that because often client involvement is reduced to, and consists of, the residents meeting and a concern with how to make it 'work'. We will come back to this phenomena in the final chapter, but for now I would see residents groups not as the starting place but as the icing on the cake, and if we want to make them 'work', we need to begin with making our day-to-day interventions 'work'.

However, the most important part of the Braye quote to me is the final sentence, that to foster client participation can be the best, and sometimes the only way of intervening. In a previous work (Seal, 2005), I detailed how the task of resettlement of clients from supported to independent living is as much about building people's self-esteem, self-belief and the feeling that they have an impact, as it is about practical things like finding new accommodation and income maximisation. Lemos (2006) recently saw the building of social skills, and a sense of responsibility, as the keys to people changing their problematic behaviour. Hence the seventh theme of the book, that client involvement is the most efficient way of achieving these non-practical goals of clients work.

However, this view is not universally held. A counter argument I have heard is that, even if client involvement is an effective way of working, we are measured by initiatives like *Supporting People* in terms of throughput and outcomes, not client involvement. I would say that if client involvement is the best way of achieving these outputs then the challenge is to create that argument. A recent report by the Welsh assembly supports this view:

> *Many supporting housing organisations, aim to enable clients to become more independent, by involving clients in giving feedback on the services they use is consistent with this aim. This may be seen as a first step to participation in the wider community and may have other benefits, increasing clients' skills, confidence and control of their lives.*
>
> (Welsh Assembly, 2004: 6)

I will further argue in the next chapter that *Supporting People* already recognises this argument as client involvement is imbedded in the standards and is, in fact, one of the determining factors between an organisation getting a 'C' and an 'A' grade.

However, as with all the other perspectives, there are issues with the personal development view, particularly if it is used in isolation. In emphasising the process of participation we can be in danger of saying the product does not matter. Braye, citing Arnstein, recognises the potential dangers of this approach, calling it the therapeutic model. She traces how it is the feature of much policy guidance, 'emphasising the dignity and respect to be sought between client and provider, without any attempt to change the balance of power within it' (Braye,

2000). She also notes how Bowl (1996) observed that professionals found the therapeutic justification for client involvement the most palatable. Perhaps this is because it is the least challenging to them. The need for organisational change and the idea that services can be a part of the problem is again neutralised – these notions are very much challenged by the final, critical, model of client participation.

Critical perspectives

> *Many clients are not merely wanting greater involvement in the service. They also fundamentally challenge the dominant paradigms upon which provision is based.*
>
> (Braye, 2000: 17)

This final perspective on client involvement I have called the critical perspective because, as Braye indicates, it criticises not only services for what they do but the reasons for their existence. It calls for a radical overhaul of the whole system. We will see in the next chapter that this perspective has more of a history and tradition in other care sectors, although it is by no means absent in supported housing. In training, workers have often derided clients for making comments like 'I pay your wages', or 'you're only keeping me here to get your rents paid'. Apart from the fact that clients may have a point, the workers also missed the possible significance of these statements.

They could be forms of resistance, albeit in a symbolic way (Hegbie, 1977) that are calling for dialogue. As an example, the last book I edited (Seal et al., 2006), contained many accounts of how homeless identities are continually created and contested by clients through and against the services that are meant to serve them. My point here is twofold. Firstly, we ignore these forms of resistance, and the thoughts behind them, at our peril. They can explain and determine some of the behaviours of clients, particularly when, through client involvement, we open the previously closed doors of power a little. We may label their non-attendance as lack of motivation, it may be a form of resistance, particularly when they said they would come.

We will come back to the subject of sabotage several times, as it is a commonplace phenomenon. Secondly, clients may, again, have a point – the system has 'used' and occasionally damaged them. A recent piece of research I conducted with the supported housing sector revealed the extent to which the current regimes also damage workers (Seal, 2007). We have some of the highest burnout rates in the care sector, high rates of staff turnover, low levels of retention and inadequate mechanisms of support. This is why my eighth theme of this book is that we should seek to have alliances of clients and workers to improve the sector for us all. However, we may meet resistance in this, not least of which may be from clients, as Marsh et al. note with regard to the mental health survivor movement:

> *There is a debate within the user movement about whether engagement can ever achieve significant change, or whether users will always be co-opted into the service of a disempowering and inhumane system.*
>
> (Marsh et al., 2005: 21)

I believe we can and should try and build alliances, as I said in my introduction. I will expand on this as the book unfolds, but it is an alliance workers will need to earn and should not take for granted.

Conclusion: what rationale

Some authors (Forbes and Sashidharan, 1997; Braye, 2000; Beresford and Croft, 1993) contend that these different perspectives are incompatible and contradict each other. However, authors such as Barnes and Wistow (1994) find that in practice these models can and do exist side by side, although authors such as Bowl (1996) view this as a negative thing, saying that this is ultimately a fudge. As the reader may be able to guess from my first theme, I would view working with fudges as a part of getting one's hands dirty (Alinsky, 1968). All these perspectives have a point, and an audience, and we would be partial not to encompass them all to some degree. Even when we propounding a particular rationale, we should not forget the lessons from them all.

I remember discussing with a group of clients at a Groundswell conference their feelings about the event. There had just been a workshop on 'living on nothing' in a tepee and another on home permaculture in an open space in a field. A comment from an individual in my group was that while this was very interesting, he just wanted to get his own flat, get back to a normal life, and be treated decently along the way. While I may question his argument, this was his reality. Every client does not want to be an activist or have the emotional commitment to embrace the critical perspective. Involvement may just be about building enough self-belief for them to move on, but with the hope that others will be given the voice so that the path will be easier for those that follow on from them.

The point for those who are initiating client involvement initiatives, and the workers who will need to support it, is to place importance on creating a rationale. It will need to encompass the balance of these perspectives that reflects the interests, needs and understandings of their client group, as they understand it, at any given time. Then they should seek to articulate this rationale to the clients, preferably involving them in the debate and its proselytisation, at the earliest opportunity. More pertinently, they should recognise, and seek to ameliorate, the barriers to doing this, the subject of Chapter 4. They will also need to appreciate the power dynamics between the different parties, the subject of Chapter 6. If the parties think that these power differences are negligible, then they should try having an honest conversation about how far workers trust and respect management positions on the issue of client involvement.

2

Client Involvement in Context: Lessons to be Learnt From Developments in Social Housing and Other Care Sectors

While service-user involvement is very well established in many areas of health and social services, it is only in recent times that the concept has risen to prominence in the field of homelessness . . . there is a dearth of research on service-user involvement in homeless services.

(Velasco, 2001: 8)

While Velasco's comment refers specifically to the homeless sector, I think it has resonance for the wider supported housing sector. The expansion of the field under *Supporting People* has meant that there are many new workers who feel that client involvement is underdeveloped in their services (Seal, 2006, 2007). This chapter will explore what lessons can be learnt from other sectors that have undertaken client involvement for some time. According to some authors (Cameron et al., 2005) supported housing is meant to be about crossing the divide between housing and care. It would therefore seem sensible to look at examples from both sides of this 'divide'. From the housing sector the chapter will examine the history and influence of the tenants' movement on the development of social housing. From the care sector it will explore the history and impact of user led initiatives on mental health services and mental health debates.

In addition, it will explore how agencies and policy makers have changed how they view and have historically constructed their 'clients'. We will also look at how client movements have emerged, explore the significance of the battles they have fought, explore the emerging philosophies they have adopted and examine the internal conflicts they have faced. This chapter is but a starting point for this debate as we shall explore the similarities and differences between our own, these, and other sectors throughout the book, highlighting the challenges their experiences pose.

Lessons from the tenant's movement

We want to give power to local people to improve their own areas, with greater influence over decisions about where money should be spent and the priorities for their own community. The past shows all too clearly that imposing solutions from outside doesn't work; but that where people are able to work with the local authority or other service providers they can be genuinely empowered to make a difference.

(John Prescott, 2005)

Tenant participation has developed in Britain as a result of two conflicting forces – on the one hand, the tenants' movement with their belief in participatory democracy and empowerment – on the other hand, the government agenda of consumer choice, set within the context of a belief in the free market and the withdrawal of the welfare state.

(Cooper and Hawtin, 1998: 4)

As the quotes above indicate, the intent behind tenant participation, from both the tenants' and the government's perspective, is contested. These tensions have historical precedence and legacies that will be the subject of this section. Prescott reminds us in *Sustainable Communities: People, Places and Prosperity* (2005) that the involvement of tenants in social housing is viewed by the government as a cornerstone of good practice. Yet Cooper and Hawtin remind us that the ideological construction of tenants which lie behind these policies, are not always clear. I will contend that the assumptions of policy makers about 'the community' and 'tenants', and the structures they have created for its involvement have changed as the underlying ideologies of policy makers have changed:

The strength of the tenants' movement has been directly related to perceived threats to tenants. The movement at its strongest is reactive rather than ground-breaking. It seeks to defend the rights tenants' have far more than it seeks to create new ones.

(Smith, 1992)

I would also like to investigate Smith's claims that the tenants' movement has largely mirrored these developments. As Smith (1992) notes, the modern tenants' movement is generally traced back to the Clydeside rent strikes of 1915, although it had precursors in the general demands of the labour movements in the 19th century for the raising of living standards for working class people (Grayson, 1998). The provision of public housing grew in the inter-war period as a response to housing need and tenant lobbying after the First World War. It was accompanied by the first wave of systematic tenants' actions culminating in the development of the National Tenants' Federation in 1930 (Grayson, 1998).

In the aftermath of the Second World War, there were many examples of direct action by tenants and non-tenants. Over 40,000 families occupied former army camps and empty homes from Yorkshire to the South coast in a wave of squatting. Tooley (1998) saw this as a reaction to the inaction of local authorities to the wholesale destruction of housing in the war. There were still living memories of the failures of the inter-war 'home for heroes' housing policies of the Tories. Labour was returned with a large majority and the promise of government intervention on housing. In the after war period, up until 1965, there was a rapid expansion of local authority house building. Stewart and Taylor (1995) identify two characteristics of these interventions. Firstly, there was a genuine desire to tackle the devastation of war and there was recognition of the need for slum clearance. Secondly, there was a growth of industrialised house building techniques and new town planning systems favouring the separation of residential and industrial land use and new residential developments.

This is significant, as the move away from traditional social networks to estates with few facilities meant the growth of tenants' associations into new areas such as tackling social educational and housing management issues. In the wake of these building programmes, tenants' associations developed on the new council estates and new towns. The National Association of Tenants and Residents (NATR) was formed in 1948. While their emphasis, initially, was very much on self-help and education (Thomas, 1983), a legacy of their roots in mutual aid societies, they engendered a growing awareness that the welfare state had not abolished poverty and that this poverty was geographically concentrated in the new housing developments. This caused two reactions: policy initiatives that sought to deal with the 'deprived areas' and the increasing politicisation of tenants' groups (Goetschius, 1968).

These government initiatives, such as the community development programmes, built on the American 'war on poverty' models. These models were in turn based on the ideas of writers such as Harrington (1962) who said that there were cycles of deprivation in estates, but also that there were external cultures about poverty that pathologised those who could not deal with poverty or dig themselves out of it. Harrington felt that both of these trends needed to be countered. Education and self help were again emphasised in the form of initiatives such as Educational Priority Areas, Urban Programme, Personal Social Services and early versions of the Community Development Projects (CDPs). The 1960s also saw a resurgence of tenant action within the private sector, such as a rent strike against market rents in St Pancreas, and other London tenants' groups went on rent strike against private 'Rachmanite' landlords (Grayson, 1998).

Later work of the CDPs prompted the government to accept that some of the issues were structural rather being something to do with the estate inhabitants themselves. However, the structural failures were assumed to exist at the local macro level rather than at national or international level that the work of the CDPs pointed towards. Three characteristics of government sponsored tenant participation were identified at this time:

- *Participation was seen as a remedy for the failings associated with the development of bureaucratised, professionally orientated housing institutions.*
- *Planning and re-development became the focus of participatory initiatives in the face of large-scale re-design of post war estates. (Gyford, 1976)*
- *Self-organisation of tenants' groups tended to continue to focus around class reflecting the strong labour movement orientation of estates.*

The first two characteristics led to accusations, from those with the aforementioned critical perspective, that the language of participation became a focus for sustaining administrations and incorporating more radical elements (Dearlove, 1974; Craig, 1989; Cohen, 1985). Some authors are less critical but still acknowledge, at least in ideological terms, that modes of participation were far more about social planning than coming from any belief in participatory democracy (Henderson, 2005; Twelvetrees, 2001).

Much change happened in the period between 1975 and 1992, and there was a break from the post war consensus in housing, particularly with the government embracing ideas of the New Right about tenant participation, whereas some local authorities embraced some of the ideas of the New Left. These developments led to the embracing of new forms of participation. These had two characteristics.

- *Recognition of new identities – new grant strategies broke with the homogeneity of class and developed modes of participation that reflected race, sexuality and gender in the forms of race and women's units as well as grants to community organisations representing communities of interest rather than geography.*

- *Decentralisation – small neighbourhoods became the focus for administration, with direct monies going to support community participation as opposed to supporting planning structures.*

(Burns, Hambleton and Hoggett, 1994)

Some authors (Meekosha, 1993; Stewart and Taylor, 1995) saw this as a negative development. This recognition of difference actually caused fragmentation. The practice of community and tenant work, placing emphasis on working with new focuses such as identity and diversity, but operationalised in a monetarist framework with very different notions of decentralisation, actually compounded this fragmentation. For the Thatcher government tenant participation was to be achieved though 'empowering residents directly through market mechanisms' (DoE, 1982). People were to be empowered as consumers rather than citizens; participation was to be individual and not collective (Stewart and Taylor, 1995). In terms of the regeneration of 'problem areas', there was much greater emphasis put on property led regeneration and the need to create favourable climates for business growth, in the belief that benefits would 'trickle down' to all.

Characteristics were privatisation, quality assurance and increased accountability for public services. Empowerment was seen as 'the ability of the individual consumer or their proxy purchasers to participate in the public service market place' (Du Guy and Salaman, 1992). Measures that were brought in during this time reflect this as they included making people owners rather than tenants, the sale of council houses, the establishment of a variety of landlords (housing associations, co-ops, housing action trusts (HATs), the development of rights for tenants in terms of repairs etc., and the emphasis on regeneration programmes.

I noted in my previous book how, instead of engaging with political structures via local authorities, the supported housing sector grew in the voluntary sector (Meekosha, 1993; Seal, 2005). Within the tenant movement new communities who did engage were vulnerable to being picked off or set against each other (Stewart and Taylor, 1995). There was also a tension between these two tenant movements. While monies went to new communities through the voluntary sector, by decentralising, the community of place again dominated communities of interest in regeneration programmes. The emphasis was on neighbourhood-privileged geographical communities, excluding those who gained their identity from other sources (Burns, Hambleton and Hoggett, 1994). Burns et al. (1994) also saw the whole project as ideological rather than democratic in that it concerned the ideological clash between central and local government. This 'rainbow coalition' was actually about protecting communities and services against the conservatives.

In the face of this, tenants' organisations went into decline until 1988 when a wave of tenant protests against Tenants' Choice legislation, anti-sell off and anti-Housing Action Trust protests led to the formation of new tenants' organisations. In the 1990s there were mass tenant rallies against compulsory competitive tendering of housing management. The Tenants and Residents Organisation of England (TAROE) was formed from merger of NTRF and NTO.

The picture today seems to be a mixed one. In the mid-1990s, first with the City Challenge programme and then the Single Regeneration Budget Challenge Fund, the emphasis changed again. The emphasis now was on partnership working, in which 'representatives of all key sectors and stakeholders' were obliged to join in preparing regeneration proposals' (Burton, 2003). This emphasis has intensified under New Labour with 10 per cent of monies being dedicated to capacity building, and schemes needing to show active community involvement before funding is granted. Indeed, some authors (Hogett, 1997; Driver and Martell, 1997), would argue that community has replaced class as the driving motivation behind New Labour.

The conceptions have moved from the radical position of the failure of local authority corporate structuralism through New Right quangoism and the sidelining of Labour city municipality in the 1980s to the democratic renewal debates of today with the local authority viewed as 'enablers' (DETR, 1997). Views of tenants have consequently shifted from seeing themselves as a symptom and victim, with the priority being to address wider structural inequalities. Thatcherite policies returned to being the pathologised subject of regeneration, whereby the community needed regenerating, necessitating an enemy within; e.g. crime, skills shortage, drugs, homelessness, the young, etc. (Glenester, 1992). Currently, the community is viewed as the agent of regeneration and change. 'Communities are now increasingly keen to do it for themselves' (DETR, 1998).

Tenants' organisations, as I said in the introduction, have reacted and mirrored these developments. They have sometimes defended their existing members' rights and at other times they have been at the forefront of pushing issues of social justice. They have also bought into local and national government agendas. The Tenant Participatory Advisory Service (TPAS), in their account of the history of tenants' organisations since 2000, reflect this. During this time tenants' organisations and the trade union backed Defend Council Housing won some high profile anti-transfer battles. New Labour launched Arms Length Management Organisations as an alternative to transfer that win the support of many tenants' federations. By 2006, the amount of housing managed by Registered Social Landlords, including transfer organisations, out-numbers council homes for the first time. Some major tenants' federations lose their funding as landlords switch to the less problematic option of involving customers through market research. More recently, Regional Tenants' Federations are set up to mirror the government's new regional structure of housing strategy and investment.

Mental health and survivor movements

> *Psychiatry can so easily be a technique of brain-washing, of inducing socially acceptable behaviour by (preferably) non-injurious torture.*
>
> (Laing, 1967)

> *Politicising oneself by joining with other survivors in political actions is an excellent antidote to the powerlessness that psychiatry induces in its subjects. Becoming active in the struggle against psychiatry (and other forms of injustice) . . . is a good alternative to the helplessness psychiatry encourages.*
>
> (Masson, 1989: 34)

The 'struggle against psychiatry' that Jeffrey Masson describes has a long history. It could be described as the history of client involvement. As Mind says: 'as long as there have been psychiatric institutions there has been a movement against the injustices suffered within them' (Mind, 2003). However, similarly to social housing, the forms of the client movement, or survivor movement, and the positions it has adopted, have shifted, as have constructions of mental health and its 'treatment'. I think it is therefore important, initially, to consider how the treatment of people with mental health issues has changed.

Various authors trace attitudes towards mental health back to prehistory. However, their views are contested. Darton (2004: 1) says: 'in prehistoric times there was, as far as historians can tell, no division between medicine, magic and religion'. He takes the view, as does McKenna (1999) that those who displayed mental health symptoms were revered as shaman and had god given insight. Others (Mora, 1985; Sue et al., 1990), take the view that mental health was associated with illness or at least a disturbance in the balance with the spirit world, evidencing trepanning, the drilling of holes in the skull to 'let' the spirits out, as an early treatment. All these views are obviously difficult to verify, and are possibly evidence of the vested interests Sedgewick (1982) identifies in *Psychopolitics.* However, they are useful to identify as models, as they have repercussions in modern views.

The ancient Romans and Greeks were largely characterised by a similar view of the person being possessed (Mora, 1985). However, Hippocrates (460–377 BC) and Plato (429–348 BC) were the first to develop a more organic explanation of mental illness. Hippocrates believed that the cause of mental illness was an imbalance in the interaction of the four bodily humours (Mora, 1985), and it should be treated with proper diet, drink and abstinence from sexual activity (Davison and Neale, 1997). Plato was the first to see mental health as having a psychological dimension, believing that the cause of mental illness is a person's ignorance of their psyche, the force that keeps the human being alive, which in turn led to self-deception (Mora, 1985). Such mind-body distinctions were to become a recurring feature of conceptualisations of mental health.

The medieval view of mental health is seen as being characterised by contradictions by many authors (Darton, 2004; Mora, 1985). On the one hand, many monasteries followed the writings of the Greeks such as Hippocrates and treated it as having a biological cause; for example, Bedlam was founded in 1377 as the first dedicated asylum for the insane. However, Pietro Albano (1250–1316) was burned to death by the Inquisition for 'minimising spiritual principles', in his attempt to unite Aristotle's thinking with the medical facts. In other parts of the world Moslem scholars (Mora, 1985), believed that the insane person is loved and particularly chosen by God to tell the truth and some were even worshipped as saints. Phazes (865–925), chief surgeon of the Bagdhad hospital, guided by the writings of Galen and Aristotle, even made use of forms of behaviour therapy.

The restoration period of the 15th, 16th and early 17th centuries seems to have been universally viewed as a step backwards in terms of thinking about mental health (Darton, 2004; Mora, 1985) with the rise of the Inquisition and the publication of the *Malleus Maleficarum* (The Witches Hammer, 1486). People with issues of mental health were frequently persecuted and accused of being witches. The cause of mental illness was attributed to possession by the devil. However, later in the 17th century, philosophical and supernatural causation of mental illness was rejected (Mora, 1985). This did not necessarily mean that treatments were any more benign. Darton (2004) notes the emergence of a crude behaviouralism, with the notion that 'if mad people behaved like animals, they should be treated like them'. Thomas Willis, a neuro-anatomist and doctor, speaking of treatment of the mentally ill, said:

> *Truly nothing is more necessary and more effective for the recovery of these people than forcing them to respect and fear intimidation . . . maniacs often recover much sooner if they are treated with torture and torments in a hovel instead of with medicaments.*
>
> (Willis, quoted in Roberts, 2007)

It is during this time that an early user movement emerged. In 1620, a 'Petition of the Poor Distracted People in the House of Bedlam' was delivered to the House of Lords complaining against the inhumane treatment of the Bedlam Asylum inmates. They were forced to 'entertain' the public in exchange for food and clothing and were frequently shackled and subjected to other forms of physical 'treatment' and restraint (Mind, 2003). The response to these protests goes unrecorded.

The 18th century saw the development of new public asylums to house people with mental health problems. Previously, most provision had been in private institutions for the rich, and houses of correction and poor houses for the poor (Danton, 2004). However, the treatments were still barbaric, treating people as animals, with drastic, supposedly biological, 'cures'. Therapies at this time included water immersion 'to keep him under water as long as he can possibly bear without being stifled' and the spinning stool, which spun the patient round until he was dizzy, the spinning apparently rearranging the brain contents into the right positions. Another was a form of drama therapy, called 'non-injurious torture' that involved lions' dens and executions, invoking the persecution of early Christians. Early forms of ECT were also brought in by Benjamin Franklin in 1757.

It was not until the early 19th century that mental health started to be conceptualised psychologically again, with treatments being consequently more humanistic. In Italy, Vincenzo Chiarugi (1759–1820), specifically stated that, 'it is a supreme moral duty and medical obligation to respect the insane individual as a person' (as quoted in Mora, 1985). In England, William Tuke (1732–1819), called patients 'guests' and sought to create an atmosphere of understanding, free from any medical restraint (Mora, 1985). In France, Philip Pinel (1745–1826), created the first open treatments, where people were not locked up. However, many, particularly the poor, were not so lucky and continued to be locked up in appalling conditions (Danton, 2004).

Positively, with new understanding, there was the start of public outcries at the conditions in the asylums, coinciding with the formation of the first recognised modern survivors' movement. The Alleged Lunatics Friends Society, a lobbying and campaigning organisation, was formed by 'ex-patients' in 1845 and is credited with extricating the poet John Clare from a Victorian asylum. There were also periodic riots in Edwardian and Victorian asylums that were some of the first instances of direct action from clients against the injustice and oppression of the psychiatric system (Mind, 2003). In the mid-to-late nineteenth century there were two developments which represented a step backwards in the treatment of people with mental health problems. First was the development of social Darwinism. In some hands, Darwinism led to a pessimistic biological determinism about mental illness. At its extremes mental illness was seen as a hereditary strain to be eliminated. Darton notes that the big change between the 1845 and 1890 Lunacy Acts was a return to locking people up and keeping them segregated. Secondly, Pasteur's theories about viral infection led some doctors to concentrate on biological causes, and medical interventions, once more.

More modern developments, from the end of the 19th century till the late 1950s, had three influences; the development of psychology, the popularity of eugenics and the search for organic treatments; the latter two of these can be seen as a continuation of the aforementioned Darwinistic and biological trends. Darton notes that the term psychology began to be used as meaning the scientific study of mental phenomena. Freud and Janet developed alternate models of the human psyche, and how to treat them. Freud's ideas went on to form the basis of modern psychoanalysis. In the 20th century, Gestalt theory and behaviourism or stimulus-response theory have come to the fore. These two approaches begin to merge in the techniques of cognitive behavioural therapy.

At the same time, Roberts (2006, 2007) notes the development of Eugenicist ideas, the breeding of 'healthy human beings', with the formation of the Eugenics society in 1909. The

Royal Commission on the Care and Control of the Feeble Minded (1904–1908) reported that 'mental defectives were often prolific breeders and allowing them so much freedom led to delinquency, illegitimacy and alcoholism' (cited in Roberts, 2007). They rejected sterilisation as a solution, and called for separation and control. Roberts also notes that Churchill was a strong supporter of sterilisation. His proposals for the forcible sterilisation of 100,000 'moral degenerates', including the poor and 'criminals', were kept secret until 1992. The eugenicist approach reached its zenith in Nazi Germany. In July 1939, planning of the 'T4' programme of 'mercy killings' of the insane began. Experimental gas chambers were tried out at Brandenburg euthanasia centre in late 1939. An estimated 80,000 to 100,000 people were killed before the T4 programme was 'stalled' in August 1941 after public protest. As late as 1947, physicians such as Tredgold were making comments such as that below in medical text books:

> *With regard to the 80,000 or more idiots and imbeciles in the country . . . In my opinion it would be an economical and humane procedure were their existence to be painlessly terminated . . . It is doubtful if public opinion is yet ripe for this to be done compulsorily; but I am of the opinion that the time has come when euthanasia should be permitted at the request of a parent or guardian.*
>
> (Tredgold, 1947: 491)

At the same time, Danton notes that the search for organic causes and treatments for mental health problems continued. This search was spurred on by the successful identification and treatment of conditions such as phenylketonuria and thyroid conditions. Eugen Bleuler (1898–1927) coined the term 'schizophrenia' in 1908 (Shorter, 1997), and his theories on the biological cause of schizophrenia are still widely accepted today and treated with psychopharmacological substances. Deep sleep treatments became popular, initially using bromide and later barbiturates. Similarly, insulin coma therapy was popular until the 1960s, in which patients were given insulin to induce a coma and convulsions, and then brought round with glucose injections. ECT (electro convulsive therapy) and psychosurgery (including lobotomies) were also being practiced and have come under some criticism then and since (Danton, 2004).

More recent changes have been the closing down of the old mental health institutions and the development of the anti-psychiatry movement. The former was heralded by Enoch Powell in 1961 when he made his 'water tower' speech at a meeting of the National Association for Mental Health, later to become Mind, announcing the proposed closure of the large psychiatric institutions and the development of 'care in the community'. The main initial movers in the anti-psychiatry movement were Ronald Laing and Thomas Szasz, informed by the publication of Foucault's *Histoire de la Folie* which told the 'history of unreason in an age of reason'. They argued that as a society we had chosen to construct mental illness in a paranoid way that reflected our own insecurities, and we constructed the people who displayed it as somehow 'other'. In America, Thomas Szasz published *The Myth of Mental Illness* in 1960. He argued that the states of mind described as mental illness are not 'illness' but actions for which the mentally distressed person must be held responsible. He also took the view that any psychiatric diagnosis is a licence for coercion and the exercise of psychiatric power.

R.D. Laing, published *The Divided Self: An Existential Study in Sanity and Madness* in 1960, in which he contended several things. Firstly, that an existential-phenomenological psychology is required for a valid study of the human mind, and that we need to look at the whole situation of the person, including an analysis of the role and personality of the therapist. Secondly, he contended that the apparently incomprehensible language of madness is, in fact, comprehensible. As an illustration of the former, he introduced the idea of 'ontological security', by which he just means being secure in one's own being. He also calls it having a sense of being a whole person. Certain people in certain families, he argues, do not develop feelings of ontological security, and this can result in schizophrenia. In terms of the latter, the role of the therapist is to understand the code of the patient and work with the person to develop new languages and signifiers.

It was also in this period that the organised mental health service user/survivor movement developed significantly. Mind see the movement as being rooted in the civil and welfare rights movements of the 1960s, emerging alongside the Gay Liberation and Black Civil Rights movements of that time (Mind, 2003). In the light of the writings of the anti-psychiatrists 'many users were no longer prepared to accept the labels and restrictions that psychiatry placed on them' (Mind, 2003). One of the earliest groups was PNP (People Not Psychiatry: People Need People). Its aims were threefold:

- *To provide a supportive network of friendship based on the acceptance of each person as a unique individual, each one with a life-style that is valid for him/her.*
- *To provide a physical environment (houses or houses) where a variety of activities can be pursued by various sub-groups within the wider network.*
- *To bear witness to the fact that there are valid values and life-styles other than those proposed by the establishment.*

In these aims we see a clear challenge to established definitions of mental health and an alliance with the anti-psychiatry movement. This alliance has been one of the points of contention within the movement, as we shall outline below. Since then a variety of groups has emerged including the Mental Patients Union in 1973, Prompt (Promotion of rights of mental patients in therapy) in 1976, Survivors Speak Out in 1987 and Mad Pride in 1999. Authors such as Campbell (1996, 2002) and Bertram (2002) identify several common trends and points of contention within the movement as well as common reactions and obstacles the movement has faced from others. It is these trends that I want to explore further as I think that they have implications and parallels for the supported housing field, and the direction client involvement could go in. The trends that Campbell and Bertram identify in common are:

- A questioning of a number of concepts used in mental health services.
- Confronting the way in which mental health service users are described, both within the service system and in society as a whole.
- A fight against clients being seen exclusively in terms of their diagnosis, regardless of whether they accept that medical classification of their problems is valid or not.
- The right for clients to self-define; even when this becomes problematic.

Campbell also detects several points of contention:

1. *The relative importance of rights.* While he feels that a belief in civil rights for people with a mental illness diagnosis is inherent in service user/survivor action, 'in actuality, this belief seems to have played a secondary role in the movement, except in regard to the Mental Health Act.' Campbell notes how the focus more often has ended up being on consumer and patients' rights, expressed typically in the production of charters (the first being done by the MPU in the 1970s) for users of mental health services. The problem Campbell sees with such charters is that they often miss out on structural discrimination and more radical critiques, focusing on individual behaviours of workers.

2. *Alliances within professionals.* Campbell sees the influence of the anti-psychiatry movement as contested but undeniable. 'The possible intelligibility of mad persons, the possible value of their insights and agonies ... are among the respectful declarations that users and survivors warmly welcomed and frequently seek to build upon' (p221). However, he also points out that getting mental health debates labelled anti-psychiatric now guarantees marginalisation (Bertram, 2002). He sees a pragmatism since the 1985 Mind conference (From Patients to People), and the growing influence of civil and consumer rights, although as we have discussed above, the latter is somewhat problematic.

3. *The language and structure of oppression.* Campbell identifies certain terms like 'mental health service consumer', 'mental health service user', 'mental health service recipient' as not having come from the survivor movement, but are part of the consumerist move in services, the problems of which were explored in Chapter 1. He notes that 'activists seem to see themselves as service users rather than citizens' (p207). He also notes that while we should not make a simple equation of client users groups are reformist, and survivors groups are anti-psychiatry, they do point to real divisions in the movement.

4. *How to organise the movement.* Campbell again draws attention to the practical difficulties of action and organisation. He sees this largely as a division between localised and national actions. Small groups have historically been the dominant force, stemming from a philosophy of localised and decentralised actions being most relevant. However, they suffer from the insecurity of inadequate or short-term funding and the need to continually train new people in the skills of running a group and to adapt to and find support for key members going through distress. More recently national groups have been on the rise. He is concerned whether there are too many groups, that they are not clear about what their role is, that they overlap and that none of them are sufficiently strong. Yet he recognises that: 'a strong, representative voice at national level, something the movement has hitherto avoided or been unable to create, could be a necessity for continued success in the next decade'.

Finally they identify common obstacles, or reactions, that the movement has faced from others. I think these are particularly important as:

1. *Stories versus Understandings.* Campbell notes how input from clients is now widely accepted as a necessary part of planning and managing services. However, what evidence is accepted is a moot point. As Campbell says 'Accepting the idea of someone with a mental illness diagnosis as a consumer of services able to reflect on such consumption is one thing. Accepting that person as an agent able to reflect on their mental distress and to provide valuable understandings of it is quite another' (p234). I am reminded of the growth of reports in the last ten years of clients in supported housing offering their stories, with the analysis of them being done by researchers or left to the reader.

2. *Concerns about representativeness.* Campbell notes how there is often a concern about being representative, normally when those with the power do not like what is starting to be said by representatives (McGreggor, 1980). I have always wondered at people being overly concerned with whether they are talking to the 'real users', and at what point they do this; again, an issue we will return to.

3. *Fear of the professional user.* He notes leading mental health professionals' concerns about creating or sustaining 'the professional user' but sees this as a red herring. He sees this as a smokescreen for the fact that 'it is still not legitimate for service users/survivors to

self-organise – like other stakeholders in the field.' An argument I have heard in this field is that clients in supported housing are different from those with mental health issues. The latter is largely permanent while many in supported housing need that housing for ever. The argument is linked to one I will discuss in subsequent chapters about client involvement resulting in clients becoming more dependent on services. Without getting into the debate about whether mental health issues are permanent or not, I have noted elsewhere (Seal, 2007) that for many people who have been in support housing for some time, this becomes a part of who they are. I also think that we should reflect on when we start applying terms like 'professional user/client'. I argue in subsequent chapter that we often only question the legitimacy of a client when we do not like what they say.

4. *Service users as providers.* Campbell notes how the work of survivor movements has started to challenge professional (expert)-patient (recipient) relationships and proposing alternatives. He sees it as central to such developments that people with a mental illness diagnosis can be providers as well as recipients of care. He found that workers were often very threatened at the prospect, and gave several examples of contradictory responses agencies gave, even seeing it as legitimate for people with mental health issues to teach nurses, but a questioning of whether they can become one.

Conclusion

What I think we learn from the section on social housing and the tenants' movements is that the position and expectations of 'the community' and tenants have changed according to prevailing political ideologies. The early development of the survivor movement in mental health seems to be similar, although until more recent times the opportunities for self-organisation were limited. Whether Smith's claims in the earlier quotation that the develop-ment of the tenants' movement has been largely, but with notable exceptions, a 'reaction' to those ideological shifts, is true, seems more of a debate. In a recent paper (Hennesby and Seal, 2007), we saw the client and tenant movements as being more than just a reaction to ideological changes, they impact upon these ideologies and help shape them.

Analysing the above developments we saw a pattern of initial exclusion, the debate about mental health being the exclusive realm of the professional, or, in the case of housing, the idea of a tenant inputting into housing being seen as a challenge to the notion of private property. This was followed by a reaction, or rejection of these ideas by clients often accompanied with radical action. Next there was the parallel but separate development of new ideologies, and their practical application, such as public housing or, in the case of mental health, the anti-psychiatry movement and notions of self-help and self-advocacy. Finally, there came attempts to bring these models together, but with battles over what lessons should be drawn from previous periods.

In the previous chapter we explored the different ideological pulls that the clients' movement is facing in supported housing. The question seems to be, for me, the degree to which we simply follow the prevailing ideologies of the policy makers and agencies, or seek to form them. In the introduction I mentioned the different roles for client involvement being to fight it, fix it, escape it and replace it. I also made the claim that Groundswell has moved between these roles as seemed appropriate. Interestingly, the pattern of the development of client involvement has been similar to the ones described above. In the last ten years we have moved from a position of trying to develop an alternate voice, through developing alternative models and supporting self-help, to a current emphasis on working with homeless agencies to improve their services. The debates we have about the ethics of this are similar to those mentioned above.

On a more practical level, Campbell and others provide some interesting insights into the dynamics of how the clients' movement has developed. I think anyone seeking to champion client involvement should take stock of the unifying factors, take note of the points of contention, and prepare themselves for certain reactions from others. Campbell (1999, 2002) feels that one of the unifying aspects of the survivor movement has been its emphasis on self-advocacy. He feels that there are certain principles that underpin this belief in self-advocacy, which I think act as a starting point for developing client involvement in supported housing. They are:

- *A belief in the essential competence of people with a mental illness diagnosis.*
- *A belief in the value of self-help and collective action.*
- *A belief in the value and possibility of self-organisation by service users and survivors.*
- *A belief that people with a mental illness diagnosis may have special expertise to offer society as a result of their personal experience.*

I have used these ideas to underpin the principles for client involvement in supported housing in a later chapter. Positively, if I look at the initial statement made by Groundswell, an umbrella group supporting self-help and user led initiatives in supported housing, about its position on client involvement on its formation in 1997, I am heartened, for I think it contains many of the elements named above, such as:

Homeless and socially excluded people are not 'the problem' – they must be part of the solution. They hold the key to solutions in their experiences and knowledge and have a right to the information they need to make informed choices about their lives. We can build communities and create positive change by acting together.

(Groundswell, 1997)

However, the question remains about how we can best take this aspirational statement forward for it to become meaningful.

3

Policy Imperatives and Supporting People

Government policy continues to recommend client empowerment strategies and involvement of service users in the planning, delivery and monitoring of services. Yet, service users are facing increased stigma and discrimination through distorted media portrayals, coercive practices such as community treatment orders and the new 'mental health act from hell'.

(Critical Mental Health Forum, 2002: 5)

Client involvement is a political priority and is seen by many policy makers, regulators and funders as indisputably a 'good thing'. Demonstrating that service users are involved in shaping a service is now frequently a condition of funding or continuing support for a project. It is therefore likely that some activities directed at involving service users do not flow from a genuine commitment to listening to and responding to service user views but from a desire to satisfy grant conditions.

(Cameron et al., 2005)

A key element of Supporting People is the commitment to ensuring that people who use housing with support are effectively involved in shaping provision and evaluating its scope and quality.

(Godfrey et al., 2003)

The above quotations remind us of the fourth theme of the book, that behind the apparent consensus that client involvement is 'good', contradictory messages and priorities are prevalent in the policies about client involvement. They also illustrate to me that we ignore policy and its potential impact on services at our peril. The Cameron et al. quote, in particular, shows the relevance of policy for day-to-day service provision in that what is driving an agency to undertake client involvement can be flawed from the start. This chapter will explore the policy drivers for agencies to undertake client involvement in the supported housing sector, and explore how they can be used as leverage. The aim is to see how they can work for us, rather than against us, us being those who are trying to develop a strategy for client involvement in an agency.

The chapter will pay particular attention to evaluating the perspectives on client involvement that underpin these initiatives and the extent to which they have potential to achieve what they seek to promote. I do not intend to re-rehearse some of the historical policy debates of the last chapter. I will instead be looking at the policies as they exist today. There are also specific themes and tensions that will emerge in considering the impact of policy: the tension between national directives and local interpretation, competition between different client groups, competing policy priorities and the impact of market forces. I will contend that these factors can end up making bad local authorities worse, difficult if they are the administering authority for your funding, and can cause 'policy drift'. The specific policies I will examine are Tenant Participation Compacts, the Housing Corporation Charter, Best Value and, in particular, *Supporting People*.

A positive starting point for examining social policy is the Council of Europe's European Social Charter (1961, revised in 1996) which this government ratified in 2000. Of particular interest is article 30 – The right to protection against poverty and social exclusion. It states that 'with a view to ensuring the effective exercise of the right to protection against poverty and social exclusion, the parties (governments) undertake':

(a) *To take measures within the framework of an overall and co-ordinated approach to promote the effective access of persons who live or risk living in a situation of social exclusion or poverty, as well as their families, in particular, employment, housing, training, education, culture and social and medical assistance.*

(b) *To review these measures with a view to their adaptation if necessary. So, the measures to be taken do not explicitly include the participation of the persons concerned, but rather the possibility to 'review these measures with a view to their adaptation if necessary', in order to promote such participation.*

(Council of Europe, 1961: 12)

Of significance is the second phrase which makes clear that governments should not just consult with people in poverty about the 'necessary measures' to alleviate their poverty, but governments should ensure that the measures undertaken have participation as an integral and permanent feature. These statements seem to indicate that opportunities need to be developed by European countries for meaningful participatory developments to take place. However, as indicated by the policy, what flavour the social policy of a particular country adopts will vary, as mentioned in the introduction. How successful this government is in this endeavour is a moot point, as we shall see below.

I will now turn to policies regarding tenants in local authority accommodation and housing associations. While these initiatives and policies are largely aimed at social housing tenants, they also have implications for tenants of supported housing, not least because under *Supporting People*, housing associations and local authority housing departments are major providers of supported housing services (Godfrey et al., 2003).

Tenant participation compacts: local authority imperatives

In June 1999 the DETR issued their National Framework for Tenant Participation Compacts, which is meant to be used as a toolkit 'to help councils and tenants develop, implement and review compacts' (DETR, 1999). Before Compacts, the involvement of tenants in the major decisions over how housing services were being delivered varied widely. Individual landlords largely determined the amount and quality of tenant involvement. The government saw TP Compacts changing this in two ways. Firstly, by spelling out the basic principles of tenant involvement it hoped to raise minimum standards. Secondly, by empowering and informing tenants about the options available and highlighting good practice, the government expected tenants to be able to choose the level of involvement they wanted for themselves. They outlined two kinds of Compacts. The first were district-wide agreements between the local authorities and tenants. These should be introduced alongside local compacts covering estates or other coherent areas. The second are compacts developed by local authorities and tenants that relate to different groups of tenants, e.g. young people, elderly people, etc., rather than just area based ones. All compacts should conform to the core standards and local compacts should contain as much as is seen by local tenants as relevant to those particular areas. Tenant empowerment is defined in the Compact as:

1. *Making tenants aware of all the options for involvement in and delivery of housing services.*
2. *Providing tenants' groups with the skills and support necessary to choose what level of participation they want.*
3. *Providing a flexible framework that allows tenants to increase their involvement where and when they choose.*

(DETR, 1999: 9)

Enthusiasm for these initiatives was generally high, with the chief executive of TPAS (Tenant Participatory Advisory Service) commenting: 'The introduction of best value and tenant compacts offers a tremendous opportunity for tenant participation to make a positive impact' (Morgan, 2000), but warned a fair judgement of compacts must lie in the future. Several authors have identified factors that should be taken into consideration when we make these judgements. For some (Cooper and Hawtin, 1999: 5), the success of the tenant participation compacts will depend on the first theme I mentioned, how the regulators reconcile local needs and national standards. Compacts are not meant to be prescriptive about how tenants and landlords should operate the compact or how meaningful involvement is to be defined and delivered. As they say in their opening guidance: 'It is very important that Compacts are locally negotiated and reflect the needs of tenants in each local authority' (DETR, 1999: 2).

However, while this may seem to be responsive to local needs, without some national standards there is the danger of discrepancy between areas with sympathetic local authorities and already active communities, and antagonistic local authorities with weakened and more fragmented communities. Somerville (2004: 12) feels that while a TPC could 'stimulate collective action on the part of tenants, leading to genuine influence over council housing management', they could be used as a regulatory device for a local authority's management of its tenants. In the case of supported housing the dangers would seem to be particularly acute, where we may well be behind in the development of tenant action. There is also the danger of 'mainstream' tenants being set up against tenants in supported housing. Working at the turn of the decade for Camden Homeless Forum, the council set up a participation and consultation event for tenants, prior to changes in their allocations policy. They structured the event around the question of whether their allocations policy should 'serve' the 'local' population or continue to 'shoehorn clients with support needs into existing communities. Somerville (2004: 23) sees the issue in terms of power, with the New Labour model of empowerment ignoring the potential for local authorities to manipulate their tenants, or different groups of them, and take advantage of those who are not active. The contextual variation depends mainly on the attitudes of the powerful, but also on the degree of self-respect of the tenants and residents concerned.

The London Housing Unit (Sinclair, 1999) feels that increased funding for local authorities and new legislation is required if tenant participation under the government's new compacts scheme is to succeed. Developing this theme, Millward (2005) feels that under tenant compact proposals, tenants could be the first to suffer if financial penalties are imposed on local authorities with a poor record of tenant participation. This would have the effect of compounding the problem. Somerville (2004) feels that as well as implementing compacts, councils must also make sure tenants will be given full opportunity to be involved in local government under the new cabinet style arrangements. He, along with others (Curtice, 1999; White, 2004), see the new arrangements as an erosion of democracy that would have the effect of making compacts superfluous. Similarly, the Tenant Participation Advisory Service (Morgan, 2000) feels that compacts must not be seen as a panacea and that tenant participation must be a common thread that runs through local government modernisation.

There are other social housing policies relevant to client involvement; in fact, they are numerous. A couple are worth outlining, even if it is simply for the reader to quote them to try to gain leverage with a social landlord, as they are all subject to them. The first policy is the 'Housing Association Regulatory Code' and the Housing Association Charter. The code has several points relevant to those seeking to increase participation:

2.5 Housing Associations must seek and be responsive to residents views and priorities.

2.5.3 Enabling residents to play their part in decision-making.

2.5.4 Providing opportunities for residents to explore, and play their part, in how services are managed and provided.

2.5a The association is effectively accountable to its stakeholders. Current information about its activities is widely available to residents and other interested parties.

2.5c The association considers a range of methods and opportunities to consult and obtain feedback from residents. It seeks to make an agreement, developed in partnership with residents, setting out how they will be involved, consulted and informed and how this will be resourced, measured, monitored and reviewed.

Similarly, the Housing Association Charter says that housing associations must:

- Make sure their services are shaped around customers' needs.
- Seek the views of residents and respond to these views.
- Allow residents to play a part in the decision making.
- Ensure residents are given opportunities to play a part in how services are run and standards are set.

Secondly, Best Value is worth a mention, if only because it identifies clients in supported housing specifically. Importantly, it states that local authorities should not undertake the pitting of one section of the community one another.

> *Where people with care and support needs live in mainstream social housing, it is important for housing departments to take account of their views . . . are sufficiently flexible and sensitive to their needs and that new housing services are developed in a way that can respond to needs across the whole community, including those of vulnerable groups . . . Including residents with special needs in the wider consultation with tenant and residents groups can be a positive way of bringing the concerns of one group to bear on the other.*
> (DCLG, 2001: s 32)

Of particular interest is a report by Joseph Rowntree (Evans et al., 2002), examining how, in Wiltshire, disabled people undertook a best value review of direct payments and the arrangements made by the county council. Importantly, as we have seen and shall come back to, they had an established track record in Wiltshire of action and advocacy, supported and through the Wiltshire and Swindon Clients' Network. In the appendix of the report the authors detail how they creatively used the four Cs (Challenge, Consult, Compare and Competition) creatively. I think this part of the appendix is worth repeating in full.

Challenged
They challenged how Wiltshire County Council's Direct Payments scheme assists independent living.
They challenged care managers record regarding the service to direct payments users versus other users.
They challenged the effectiveness of social services systems in enabling service users.
They challenged policy against best practice in delivering the service.

Consult
They surveyed users of the support service for independent living.
They surveyed care management team views.
They consulted direct payments users regarding systems and practice.
They consulted users and care managers about policy issues.

Compare
They compared cost of care management support to direct payments users with support for users of direct services.
They compared support service for independent living with other centres for independent living.
They compared care management within Wiltshire County Council with care managers in other studies.
They compared costings with costings information from previous research.

Compete
They opened up support service for independent living to competition from other Centres for Independent Living.

(Evans et al., 2002: 34)

Other policies relevant to client involvement in supported housing

As mentioned in the introduction there are numerous policy initiatives that will impact on the promotions of client involvement in supported housing, but we do not have time to cover them in detail. However, I think it is still worth signposting the reader towards other policies and initiatives that may be helpful.

Community development and regeneration

The *Together we can* initiative (*www.togetherwecan.info*) has four strategic priorities that link into client involvement. Citizens and Democracy; Health and Sustainability; Regeneration and Cohesion and Safety and Justice.

Making it Happen in Neighbourhoods, the National Strategy for Neighbourhood Renewal Four Years on is a good summary of some of the major issues surrounding Neighbourhood Renewal debates.

All local authorities are required to produce a community strategy. A good document to start with is the *Process Evaluation of Community Strategies and Plan Rationalisation: Annual Report 2006*, dealing, as it says, with matters of process as well as outcome.

Health

Creating a Patient-led NHS: Delivering the NHS Improvement Plan (2005) along with the guidance, *A Stronger Local Voice: A Framework for Creating a Stronger Local Voice in the Development of Health and Social Care Services* (2006), and specifically regarding primary care, *Public and Patient Involvement in Primary Care* (2002), are useful documents of relevance to client involvement.

Homelessness

Sustainable Communities: Settled Homes; Changing Lives (2005), *More than a Roof* (2003), and local guidance on developing homeless strategies, *Homelessness Strategies: A Good Practice Handbook* (2002). All contain sections, or elements of sections, saying how clients should be consulted in the implementation of their recommendations.

Supporting People

> *The Supporting People Programme offers vulnerable people the opportunity to improve their quality of life through greater independence. It provides housing related services which are cost effective, efficient and reliable and which complement existing care services. Supporting People is a working partnership of local government, service user's and support agencies.*
>
> (Godfrey et al., 2003: 3)

On 1 April 2003, the *Supporting People* programme was launched. As Homeless Link have noted, it 'is the first national co-ordinated programme to deliver 'housing related support' for vulnerable people' (Homeless Link, 2000: 2). The DCLG (Department for Communities and Local Government, formerly the Office of the Deputy Prime Minister), has the main responsibility for the *Supporting People* programme. It allocates a *Supporting People* grant to local authorities (LAs), and monitors their performances. LAs are responsible for implementing the programme within the local area. They contract with providers for the provision of *Supporting People* services. These can be within the statutory, voluntary and private sectors. A Commissioning Body (a partnership of local housing, social care, health, probation and other statutory and voluntary services), sits above LAs and advises and approves a *Supporting People* strategy that needs to be produced annually. There are therefore two avenues for client involvement through *Supporting People*, at the monitoring and strategic planning stages. Positively, guidance has been provided for client involvement in both, and in the case of the former, a need to show that the organisation is embracing client involvement is embodied in the standards by which organisations are monitored. As *Supporting People* monies is likely to be the funding source, and hence driving force, behind provision for some time, I want to explore its possible impact on client involvement.

Supporting People: The Quality Assessment Framework

The Quality Assessment Framework (QAF) is one of the mechanisms used in *Supporting People* service reviews, which itself is one of the ways in which services providing support services are monitored and evaluated. The aim of the framework is to 'assess the quality of services . . . and to encourage and facilitate the raising of standards within the support services sector' (ODPM, 2002). Brafield (2003) identifies that the QAF aims to bring together 'the merging demands of the Housing Corporation, Audit Commission, Best Value, etc.', and that this includes that the influence of clients in housing related support services needs to be demonstrated. To accompany these standards, the ODPM produced the *Guide to Client Involvement for Organisations providing Housing Related Support Services* already mentioned. In it, the ODPM defines four levels at which clients can and should be making contributions:

1. Dialogue/information.
2. Day to day running of the organisation.
3. Planning and policy in the organisation.
4. Service management.

These principles are then integral to, and integrated throughout, the standards in the QAF. The standards are organised into six core ones (needs and risk assessment, support planning, health and safety, protection from abuse, access, diversity and inclusion and complaints), and four supplementary ones (empowerment, rights and responsibilities, the service and organisation and management). During reviews, agencies are graded, and from 2006 have graded themselves on these standards from a D (failing) to an A (excellent). C is seen as the minimum standard, and something to develop from. There is potential for client involvement through both the core and supplementary standards. The first set of supplementary standards, concerning empowerment, specifically addresses client involvement and gives ample leverage for client involvement. The section headings, as outlined below, demonstrate this:

S1.1 Service users are well informed so that they can communicate their needs and wishes and make informed choices.
S1.2 Service users are consulted about the services provided and are offered opportunities to be involved in their running.
S1.3 There is a commitment to empowering service users and supporting their independence.
S1.4 Service users are empowered in their engagement in the wider community and the development of social networks.
S3.2 The service is flexible, sensitive and responsive with the aim of maximising service client's dignity, independence, choice and control over their own lives.

(ODPM, 2004b)

It would be tempting to concentrate on these explicit standards as a vehicle for client involvement, but I believe that this would be limiting and would miss the potential power within the standards. The problem with the supplementary standards is that they are precisely that. Most practitioners describe how their agencies have been concentrating almost exclusively on the core standards and this is demonstrated by practitioners' working knowledge of the core standards, but lack of knowledge of the supplementary ones. Indeed, the guidance is explicit about how the initial reviews have concerned the core objectives only (ODPM, 2004a). Even after that, which supplementary objectives are to be used as a measure for an organisation are a matter of negotiation, as such empowerment as a measure could all too easily become squeezed or marginalised.

However, if we examine the core standards we see that client involvement is embedded in them, something the guidance is indeed explicit about (ODPM, 2002). I further contend that the biggest factors that make the distinction between an agency getting a 'C' and an 'A' grade in the different standards is, firstly, the degree to which they involve clients in their processes, and secondly, how successfully they involve and work with other agencies. It is the former that concerns me here. As a general trend, at Level C the standards expect clients to be informed, to demonstrate understanding and occasionally feel they have a choice over things. At Level B, clients are expected to have an active involvement and a say, at least on a day-to-day level. At Level A the standards expect clients to be involved at a strategic and policy development level.

For example, the core objective 1.1 concerns needs and risk assessment. At Level C they have to demonstrate such things as 'The written procedures describe how service users' views are to be incorporated, 'Where prospective service users disagree with any outcomes of assessment or reviews their views and reasoning are recorded', and 'Service users confirm that their views have been listened to and taken into account'. Level B largely concerns appeals and more active involvement including standards such as clients being given written details of the appeals process which explain who will be involved, when and where the appeal will take place and that 'Support plans incorporate specific intended outcomes which have been agreed with service users'. Level A demands strategic involvement such as reviews of support needs, considers how successful the service has been in assisting service users in realising their plans, targets or aspirations, and how this information is used to improve services.

Similarly, 1.3 concerns Health and Safety. At Level C the standards are that 'Concerns are documented and illustrate that service users understand and participate in health, safety and security risk'. At Level B that 'Assessment records record the participation of service users.' And at Level C that 'Service users are involved in review of health and safety and security policies and procedures.' It would therefore seem that advocates of client involvement would be well advised to start with the core standards. I would also contend that to do so is more likely to embed client and client involvement, rather than its being seen as something additional and 'supplementary'.

The involvement of clients at a strategic level in the Supporting People Initiative

Pay particular attention to very vulnerable and 'unpopular' groups, be based on Best Value principles and the Communities Strategy and could provide the basis for longer term arrangements for stakeholder involvement.

(ODPM, 2002: 6)

Aim for meaningful involvement and participation throughout strategy development processes. Do this by going to different service users and appreciating differences and needs, not setting up one off events.

(ODPM, 2005a: 12)

We can see from these earlier and later pieces of guidance that there is at least the intention to have meaningful involvement of clients at a strategic level. However, there is no compulsion to have it so, or more to the point, there are few adverse consequences if strategic authorities do not involve clients. As the Audit Commission noted recently: 'Although there is strong support for client involvement by the ODPM, the best local providers and the best authorities, no one has an automatic right to a service. Many are not in a position to push for their needs against those of others' (Audit Commission, 2005). They conclude that while more local determination may be desirable in many areas, on the subject of client and carer involvement, more of a government steer is needed (Audit Commission, 2005). Until then I would recommend the two reports by Helen Brafield for ROCC in Hampshire *Consulting With Hard To Reach Users of Housing Related Support Services at the Strategic Level for 'Supporting People'* and its accompanying guidance. I think, in finishing this section, her top ten tips for commissioners are worth repeating here, as I will come back to them later in the book:

- *Prefer independently collated views, statistically valid surveys etc. If this is not an option they can set standards for providers to meet if they are consulting on their behalf.*
- *Offer choice of methods of consultation in order to engage clients i.e. flexible times/methods of involvement and consultation including development of current District Inclusive Forums and working groups.*
- *Accept the validity of creative writing, drama, video, etc. as complementary qualitative information.*
- *Go out and see clients in their services.*
- *Offer practical partnerships for like agencies to set up independent client groups.*
- *Pay for consultation structures to be set up and run.*
- *Be clear about expectations, role and weight of views.*
- *Accept some clients are happy for staff to speak for them.*
- *Offer payment/reward for contributions.*
- *Set up mechanism for sharing good practice and establish common quality standards of client involvement in strategic planning.*

(Brafield, 2003: 8)

Arising issues: local and organisational policy slippage

Policy slippage is the gap between the intent of policy in legislation or government directives, and the implementation of such policy.

(Thompson and Wilson, 2005: 1)

There are many issues we could discuss about the difficulties that have occurred under *Supporting People*, with the lack of infrastructure for organisational change under conditions of often rapid organisational expansion being a major one (Van Doorn and Kain, 2006). However, in the context of client involvement, and given the discussion above, I think policy slippage is the most pertinent. Policy slippage is a well-documented phenomenon (Thompson and Wilson, 2005; McGregor and Sue, 1996) and it is where, in the process of implementation, the meaning of the policy changes. I think this is true of the implementation of *Supporting People*.

One consequence, which I have heard many workers in training relaying, is various myths about what the policy, in our case *Supporting People*, is making them 'do'. Examples might include that they have to have a residents' group, or that they have to allow clients into their staff meetings, or that they must have a client on the interview panel (who often end up being tokenistic and marginalised, a phenomena to be discussed later). If we refer to the standards themselves, we see that there are no such compulsions at all. The closest the standards come to recommending such things is in the Level A standards where it says: 'Forums and opportunities are available that enable clients to come together, to share experiences and determine what will meet their needs' (S1.2.2). Even in this case the guidance on client involvement is explicit that:

> *Evidence requirements in respect of service user involvement may need to be interpreted differently depending on the circumstances. Providers should be able to demonstrate that there are processes in place which are broadly equivalent to those required by the QAF (i.e. in terms of the results they aim to achieve) but which are more appropriate to the particular service users with whom they are working.*
>
> (ODPM, 2002: 13)

Part of the issue here is linked to the aforementioned theme of tensions between national directives and local interpretation. As one example, the diagram below illustrates the channels of communication and negotiation around *Supporting People*, the QAF standards and the local interpretations/strategies that pertain to them in Hampshire (this diagram only illustrates the direct and most *obvious* influences). Given this level of complexity we can see that there is scope for a myriad of interpretations of the standards and priorities within them. The two-way arrows are also somewhat optimistic given the competing agendas and strategic pressures that will come to bear on that interpretation.

Given the above it is no wonder that myths arise about what exactly *Supporting People* is expecting of organisations and workers. This would seem to be exacerbated by two factors (described by practitioners on courses); firstly, that local flexibility quickly becomes rigid and standardised and secondly, that there is a lack of communication and consultation between staff and management on the interpretation and implementation of standards.

Many practitioners and managers have reported, on training, how the review process has been problematic with rigid interpretations of how standards within the QAF are implemented. This seems to be one of the sources of rumours that organisations 'have' to have things like residents' groups or newsletters etc. This seems to be in spite of the fact that the guidance for authorities is clear about the importance of flexibility as illustrated below (a passage the reader may want to quote if they are encountering such difficulties):

> *There will be the necessity for Administering Authorities to use their discretion and judgement in applying aspects of the QAF to particular services and to take a pragmatic approach in assessing the evidence to comply with the QAF standards. The Administering Authority must understand the underlying principle of the QAF by asking what the framework is looking for and then determine a suitable interpretation that can be applied to the service in question.*
>
> (ODPM, 2002: 12)

So far we have noted this phenomenon, we now need to explain it; it is not good enough to just put it down to individual workers or its being an inevitable aspect of bureaucratisation (Midgely, 1986), although the later would seem to be a factor. Hanseth et al. (1996) note how in public policy there is a tension between the drive for standardisation and quality assessment and the need for local interpretation. In the case of *Supporting People* this tension is inherent.

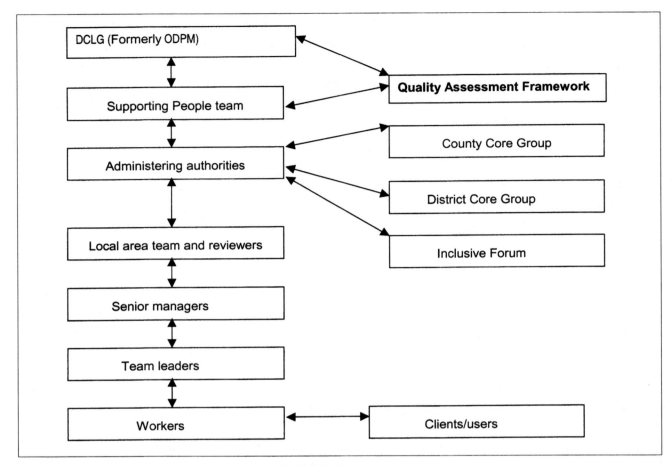

Figure 3.1 Channels of communication (Brafield, 2003)

While the aims mentioned earlier place an emphasis on the needs for standard and quality assurance, there is also an emphasis on flexibility and local interpretation of the QAF, as we have explored with other policies.

What seems significant in this case is the degree of local interpretation at a strategic level, as illustrated in the above diagram. It may be that such a degree of emphasis on local interpretation and priorities at this strategic level is counterbalanced by more rigidity at the organisational level of interpretation of the QAFs. In a similar vein, such local strategic priorities may necessitate a rigid interpretation of the standards to fulfil such set agendas. In a previous work (Seal, 2005), I explored how Jenny Edwards from Homeless Link (Homeless Link, 2000) feared that the recent cuts in *Supporting People* funding would mean that local authorities would be under pressure to cut funding to more high cost services – for example, to people with multiple need and complex issues, such as homeless people, who are less politically popular. The fact that such services are often situated in the voluntary sector exacerbates this tendency, as the local authorities' priority will often be to protect its own services. A rigid interpretation of the QAFs would be one way of achieving this.

On the other hand the tendency of the sector and workers to both distrust and resist evaluation and to avoid recording is a factor (Seal, 2006). Given that one of the main thrusts of the QAF, justifiable in my opinion, is that we should evidence the good work that we do, we are not helping our case here. We have a selling job to do here and all too often I hear practitioners give tales of being reactive rather than proactive, defensive of their practices rather than promoting of them. If we do not justify our practices and promote what we think is good practice in interpretation of the standards then interpreters of policy will go for what is obvious and understandable to them. On my courses I often make a plea for being more articulate about why we do what we do in the service of our clients, particularly when it deviates from a more obvious interpretation of the standards. One of the greatest tragedies I find about good client involvement is that it remains unacknowledged.

The second issue is the lack of communication and consultation between staff and management on the interpretation and implementation of standards. In all my training courses, including those on client involvement, I am startled by how few front line workers have a working knowledge of the QAF standards. I think this is the second source of the cries of 'Supporting People says we have to do this'. The guidance to the QAFs says that QAF can be used to promote a shared understanding of services and to create an environment in which informed planning of quality improvements can happen (ODPM, 2002: 9). To my mind this should mean that staff and management work together to understand, improve and evidence the good work that they are doing. The standards are punctuated with phrases like 'as appropriate to the client group' and the staff need to be involved in defining what this means, as they work with and have more intimate knowledge of the client group and what they will be responsive to.

All too often I hear tales of how front line worker involvement has been minimal in the operationalisation of standards. Workers are oblivious until they are suddenly told about changes in policy and procedures, often accompanied by new paperwork that people are told they have to use as they meet the standards. In the case of client involvement this takes the form of the myths already mentioned, of groups to be run and surveys to be conducted. As we shall explore in subsequent chapters, to operationalise something in such a way is often doomed to failure, or at least will mean workers have little ownership of the new processes. Many workers report struggling with, and often abandoning the new paperwork, and ignoring the new policies, citing them as irrelevant to their work, and to the clients. Ironically, this will often be picked up at the review stage where workers have little working knowledge of their own policies and the clients even less so, something cited as being important throughout the standards. Workers also need to take some responsibility in this area. Resistance to evaluation and paperwork on the part of workers (Seal, 2005, 2006), all too often means that they are happy to leave policy and paperwork to managers, even when they reject the end product. I think that a little more give is needed on both sides.

Conclusion

Hopefully, I have explored how many policy initiatives have the potential to support and act as leverage for those wishing to promote client involvement in supported housing. Returning to my opening quotes and recounting some of the points I have expanded upon in the chapter, the potential for policy slippage for *Supporting People* and all the other relevant initiatives, at regional, local and organisational levels is very real. Also real is the potential for the policy to be used for other ends, and for those agendas to skew its interpretation in certain ways that can bring pressure to bear at the level of individual providers. Finally, while working with it, I think we should retain a healthy cynicism for the intent and principles behind policy. Most of the policy initiatives over the past few years have made claims to have involvement and empowerment at the heart of them. However, as Groundswell has said, the trouble with client involvement is that it is hard to say you disagree with it. Unfortunately, this also means it can be easy to pay lip service to.

We explored previously how New Labour has a largely consumerist interpretation of involvement. Such emphasis on information, consultation and choice can be seen in the supplementary standards for empowerment in the *Supporting People* QAF. Critical perspectives, with more emphasis on the inequalities of power are not present. I spoke earlier in the chapter of Somerville and Chan's comments about the ignoring of power relationships at a local authority level. They level the same criticism at a governmental level. They suggest that to promote client involvement, but within distinct parameters, can be as much about containment as it is about empowerment.

> *The unspoken agenda here is clearly that of the maintenance of the status quo in terms of corporate power and class divisions. Individual rights are matched by individual responsibilities, and state duties are matched by individual duties, but what is missing from the whole approach is a matching of (national) state power by (national) state.*
>
> (Somerville and Chan, 2001: 8)

Indeed, if we examine the guidance of some of the policies mentioned, such containment is explicit, although couched in the terms of 'not letting clients down by allowing them to have unrealistic expectations.' As we can see from the guidance there is little acknowledgement of the power differential, or allowance of discussion about why the parameters of the debate are such as they are.

> *It is important too for service users to be clear about their priorities and to take a responsible attitude in recognition of the competing demands that authorities need to balance within the resources available to them. Authorities need to work with service users to develop a shared understanding of each others requirements and constraints. This will be important in avoiding unrealistic demands being made by service users.*
>
> (DCLG, 2001: s 35)

Part Two

Barriers Against, Principles Underpinning and the Power Dynamics of Client Involvement

4

Barriers to Client Involvement in Supported Housing

Historically, the two biggest barriers to client involvement in services have been professional attitudes and service's traditional inability to distinguish between 'consultation' and 'information'.

(Bryant, 2001: 5)

Workers often feel that homeless people are particularly hard to consult, because they may have chaotic lives, have other priorities, drop out of the service or leave it quickly. It is not clear whether homeless people are harder to consult than, say, young people.

(Welsh Assembly, 2004: 22)

When examining professional attitudes, such as the above, it is worth considering which of these are real or imagined barriers, conscious decisions or subconscious attitudes born out of the fear of challenge or change.

(Brafield, 2003: 8)

I remember training recently with a group of managers in Dublin on the subject of client involvement. I asked them the same question that this chapter seeks to explore, 'What are the barriers to effective client involvement?' The answers they gave did not surprise me. Many of them will be explored here, and included such things as resources, communication, client motivation, etc. However, it was the chief executive of the organisation who made me think. He just pointed at his head and said that the real barriers to client involvement were there. If there is one message I want to get over in this chapter it is that. As the quotations above illustrate, many of these barriers we perceive about client involvement are not the practical things we perceive them to be but are psychological and attitudinal. In my experience, the biggest barriers are actually fear and lack of trust, often wrongly labelled as mis-communication. Bryant gives a good example of this that we will explore later. The quote from the Welsh assembly is also telling. Many barriers, especially those of our own making or ones that are actually masks for other things, can very easily slip into being excuses, excuses for not doing anything. And that simply is not good enough.

This chapter will examine barriers to client involvement both horizontally and vertically. By vertical barriers I mean those barriers that may be particular to certain stakeholders, be they clients, front line workers, managers, the whole organisation and the sector. The wider political context has hopefully been adequately explored in the previous chapter. I will conclude by examining those horizontal barriers that go across different stakeholders such as resources and certain cultural and attitudinal barriers.

I am reminded of a discussion I have had with my co-trainer Jimmy, who you will hear more from in the conclusion to the book. We often discuss how agencies and workers seemed to make client involvement so complicated, intractable and alien, when in fact it is a fairly basic idea; that you ask people what they want and involve them in getting it. Brafield's comment above says volumes about why agencies and workers make things difficult in this way; if we are challenged by something we make it so complicated that it becomes impossible.

What this chapter will not do is to identify ways of breaking these barriers down. This is mainly because I think this is what achieving meaningful client and client involvement is actually all about, breaking down these barriers. Once we remove such barriers I think we are most of the way there. However, this is no easy task and it is therefore in removing the barriers that the majority of the work lies. Indeed, the rest of the book is dedicated to this task. It is only in Chapters 8 and 9 that I turn to the levels, techniques and methods of involvement, everything before builds up to this point and is about breaking down these barriers. This chapter therefore sets an agenda for the barriers people promoting client involvement need to take account of and ameliorate, before they even start considering what they want to involve people in.

Barriers for clients

. . . (regarding past failures in client involvement) Clients may have been interested, but anxious, or lacking in confidence, or suspicious about your motives. If this is the case, you will need to address these issues.

(Welsh Assembly, 2004: 23)

They will also come under pressure from other service users making it difficult for reps, for example, to set boundaries, that other residents can recognise. Unlike staff, they cannot leave their 'work' behind them out-of-hours.

(Novas-Ouvertures, 2004: 10)

There could be concern amongst clients that speaking out may have an adverse effect on how they are treated, that they may experience pressure or discrimination from the service provider or other clients – Personal confidence does have a part to play in motivation as often clients have expressed the view that they are embarrassed to ask for clarity of jargon, or concepts.

(Brafield, 2003: 12)

These quotes illustrate a multitude of barriers to client involvement, and I will return to them as I examine the barriers in turn. Clients will often have a suspicion about agencies and their motives for undertaking client involvement. As we discussed in the introduction, this can often be because agencies are not clear about why they are doing it and give out mixed messages about their motivations and intent. Following the second theme of the book, it is also because they have become disillusioned through previous experiences. This can then be compounded by workers labelling them as unmotivated, unrepresentative etc, something we will cover in the next section. In the face of this, it is no wonder that clients develop a cynicism about workers and agencies genuineness around client involvement.

However, I think clients' suspicion of agencies' motives, particularly for those 'hard to reach' clients, goes deeper even than this. We have talked about how clients in supported housing are not homogenous. However, Rowe found a common factor, for those who have been through the circuit a few times, of a 'complete break in trust with others, an obliteration of any remaining shred of a social contract between them and others' (Rowe, 1999: 82). Similarly, Geddes (2007) sees a characteristic of the refugee experience being a similar lack of trust, particularly of those who have power over them or associations with government officials. I remember running a consultation event for a local council on various policy initiatives. They wanted to reach several client groups including refugees and an event was run with a group of refugee women. For all the other client groups the model had been to get the clients to speak to councillors directly. However, despite numerous assurances, the group did not feel safe meeting such 'officials' directly, and we had to work using intermediaries.

Another barrier is how client representatives may be viewed by other clients. Jimmy, my co-trainer, both ex-homeless and an ex-drinker, saw the mentality of clients as a big barrier. There was a real feeling of mistrust of agencies and a 'them and us' mentality towards the 'straight' world, of which agencies and workers were seen as a part. It was a mentality borne out of institutionalisation. This would seem to link to the points made in both the Novas-Ouvertures and the Brafield quotes above. Those clients who engage in client involvement, often in the form of becoming representatives, are in danger of being labelled as having sold out, or at worst of being spies. On the other hand, representatives may fear being blamed by other clients if things go wrong. They may have too many expectations and demands placed on them, from both clients and services. These fears may well be based on people's previous experiences. Recently I was involved in discussions with clients' representatives in Ireland who reported such phenomena, with clients feeling bombarded by other clients and often transference of resentment if things do not happen immediately. The issue of agencies, and specifically managers, having too many expectations is one I will come back to. However, it is worth noting it is common for those clients who do get involved to do far too many hours and burn out.

The fear clients have about discrimination from the agency for speaking up, mentioned by Brafield, could stem from their inherent lack of trust in agencies, but may also have a basis in reality. In two recent pieces of research on developing client involvement (Groundswell, 2005; Kaur and Seal, 2006), clients who became reps saw themselves as putting their heads above the parapet, with an acceptance that there might be real consequences for them. Again, these worries may not be unfounded. Many studies have shown that people who 'speak up', even when they have been appointed to do so, are more likely to get labelled as a 'trouble maker' (Campbell and Wilson, 2005; Mind, 2004). Mind (2005) talk about how in the mental health field to question the services one is given often leads to one being labelled as non-compliant. Clients have talked to me in training and in research about how it can often take subtle forms in supported housing. Once a client starts questioning the service in what is not seen as 'the right' or 'a constructive' way, they can start being labelled as 'creating a bad atmosphere' or 'being a bad influence'. More subtly, it is at this point that their representativeness may be questioned. All are labels that, once one has been placed on a client, have personal consequences in supported housing.

Finally we can draw from the second half of Brafield's quote that confidence, self-esteem and self-belief can also be issues. I have covered in other works (Seal, 2005, 2006, 2007a) that those in supported housing often suffer from low confidence, low self-esteem and negligible self-belief. However, I contend that agencies and workers often leap to these issues first, and the more negative ones of apathy and lack of motivation in clients. I think this is because they are issues that can be located in the client rather than the agency, and means agencies avoid having to look at themselves too deeply. The other day I was discussing with a group of trainers the dynamics of being brought in, by agencies, to deliver support to client groups. We talked about how managers, who normally commission us, are occasionally a little misguided about the training needs of their workers. However, we thought that when it was training for clients this phenomenon was more extreme. We were normally asked to deliver training around confidence building and self-belief etc. In contrast, more often than not, the clients wanted to talk about all the other issues I have mentioned, lack of trust, fear of consequences and why this time the agency meant it when their previous experience of them was to the contrary.

Barriers for workers

Power is not an issue between clients (and workers) and client involvement is a distraction.

(Seal, 2007: 156)

Workers do have serious concerns that people become dependent on the hostel and they see that as detrimental to resettlement . . . (However) there is a need to experience and enjoy a positive period of dependence, in a reliable and secure environment where they can feel heard, and contained, before taking steps to move on into their own individual accommodation and for that move to be a successful one.

(Wyner, 1999: 4)

(The worker/manager culture) was based on a divisive 'them and us' attitude involving minimal contact and consultation, non-existent team work and the adoption of a 'restrictive practices mentality'.

(Smith and Wright, 1992: 34)

Perhaps the most common cry I hear on courses, from workers, is that clients are 'not motivated' or are apathetic about being involved. I believe this is mostly an erroneous construction of their own making, largely because it is an excuse for evading their responsibilities. However, I want to deal with this phenomenon in the section on the sector as a whole, as I have found it to be an endemic cry. At this point I only want to consider some of the attitudes, and the reasons for those attitudes, that may lie behind this cry.

The first quote is taken from a piece of research I was involved in recently (Seal, 2006, 2007b) exploring the views of workers in the field. Workers' opinions about the value and purpose of client involvement were mixed. As it says, 28 per cent of respondees saw it as a distraction from their real work of helping clients. This comes back to the debate in Chapter 1 about the purpose of our 'work', or more specifically, the most effective way of achieving it (I will not go over the argument that client involvement is central to achieving the goals of our interventions with clients, it is the seventh theme in the book and we will return to it many times). Positively, the research showed that the majority of workers recognise that client involvement is a means of getting people to believe in themselves, which is a key to their resettlement (Seal, 2007b). It could be argued that to have a figure of 72 per cent supporting client involvement is high, and to not to, goes against the general grain of the sector. However, as I said in that research, to have a sizeable minority opinion is potentially divisive and all too often gets played out in front of, and through the clients, compounding the aforementioned suspicions about workers' motivations. Many authors have noted (Seal, 2005, 2006; Smith and

Wright, 1992; Van Doorn and Kain, 2006), that the supported housing sector is practically orientated, seeing practical tasks as its main focus, not participatory processes.

This links into workers' view of power, which was predominantly that it was a non-issue. This is interesting, given the high prominence of power in clients' perceptions of the barriers to involvement, particularly the perception that speaking up could mean power will be wielded negatively against them. Workers blindness to issues of power is intriguing. Perhaps it stems from the aforementioned practical orientation of the sector and many workers. If we believe our role is simply about giving clients choices and helping them practically, rather than going into the more social, psychological and identity issues that other authors mention as important in our interventions (Seal, 2005, 2006, 2007b; Lemos, 2006; Dodson, 2006; Brandon, 1998), then issues of power could be seen as less of an issue. Why would people not feel able to speak to us when there are few power issues? Therefore, when they do not, it must be something to do with them, not the nature of our relationship with them. We will return to the issue of power in another chapter, suffice to say there seems to be a gulf between worker and client perceptions.

The ideas behind the Wyner quote represent an interesting spin off from this power dynamic and re-enforces the third theme of the book, that we have particular ways of constructing clients. In training, many workers and managers express a worry that client involvement may make people more dependant on the service, when what they should be doing is moving on. It is mirrored by worries that if a client becomes a little dependant on the worker then the worker has done something wrong, rather than the view that this is normal, even a sign that the relationship was a positive one (Meyersohn and Walsh, 2001). Wyner takes this further and questions the whole notion of dependency. On an organisational level, Wyner is viewing such dependency as normal, and a part of the therapeutic process. Such notions, which view coming out of supported housing and services as a process of recovery (Coleman, 2004), are very different from the aforementioned practical orientation of the sector and many workers.

The final quote is meant to encapsulate a more insidious barrier regarding workers, and a quite different take on the aforementioned power dynamic. I am always quite surprised to see that client and client involvement normally involve the two most disenfranchised parts (or at least those who feel disenfranchised), of the organisation talking to one another. If workers have a 'them and us' attitude about management and do not feel that they are listened to (Seal, 2005), then I would question whether they will able to instil any faith in the clients that they will be listened to, when they do not believe it about themselves.

In a recent piece of research I was involved in (Groundswell, 2005), some of the recommendations were to have greater involvement of, and consultation with, front line staff in service planning. We felt that if staff were not properly involved themselves, two things may happen. Firstly, they would be overt in their cynicism about management's genuineness about client involvement that would seep through to clients. Perhaps more insidiously, if they did see that the clients were actually being listened to, there was a danger of them, perhaps subconsciously but nevertheless in a real way, sabotaging client involvement. If they were not being listened to – why should the clients be? This phenomenon has been noted by many authors in many circumstances (Wilcox, 1995; Lukes, 1974; Foucault, 1986; Brandon et al., 1980), the disenfranchised resenting other disenfranchised people getting slightly more influence than previously, and it was felt quite real in this situation. I will return to the incident that sparked this recommendation in the chapter on power, suffice to say I do not think we experienced a unique phenomenon.

Before we examine managerial barriers I think it is worth listing some of the phrases workers and staff often use when questioning client involvement that embody the barriers we have talked about. These are taken mainly from Wilcox (1995) and Brafield (2003), with a few additions of my own. In training I give participants these 'excuses', and ask them what perceptions they think lie behind them and how they are going to counter them. To their credit, participants quickly become adept at coming back on such constructions. I will repeat some of their responses here.

Table 4.1 Top 10 excuses (and counters) for not having client involvement

1	Our clients just don't want to get involved.	*Everyone gets involved – the question is 'what do they want to get involved in?'*
2	We would raise people's expectations unrealistically.	*And raising expectations is a bad thing – isn't that for us to then deal with?*
3	Who is the client anyway? Aren't we all service clients.	*I think clients are pretty clear about the distinction and which side we're on.*
4	It would be too much of a burden for them.	*How is raising self esteem and being heard a burden?*
5	There just aren't the resources – it costs too much.	*What resources does it take to listen – how much do we put into things that don't work?*
6	Some people could never be involved it would be unfair.	*So we should ignore those who could get involved – we're all involved in something.*
7	We can't do it now, but we will sometime in the future.	*Great, let's talk timescales – and how do you feel when someone says they'll do it later?*
8	People just want to talk about what they can get, not wider things.	*Maybe that's because that's all they feel safe or able to talk about.*
9	It happens in our organisation all the time anyway.	*So let's start feeding that back to people better, because it's not what they say.*
10	It would be dependency creating, people just want a service.	*Giving something back is one of the first steps to getting your dignity back.*

Managerial barriers

(Of) 42 voluntary sector organisations over half the senior managers felt the biggest barrier to service user participation was clients' preferred interest in the quality of the service they received, rather than 'management issues'.

(Robson et al., 1997: 8)

Other barriers perceived were reported as service users' state of mental health, understanding of committee procedures, travelling, and lacking motivation.

(Brafield, 2003: 8)

I thought it worth distinguishing between organisations and management for it is a mistake to view them as synonymous. It is also worth noting that the barriers I mention in any particular category are rarely exclusive to them. The main thread that I think runs through both the quotes is a certain view of clients and how agencies therefore structure client involvement i.e. the third theme of this book. It constructs clients as not being interested in the strategic planning of organisations, and that they do not respond to our planning structures, such as committee meetings. It also betrays a view that behind this is a lack of motivation to go beyond their immediate needs.

Brafield (2003: 10) notes in her report the influence of Maslow's hierarchy of needs on this way of thinking, expressed via such views as 'The women have pressing needs now and no energy left for management issues'. I have noted in other books that Maslow's thinking has an undue influence on the sectors thinking, and actually serves to limit our expectations of clients and the potential levels of their thinking and interest. I also think that to say clients do not have potential interest in managerial and strategic issues is just patently untrue. Interviews with 57 homeless young people in Scotland found a desire amongst the majority for a greater say in service provision and resentment of their lack of a voice in decision making (Cummings et al., 2000). Yet a recent Scottish study found that amongst 371 organisations, none of them involved their young people in any decision making (cited in Velasco, 2001). Similarly, Emmaus UK 2000 found that 80 from 97 homeless and ex-homeless people wanted to be able to take part in day-to-day decision making in a shared living scheme (cited in Velasco, 2001). I think more pertinent are the ways in which we have tried to involve people and their experiences of wider involvement.

Implicit in the other quotes is the belief that clients need to change and learn how to respond in new ways to engage in strategic and managerial issues. I will return to the subject in the chapter on power, arguing that the way we plan and involve clients in this planning is not neutral but bound to our professional culture. The emphasis is put on the client to learn our languages, rather than for us to change them. The thought that it is clients who need to go through learning and change processes, is a lot less threatening than the thought that it is we who need to.

Organisational barriers

> Despite the interest in client involvement, most of what is currently on offer is little more than tokenism. There is evidence of a real interest in developing this approach but a lack of information about how to actually do it. This, and limits on resources, have hindered development.
>
> (Wyner, 1999: 5)

> Having provided your service users with a public platform for their views and opinions, be prepared to accept some very public criticism of your own organisation's shortcomings.
>
> (Novas-Ouvertures, 2001: 10)

Early on after its formation I remember the then co-ordinator of Groundswell, Jerry Ham, speaking at their inaugural conference and saying that if an organisation were to take client involvement seriously it had to accept three things. Firstly, that it would take resources, and that time and space were the most important of these. Secondly, that the organisation would be criticised and challenged in ways that it had not predicted and thirdly, that the organisation would have to be prepared to change, most fundamentally in how the organisation thought about itself. If agencies were not prepared to accept these things then client involvement will be tokenistic. We shall discuss at different points in the book how tokenism can manifest itself; at this point I just wanted to discuss the concept.

In terms of client involvement, tokenism can be seen as a policy of making only a perfunctory effort or symbolic gesture toward true involvement (Daly, 1998). However, this begs the question of what true involvement is and it is here that I think there are cultural clashes, as we saw in the first chapter and encapsulated in the fourth theme of this book. I think organisations often have a consumerist view of client involvement which excludes more democratic and critical forms of involvement. Barnes et al. (2003: 12) note that since the 1990s, there has been 'a growing emphasis on "markets" and private sector practices in the provision of health and social support services', both within statutory and voluntary provider sectors (detailed in Chapter 2). The significance of this is that the organisational and management drive has been towards achieving 'economy, efficiency and effectiveness' (Exworthy and Halford, 1999; Sanderson, 1999). Barnes et al. see this as having two significant impacts on client involvement. Firstly, managers have operational autonomy only within strict budgetary controls and performance targets. Secondly, it means that organisations operate within a culture that prioritises 'explicit standards and quantifiable performance targets, efficiency in resource allocation, and managerial control over the workforce' (Braye, 2000: 54). Many researchers (Fletcher, 1995; Ross, 1995), have found that managers strictly regulate client involvement to a consumer model. In contrast, Robson et al. (2005) suggest that clients only really value 'client-centred client involvement', which is more democratic and critical. Given this context, the whole approach of much client involvement, as Wyner says, is inherently tokenistic. It seems that many organisations' approaches also fail to create the resources and preparedness to change, outlined by Jerry Ham.

The point that Novas mention is related. Given a platform, clients may well criticise what they see as tokenistic client involvement. However, I think Novas are also illustrating another phenomenon, alluded to in the sixth theme of the book, that in the early stages of client involvement clients may well have a negative reaction to the agency that has involved them. In my experience this is a common phenomenon for agencies when they first involve their clients. For those who work in community and even organisational development, this is no surprise. Those who are disempowered can often develop a 'siege mentality', characterised by the mistrust that we discussed before (Hawkins and Shohet, 2006; Senge, 1990), and reactions to getting power not being one of gratitude but an outpouring of resentment, suspicion and negativity, often towards those who gave them some power. We will talk in the next chapter about how clients are often 'educated' to not believe in themselves. If our client involvement counters this, which it should, people may well get angry. Becoming aware of what power you have, and that you have been educated to not question things and not believe in yourself previously, will evoke such feelings. I would view that far from being a negative sign, some rejection and anger is a sign that the agency is doing something right, not wrong. I would go so far as to say that if such anger is not present, it could well be a sign that the client involvement is tokenistic.

Similarly, we rarely take account of group processes, even when much of client involvement is operationalised through groups. If we did we would realise that such storming is quite normal in group development (Brown, 1993; Tuckman, 1965; Johnson and Johnson, 1998), and in the development of marginalised groups, a period of rejection and polarisation is an understandable reaction to previous oppression (Cross, 2004), but also that it is a precursor to the group re-integrating and engaging in constructive debate. I think it a shame that many organisations abandon their client involvement initiatives, thinking they have failed when in fact such early reactions could be an indication that they are on the right lines, or seek ways to marginalise such 'negative' clients. We will come back to such considerations in the chapter on the process of involvement and in the final chapter on group methods. Suffice to say that organisational lack of knowledge of these processes constitutes a significant barrier.

Conclusion: sector barriers, the example of homelessness

Homelessness hostels in general could take a much more proactive and informed approach to client involvement and empowerment by incorporating ideas and processes developed by other sectors, but developing them in a way that is appropriate for the sector.

(Wyner, 1999: 45)

The attitude that doesn't recognise a client's capacity to develop and grow can only limit that growth and development, and engender a prejudiced view of what vulnerable people can and cannot achieve. If this is the case in the daily workplace then it is bound to restrict the expectations of exactly what clients can be consulted about. Such resistance needs to be worked with and broken down, so genuinely useful structures can be developed that allow and respect a client's right to participate and be consulted.

(Brafield, 2003: 8)

I have chosen sectoral barriers as the conclusion to this chapter as these are the horizontal barriers, mentioned in the introduction, that apply to all stakeholders. Sectoral barriers in supported housing would be hard to define accurately as it is such a broad field, but also a relatively new field. Therefore I want to talk about just one aspect of it, the homeless sector, as an example. This is partly because it is the sector about which I have the most knowledge and there has been recent work examining the characteristics of the sector. I also do not think that the issues facing the supported housing sector as a whole will be dissimilar.

Firstly, as noted in Chapter 2 our starting place is behind other sectors. Wyner notes that the homeless sector is one where client involvement is undeveloped and could learn a lot from other sectors. In the same vein, Velasco (2001) remarks that in the most exhaustive bibliography on homelessness to date (www.crashindex.org,uk), there were only four references to client involvement, one of which was American. In comparison, there were 54 references to access to housing and 70 to young people. Similarly, a European study on homelessness (Edgar et al., 1999), while seeing client involvement as 'a prerequisite for the development of the capacities for independent living', failed to find a single example of good practice. In terms of care leavers Big step found similar dissatisfaction amongst clients with their lack of involvement in care planning amongst care leavers (Big Issue, 2000). We also saw in Chapter 2 that other sectors have a longer history of client involvement. Yet, a common cry I hear from organisations is they do know how to 'do' client involvement, despite this wealth of examples from other sectors. This all begs the question why we do not look to the practice of others. Van Doorn and Kain (2006) recently examined the 'cultural anchor points' of the homeless sector. Several of these anchor points, and their consequences, seem relevant to this question.

Firstly, they note a culture that rejects other agencies, particularly statutory ones and professionals. While such perspectives also have a strong tradition in survivor movements (as we noted in Chapter 2), the cultural imperatives are of quite a different nature. They come from a belief in practical solutions and the importance of workers having the right attitude rather than expertise (Van Doorn and Kain, 2006). As we noted before, the former leads to a rejection of client involvement as a 'distraction' and issues of power as irrelevant (in direct contrast to the concerns of survivor movements). The later leads to burnout workers (Seal, 2006), macho attitudes, blaming others, particularly managers, *Supporting People* teams, other agencies and ultimately the clients for being 'difficult'. Most importantly here it leads to a sector culture that does not reflect on itself and its assumptions; we just 'do'. It is therefore no wonder that the homeless sector does not look to the lessons of other sectors. As Van Doorn and Kain say, organisations need to 'learn how to test the cultural assumptions out against the world around them and the needs of the client group, and enable whole organisations to adapt and change their culture in relation to meeting the client groups' needs' (2006: 128).

Brafield (2003) gives us another indication of how such cultures relate to the wider supported housing sector, and how it needs to change. Taking a 'practical' and 'common sense' view of the solution to clients' needs, something the whole sector does, labels clients as impractical and not having common sense. If the solution to clients' 'issues' were that easy, why would they need the sector at all, unless they were stupid? As Van Doorn and Kain say, such constructions underestimate the complexity of clients' issues. It also underestimates the sophisticated nature of clients' understandings of, and responses to, this complexity, when in fact these abilities demonstrate a huge potential and resource that could be worked with and be of benefit to the agency. If we have such a limited view of clients generally, this will also apply to how we view what they are capable of being involved in. I have rarely seen client involvement viewed as utilising a valuable resource but as something we should, or have to, do.

I will give an example of this sophisticated understanding that also illustrates clients' awareness of some of the barriers mentioned in this chapter. The diagram below came from a client during a drawing exercise I conducted with a residents' meeting. Residents' meetings are a typical client involvement mechanism used in hostels, normally weekly, that are optional and run by workers. Workers had complained that they found the subjects of discussion were limited to requests for objects such as dartboards, new TVs etc. The workers wanted to talk about other issues and made assumptions about why clients did not, similar to those that Brafield notes in her research, i.e. 'Clients get stuck in trivia and can't see the whole picture'. Clients were asked to illustrate 'why do clients in this hostel often only ask for things such as "Sky TV" in the "residents" meeting'. The picture illustrated this client's view that there were all kinds of barriers to more in-depth or meaningful discussions on both the part of the workers and the client but these were closed off to each other, the only thing that either party felt able to discuss was Sky TV.

Finally, I wanted to return to the idea of a blame culture as something to be avoided. Blame cultures are commonly defined as when stakeholders in the organisation blame one another for things that are going wrong (Bostock et al., 2005; Hanson et al., 2006; Marsden, 2006). I think it is a culture that is prevalent in supported housing regarding client involvement, and Van Doorn and Kain indicate as much in their research. Although, as Marsden (2007) says, it is something everyone will deny. I remember conducting training for a supported housing organisation on client involvement. I ran three training courses, one for clients, one for managers and one for workers. The managers saw the biggest barriers to client involvement as the lack of motivation in clients and that the workers were resistant to new ideas and any

---

Barriers to discussion in hostel XXXX

Workers	Clients
You scare me	You scare me too
I don't know what I'm doing	This place doesn't feel safe
If I tell you anything you'll use it against me	I'm not a grass
I don't agree with the policies either	Your policies don't make sense
I don't get on with my colleagues	I'm frustrated

Sky TV

Figure 4.1

change in their job descriptions. The workers felt that barriers were that clients were not interested and the managers would not listen to them, let alone the client, and were only doing it for *Supporting People*. The clients thought that no-one was sincere and so what was the point in engaging. This blame culture became an excuse for no one to do anything. As Marsden (2006) says, in a blame culture 'it's likely that more time will be devoted to avoiding responsibility and passing blame than will be spent on developing and promoting the business'.

For client involvement to work all parties need to start working together and breaking down some of these barrriers that lead to blame cultures. For this reason we recommend in the next section having 'champions', people who will take a lead on, and continually push for, client involvement in organisations. They will need to be at client, worker, management, senior management and board level, to stop such blame cultures emerging and persisting. This is not to say that there are no power differences and for that reason organisations also need firm commitment and leadership from the top on client involvement, something we will also explore more in subsequent chapters.

5

Principles Behind Effective Involvement in Supported Housing

The principle that users of services should be involved in decisions that affect them is now generally supported. However, problems of interpretation and practical implementation have led to frustration amongst clients and professionals alike.

(Philips, 2004: 3)

People who work in the sector tend to be very busy. This is partly because there is a lot to do, but also because people tend to do rather than reflect . . . The focus on action, however, tends to push out the space for thinking and reflection; a space where cultural assumptions can be questioned and new expertise developed.

(Van Doorn and Kain, 2006: 142)

This chapter takes the view that before we try to develop a strategy for client involvement, it is important to establish what principles should inform the development of any initiative. This should not be an academic exercise, the principles are things we should keep in mind when we are wrapped up in, or swept away by, the minutiae of practice. I think it is important to counter attitudes that see such an enterprise as unimportant. They are attitudes that I often encounter when running client involvement courses. The argument often runs along the lines of 'this is all very well but can't you just tell me what works'. While understandable, given Phillips' comments above, such attitudes miss the point for me on several levels. Firstly, they see client involvement as an event when it is as much a process, an attitude, an orientation (Groundswell, 2005; Bryant, 2003; Godfrey et al., 2003). Secondly, for client involvement to be effective, as the proceeding chapters have demonstrated, there are many subtle considerations that one needs to take account of. Otherwise what people have been told is 'what works' may not.

In countering these mindsets, it helps to know where they are coming from. Several authors have noted that workers in the supported housing sector are often of a mind to 'do for' rather than 'work with' clients (Bryant, 2001). Effective client involvement needs the latter mindset. Van Doorn and Kain (2006), and I (Seal, 2006), have noted both a worker predisposition for, and a strategic emphasis on, practical interventions. Similarly, the emphasis of the sector is on quick action, rather than basing interventions on the reflection and coherent models that client involvement needs (Van Doorn and Kain, 2006). This leads to further concerns about such approaches. As Van Doorn and Kain imply in another piece of research in 2003, the logical outcome of a strategic base on action is an equal emphasis on crisis responses. Client involvement, which necessitates a preventative, rather than a crisis response, has therefore been patchy.

A third, more philosophical concern, is the belief that such a positivist outcome is possible, or even desirable. To believe that one thing could work in all situations, or to even think we could isolate all the possible variables and come up with a formula is dangerous. I, and others (Cohen et al., 2000; Everitt, 1995), would see any attempt to apply such pseudo-scientific notions to client involvement as dehumanising and a denial of subjectivity. Furthermore, such an enterprise will only serve to hide power relations, for if the initiative does not work we will blame the tool, or the clients, and not look to ourselves.

Unfortunately, such positivist perspectives are re-enforced by a New Labour policy agenda that has emphasised Evidence Based Practice (SCYPG, 2001; Trinder and Reynolds, 2000), often in the most reductionist form by saying agencies should just replicate 'what works'. Trinder and Reynolds (2000) see the danger in such thinking, recognising that 'EBP remains firmly committed . . . to the modernist promise that phenomena can be assessed and controlled by expert knowledge'. EBP itself resists such reductionism despite being based in medical practice (Sackett, 1996), where such a positivistic, scientific perspective is understandable. There is even greater danger in applying the practice to the care field, since 'many medical outcomes are relatively easy to measure . . . in contrast, in the field of social care, outcomes are not always that explicit' (SCYPG, 2001: 15).

In the context of these concerns, the following principles are intended to aid people's critical reflections on their client involvement initiatives and help change our sector's culture from one of action orientation and of 'doing for/to' clients, to a reflective, process orientated one of doing 'with' clients. The principles are taken from a number of sources and come from a mixture of perspectives on client involvement. They are accessibility, educating people about participation, having a diversity of approaches, being comprehensive, starting at their point of interest, developing permission and protection, demonstrating potency and commitment and being conscious of space and establishing reciprocity. The practical application and limitations of these principles will be examined through looking at examples and case studies.

Believing in the importance of client knowledge – let people develop their own ideas and then speak for themselves

> *Service users have highlighted two activities as central to making client involvement work . . . (secondly) the need to make their voices heard, to be able to speak and act for themselves.*
>
> (Beresford and Branfield, 2006: 3)

> *Homeless people are part of the solution not the problem.*
>
> (Groundswell, 2006)

> *People think the only thing we know is how to moan. But they are not listening. We know what needs changing, what works and what doesn't work. We know this because we live it 24/7, 52 weeks a year with no days off.*
>
> (client quoted in Beresford and Branfield, 2006: 5)

For me, the first thing to grasp about client involvement is that it should be about supporting people to come up with their own solutions for their problems. It follows that we need to believe that clients can do this, and that their ideas, once articulated, will be as good, if not better, than ours. This belief is more than an article of faith; indeed it has a long legacy in the client movement (Barton, 1996; Beresford and Branfield, 2006; Campbell and Oliver, 1996; Oliver, 1996; Barnes et al., 1999). Such a belief goes across the consumerist, democratic and critical rationales for client involvement. However, I think the principle needs to be stated and acknowledged for two reasons. Firstly, despite some consensus on the importance of client perspectives and knowledge in the field, Beresford and Branfield (2006) describe in their report how client knowledge is still not taken seriously and is often devalued by services (for more information see Beresford and Branfield, 2006, in Refs). Suffice to say that many of the following principles are based on their findings and recommendations for how to strengthen clients' knowledge. Secondly, there are other perspectives. Client involvement could simply be about consulting one of the stakeholders in developing services. This is a view, but not one this book is based on. There are also practical implications of my stance. It means that one of our objectives for client involvement is to help clients develop their own views and be actively involved in articulating them.

Be accessible: offer practical help and skills development

Effective client involvement is inclusive and anti-discriminatory. Support and access should be provided to enable people to be engaged to the extent and at the level with which they feel comfortable.

(Godfrey et al., 2003: 16)

Service users have a right to the appropriate support to become involved and sustain, develop or withdraw their participation, as they choose.

(Bryant, 2001: 3)

. . . organisations frequently didn't understand access issues and don't make it possible for service users with a wide range of access needs to contribute on equal terms. They tend to interpret 'access' in its narrowest sense.

(Beresford and Branfield, 2006: 5)

Access works on three levels: people need to access *personal development*, to increase their expectations and assertiveness, *skills development*, to support them in developing the skills needed to participate and *practicalities*, such as child care, advocacy and transport. While the practicalities are indeed important, I will not dwell on them. This is partly because such considerations are a part of any event and are explored elsewhere. However, I would support Beresford and Branfield's contention that agencies tend to think only about accessibility in the narrow sense of practicalities, as in 'how do we get people there', neglecting other aspects. While this is not unsurprising given the previous discussion on our practical orientation, it can set up negative dynamics. I have been involved in a number of client involvement initiatives, normally events for tenants, where the concentration prior to the event has been on working out and enabling people to physically get there. The attitude towards 'why' they would want to is 'they will come if they are motivated'.

This emphasis on the practical even goes to the point that when clients do not come workers would start fetching them in a minibus from their accommodation, corralling those who happen to be around and bribing them to come. Even if this succeeds in getting clients there, having not attended to the other aspects of accessibility, they rarely find the event meaningful. It is equally important that clients feel there is a point to coming to such an event and that their opinion is one that is worth listening to. Clients may also need to develop specific skills such as being able to articulate their ideas and, depending on the structure of the involvement, speaking in public or being concise. These events often, consequently, become token, or even non-events.

Give support for those who get involved, preferably mutual support

Clients and carers can face increasingly unrealistic demands on their time. It is important that they find ways to support each other in setting realistic expectations, and are offered the sort of support that staff would have to take part in activities.

(Goss and Miller, 1995)

Service users have highlighted two activities as central to making client involvement work . . . (firstly) being able to get together to work collectively for change and mutual support.

(Beresford and Branfield, 2006)

I was in the Groundswell office recently and we were discussing an activist who had recently relapsed, in terms of his drug use, largely as a result of not being supported properly. We then starting listing all the activists we knew and struggled to find anyone who had not burnt out at some point through being involved in client involvement. As Goss and Miller indicate, should they not be offered the same kind of personal support that workers do? We have already detailed some of the demands and stresses that will be placed on activists from other clients and managers. When combined with the aforementioned feeling that if you speak up too much then there will be personal comeback or you will be labelled a 'professional client', we have the emergence of a very stressful role. Unfortunately, elsewhere (Seal, 2006, 2007a), I have detailed how the sector is bad at supporting its staff with burn out rates that are high even for the care sector. If it cannot support its staff, how effectively will it support its clients?

On top of this, clients may not see the importance of needing support and breaks. I have heard clients say that one should not need a break from something that is a passion. Only doing your hours, having holidays, keeping boundaries, not allowing your role to keep expanding, having appropriate outlets for your frustration and being allowed to have a little fun now and again are not things that will necessarily come naturally to clients and need to be learnt and taught. Many clients are effectively volunteers and so will not even have the succour of financial remuneration to ease things. While not underestimating people's skills and resilience, many clients are also vulnerable to start with, or have burn out before, or, thinking of the many drug clients I have worked with, are used to having an all encompassing lifestyle and are seeking to find another.

As well as raising awareness of these issues and developing the same supportive mechanisms for clients that staff have, or should have, we need to think out of the box. Beresford and Branfield say we need to encourage and facilitate mutual support and exchanges between clients, as this is what they value most. At Groundswell the thing that has proved most successful has been events where clients come together, either in the form of annual forums or, in particular, a programme of exchanges we have run where clients visit and then host other clients to learn and support one another.

Recognise people need education for participation

Services should be underpinned by a philosophy that clients are more capable, resourceful, gifted and enterprising than they themselves, and often others, realise.

(Godfrey et al., 2003: 29)

Inequalities in knowledge, resources and power were undeniable but conscious efforts to put these on one side to enable an honest exchange of views were crucial for enabling change.

(Robson et al., 2005: 13)

(The) prevailing consciousness is internalised by the population (and) . . . becomes part of what is generally called 'common sense' so that the philosophy, culture and morality of the ruling elite comes to appear as the natural order of things.

(Boggs, 1976: 39)

Brafield (2003) mentions an organisational frustration that clients 'get stuck in trivia and can't see the whole picture'. I have talked in other books (Seal, 2005, 2006) of Friere's (1968) concept of conscientisation. He believed that people had been educated to not believe in themselves, not to analyse their predicament and not to question wider issues. It was in the state's interest that the poor did not think about their situation, lest they do something about it. Boggs above shows how this gets subsumed in notions of 'common sense' which actually support the status quo, the ruling elite, and, in our case, the prevailing regime in supported housing.

People need to be educated to be able to examine their situation, to understand what has happened to them and why. You cannot just ask people what they want, people have to learn how to ask, analyse and question what they have first. In youth work the naive question posed to young people of what they want to do is commonly met with a response of 'dunno'. Returning to the 'Sky TV' syndrome mentioned at the end of Chapter 4, sometimes it is simpler than the picture that clients drew. Sometimes people only ask for Sky TV because that is all they know how to ask for. To learn how to articulate needs and wants takes development. This is not because people are stupid but is because many institutions that people in supported housing have been subject to have actively undermined people's confidence and belief in themselves, the capacity to think for themselves and look beyond their immediate needs. These processes need to be undone before effective involvement can take place.

This highlights a common danger in operationalising client involvement. If this education does not happen people may well just agree with what the agency wants them to. I have seen 'consultation processes' happen, say on things like house rules for shared accommodation where the clients mysteriously come up with the kind of rules they are subject to already, or even more draconian versions of them. I have also seen clients on management committees being talked out of their ideas by more articulate board members, or even simply acquiescing in any of the proposals put to them.

Have diversity: no one model will work for all

All service users have a right to choose not to be involved and to change their minds if things change for them.

(Bryant, 2001: 3)

There is no single model for effective client involvement. Clients are not homogenous and there will need to be a multiplicity of methods and ways of their being involved; this is linked to valuing diversity. Importantly, all methods of involvement will allow certain groups to dominate and this must be acknowledged. No model will work for everyone and it is important to work out whom a particular method will favour. For example, when working with homeless people I was involved in the development of 'Speakouts'. These were originally intended as a counter to the somewhat patronising annual 'sleepouts' that some charities and campaigning organisations organised whereby people sleep out for a night, supposedly to show some kind of solidarity with homeless people. Speakouts were alternative events that brought homeless people together with policy makers and politicians to discuss the issue of homelessness, and allowed homeless people to express their concerns, needs and desires.

In my experience they tended to favour vocal people and were often male dominated. This is not to say that they were wrong, just that they did not suit everyone. I mentioned in the last chapter that for the group of refugee women we were working with, this would never have worked; to expect them to meet officials face to face was not realistic. Similarly, we found that young people, and in particular young women, did not want to air their views in a public forum and instead found local councillors holding surgeries as more appropriate to their needs.

Bryant makes another point. Some people will want more, or less, active involvement and may well choose to move between the level of involvement they want over time. To give another example, I was involved in a piece of work for the housing charity St Mungos, which provides a multitude of services for various client groups. Initially, we concentrated on involvement in the running of the supported housing projects. Those in semi-supported tenancies were not interested in this and were initially labelled as being a hard to reach group for whom client involvement was not a priority. However, the project had a large element of peer research whereby we trained clients up to research into each others' perceptions of client involvement. The majority of these volunteers came from the semi-supported projects. Similarly, clients in the mental health project were less interested in the day-to-day running of the hostel but wanted to be involved in their own treatment and supporting each other. At the other end of the spectrum, there was a project for older people, most of whom would be there for the rest of their lives. It was thought that these clients would not be interested in client involvement and indeed most said that they really just wanted to be looked after, did not want to volunteer or have key working. However, they really valued a reminiscence group the project ran and in using this medium we got really valuable information about what it is like to go through the care system, how it has changed, what they had valued in services and what they thought constituted a good worker.

Be holistic: seek to involve people in all aspects of the work

Client involvement will achieve the aims of Supporting People where it is not a separate activity, but an approach to working with people that is integral to the culture and ethos of the service and the working practices of all staff.

(Godfrey et al., 2003: 17)

This, one feels, is a little idealistic and is the one that many people in training criticise. However, as Godfrey et al. (2003) say, being holistic is not necessarily about clients being involved in everything and is more a culture, in that we consider the client angle in everything we do, at every stage of an ideas development, and that to do so should be our starting point. I sometimes make a parallel with how workers and organisations have changed in their thinking about risk assessment. When I started as a worker it was rarely if ever done and only in retrospect. It then moved to people recognising that they needed to do risk assessment but they still did not really value it or make it integral to their work. It was more a case of being one task amongst many that needed to be done and was thought of sometimes as something that often got in the way of the 'real work'.

Now risk has become a thing that people consider at every level and stage of their work. When we do anything we have to consider the risk element (although this can be a source of complaint for some workers). I think this is how we should think about client involvement. I think many projects are at the second stage, thinking of client involvement as something that they need to be able to say they have 'done', rather than something that they see as integral. Hopefully, we will eventually move to the last stage, considering how to involve clients in our deliberations for any work we are undertaking.

Be bottom up: start at the point of interest for the clients

User involvement should be 'grown' and nurtured, starting from clients' immediate needs, interests and concerns, expanding and deepening in iterative fashion.

(Godfrey et al., 2003: 15)

All service users have the right to be involved at a level that they feel is appropriate to them and their circumstances at the time.

(Bryant, 2001: 3)

As my training partner Jimmy says; 'if they can't sort out the sausages, why would anyone believe they could sort anything else out'. Bryant (2001) similarly observes that 'services often ask the question "why won't our clients get involved?" A better question might be "why on earth would our clients want to get involved?"' On a base level the point is that we have to start at the point of interest of the client, rather than our own. On our training courses we ask participants to introduce themselves by saying what motivates them. The answers are various, from family to hobbies, to sport to politics. We all have interests and good client involvement will tap into them. Would we become involved in something that we are not interested in?

The point may sound obvious but I have been surprised how many agencies start at their points of interests rather than the clients. I recently worked with a London Drugs Action Team that set up a client group to specifically comment on their five year strategic plan. Perhaps this was their interest, but the fact that they brought me in because their client group was not working seemed to indicate otherwise. Often joint meetings with clients are full of agenda items from workers. Perhaps clients did not put anything on the agenda, but this begs a different question. Some clients will not be interested in strategic issues initially for the reasons explored earlier in the chapter; they cannot see their relevance. Some clients may never have an interest in these issues, as many workers do not, and I suspect many in strategic meetings do not. We will discuss this in more detail when looking at levels of involvement, where agencies have an intention to involve clients in strategic planning. For now the point is, as *Supporting People* themselves say:

Involvement should start from an understanding of, and a willingness to respond to, the immediate needs and concerns of clients i.e. what is important to them as opposed to what may be the interests and concerns of providers.

(Godfrey et al., 2003: 14)

As a counter to this, Jimmy and I are currently writing an article about the dangers of working with only the few clients who do develop an interest in these areas. In it, we outline the dangers of relying on certain clients. It can mean that we do not do the developmental work of building capacity in other clients, or look at other avenues for involvement. If we do not change our approach to engage with clients at their point of interest, we ultimately run the risk that those clients who do engage at this level become unrepresentative and burnt out.

Cultivate permission and protection

Perhaps the overarching theme that I came across in the accounts of homeless people was that of a complete break in trust with others, an obliteration of any remaining shred of a social contract between them and others . . . In early encounters, though, trust is more of an all-or-nothing proposition.

(Rowe, 1999: 67)

This principle develops on from the second principle in that as well as people needing to feel that what they have to say has worth, that they also need to feel free to say it and be confident there will not be any comeback if they do. We first encountered Rowe's thoughts on trust in Chapter 2 when we explored how much of a barrier trust can be for people in supported housing, particularly those marginalised and hard to reach groups. To develop this trust will take time; it is not enough to say 'trust me'. Many clients have a history of being let down and will not just give trust, it needs to be earned.

Given Rowe's comments, I would recommend being ultra cautious about this principle in the early stages of a project. This is why I would make the third practice theme in this book, that where possible agencies should use independent people as facilitators and advocates, preferably utilising clients and ex-clients. Clients will need spaces where workers are not present and clients can talk freely on their own and develop their own ideas. Given the discussion in Chapter 2, there may always be a level of distrust when a worker is leading a session, simply because they are workers. It does not matter how open and trustworthy the worker considers themselves to be, and even genuinely are, this is not the point. I have worked with several supported housing organisations, where there has not been some independent intervention or facilitation. Workers have assured me that there will not be comeback for clients. Even when this is true, clients still talked about speaking out as putting their heads above the parapet.

I believe that clients felt able to say these things to us because they felt we were independent. Our independence was real but also symbolically powerful. As an illustration of the importance of this independence, I will talk through the characteristic reactions I have got from clients in the initial stages of a typical piece of work I have undertaken with Groundswell. In these early stages, clients often probe the nature of the relationships between the organisation and myself and are suspicious because they are paying me. This is why we are insistent that what the clients say to us remains confidential and that we will negotiate what they want feeding back to the organisation. Some time is spent on ground rules to ensure they have some confidence in the process. Where possible we use other clients and ex-clients as facilitators. This is not necessarily because they make better facilitators. It is again similarly important in a symbolic sense, and can acknowledge the degree to which there can be a 'them and us' divide between workers and clients. Even where the aim may be to break these perceptions down, we need to engage with clients at the point where they are and work them towards being able to come together with staff.

Demonstrate potency and commitment

Effective involvement requires imagination, creativity, energy and commitment to engage people effectively, and openness to respond positively to the demands for change that flow from it . . . client involvement requires careful nurturing. Minor successes can be hard won, but they may be the building blocks for greater achievements.

(Godfrey et al., 2003: 16–17)

The long and often slow process of change was usually driven by the persistent actions of leaders, both clients and managers, to optimise the enablers of change and to overcome the barriers to change.

(Robson et al., 2005: 14)

Participatory processes should have sufficient power to achieve the agreed objectives. This may require a change in the existing power sharing arrangements.

(Involve, 2005: 12)

Potency is an interesting theme. In a previous piece of work (Seal, 2005), I noted that many clients do not necessarily want or expect world shattering changes, just that agencies do what they say they will. Clients will cease to be motivated to take part in consultation exercises if they do not receive feedback as to what has taken place as a result of their input. Clients have repeatedly said in training they felt that a 'no' decision was better than not hearing whether a decision had been taken at all. On a slightly different point, we often accuse clients of being unrealistic, but who is being unrealistic is a moot point. I remember one client saying that one of the reasons he distrusted client involvement initiatives was that they were often asked daft questions like 'what would an ideal service look like' and then they would hear nothing back. The one initiative he valued was when his complaints about the food were listened to, or at least it was explained to him as to why things were not going to change.

One of the difficulties, depending on the nature of the accommodation project, is timescale. Given the time many agencies may take in operationalising changes (Argyris, 1990), clients may move on before their suggestions are acted upon. While this may ultimately call for changes in planning structures, in the meantime this just means we change the way we put things to clients.

When undertaking consultancy with clients, I will often say that the fruit of what they are doing may not be of benefit to them, but to the clients that come after them. In the main, people are fine with this, to not think so falls back into a trap, labelling clients as incapable of altruism. Much research challenges this notion (Fry and Dwyer, 2001; Kaminsky et al., 2003; Velasco, 2001). Even if we buy into this negative view, many clients are also realistic in knowing that, unfortunately, this may not be the only housing service they go through (Seal, 2005; Randall and Brown, 2002). This can be particularly difficult in an emergency agency, where clients do not stay long. However, I know such an agency that make a point, when a client makes a suggestion that results in a change, of telling other agencies that the person still uses and their street teams, to pass on this fact if they meet the client. It is amazing how word spreads through the client grapevine about this, developing a good reputation for client involvement for the agency amongst clients.

Positively, I believe that in many agencies clients inform decisions all the time, in an organic informal way. A client may talk to a worker, which then informs that worker's discussions with their manager, which then informs that persons decisions or discussion higher up, which may eventually lead to a change in policy. Unfortunately, agencies forget to close the loop and go back to that client to inform, or even thank them. This is a great shame as such things, as Godfrey et al. (2003) say, are building blocks for other things. For this reason, in training, I get people to examine how clients already inform decisions informally, and to consider how they can acknowledge this, before they consider anything new.

I will return to the issue of power in the next chapter, and we have already considered it as a managerial and organisational barrier. I would take Involve's comments further and say that organisations should *demonstrate* that they are prepared to change, fundamentally, in how they organise and plan services. It is for these reasons that I recommend starting an initiative with a demonstration of some kind of power shift; such as creating a space on the management committee or a clients' committee. This is not because they are necessarily the answers, and indeed they may not come to fruition, but they are a symbolic gesture that the agency is serious. It is therefore important that the gesture is something that the clients see as symbolic and important, not necessarily the organisation. Indeed, as we shall see in the next chapter, it could even involve getting rid of an existing structure for involvement.

Finally, commitment also needs to be *demonstrated*, and in this case both symbolically and in reality. We will see in the next chapter how the idea that power is concentrated in senior management is a myth. However, many clients believe this to be so. Therefore, as our first practice principle states, commitment must be secured, and be seen to be secured from senior management. That they have power is also not all myth. Robson et al. see leadership as being crucial for successful client involvement, both from within the organisation and amongst the clients, and this is backed up in most reports on client involvement (Brafield, 2003; Novas-Ouvertures, 2001; Godfrey et al., 2003). Brafield notes that there are different kinds of leadership, and that an open supporting one is needed for client involvement. This is another reason for our second practice principle; that of having champions. If there is a named person at all levels of the organisation, who has received specific training and support and has a specific remit for client involvement, the open support will be there, and importantly, be accessible, for there will be more than one person to turn to. In the area of diversity, the idea of champions is common place (Stonewall, 2006). To have them challenges the view that diversity and client involvement should be everyone's responsibility. While this is true, if no one takes responsibility then such issues are not taken forward, or if they are, then it will be by interested parties i.e. champions, except that they lack acknowledgement and support and, often power.

It is crucial that there are champions at all levels of the organisation, and preferably there are more than one of them at each level. This is to acknowledge and ameliorate the truth in the criticism above. To give a specific person remit for client involvement can mean everyone else stops taking responsibility. I think the important thing is to have a critical mass of champions. It is their job to push the issues and ensure that others take responsibility.

As an illustration of what can happen without this, in many of the larger organisations I have worked with they have employed a co-ordinator for client involvement. They are normally middle-to-low rank in terms of managerial responsibility and often have a 'ready-made' client group to 'lead'. All too often this means that no one else in the organisation takes responsibility for client involvement, and that one person is expected to do everything regarding client involvement and, more worryingly, 'make it work'. I think this underestimates the level of personal and organisational resistance they may encounter in trying to do so (Argyris, 1990). They often end up feeling token and resentful, and become marginalised and burnt out, having been blamed when the resistance and lack of responsibility of others have stalled a client's initiative. Client involvement, or indeed any idea that needs change that threatens the prevailing culture of an organisation, needs to pushed for at all levels, including, crucially, a champion at senior management level.

Recognise the importance of setting, abandon the idea of 'neutral space'

> *More client-centred activity occurred where leaders created space for clients and staff to debate client involvement, to develop and try out ideas, and stepped aside to make space for individual clients and client groups.*
>
> (Robson et al., 2005: 12)

> *Washing one's hands of the conflict between the powerful and the powerless means to side with the powerful, not to be neutral.*
>
> (Freire, 1968: 98)

Broadly this is the idea that the concept of space is important but that the idea of 'neutral space' should be abandoned. Space and place has been recognised as important to how any group of people sees and defines itself (Anderson, 1991; Smith and Jeffs, 2001; Cohen, 1985). It then follows that the person who controls this space, and any space in which we try and bring communities together is an important consideration (Avruch and Black, 1991; Burton, 1987; Hoggett, 1997; Lederach, 1997). In supported housing we should take the involvement processes to the clients own space, rather than a neutral one, as this acknowledges that the power differential between the two groups is in the workers' and organisations' favour. This principle is probably best illustrated through an example, as I believe that the way we construct events, and the structures for involvement as a whole, are often done for organisational convenience rather than for the benefit of the clients.

I worked with a certain London local council who used to hold a 'homeless liaison committee', ostensibly for homeless people. It was held in council chambers, had the same structure as their other committee meetings and was controlled centrally by committee services. The council seemed genuinely surprised that homeless people did not attend. (We later found out that the usher was unlikely to have let them in anyway.) Their initial starting point was to ask how they could 'motivate' people to come. We worked with them to see that this set up was one they felt comfortable in, that they understood and which only served to intimidate clients and reinforce the attitudes they already had about the council.

The council then wanted to hold the meetings in a 'neutral space' i.e. one that was unfamiliar to both sides so they could meet on an equal footing. While this would have undoubtedly been a step forward, we argued that this still misunderstood the power dynamic.

We argued that disempowered people, at least initially, need to have this power balance redressed in their favour to feel they are getting back on an equal footing (Friere, 1968; Illich, 1977). We ended up holding the events in homeless day centres and places where homeless people felt comfortable. Homeless people arranged the structure of the meeting so that they felt comfortable, and occasionally so that the councillors felt deliberately uncomfortable. I remember at one event the young people insisted that the councillors wore casual clothes, and sat in a circle to be asked questions and that there was no agenda, whereby people talked about what they felt moved them. As a parallel we covered in the previous chapter how accommodation providers often hold client meetings at times of their own convenience and structured in a way that they understand, rather in way that privileges the clients' understanding and starting points. It is this tendency that needs to be thought about and countered.

Reciprocity: being clear how being involved has value for all parties

Service users have the right to expect respect for their contribution.

(Phillips, 2004)

People may be encouraged to be involved, and even paid for involvement, but effective participation requires them to choose to be involved.

(Involve, 2005)

This principle is based on the idea that we should be clear what clients and 'involvers' get out of the process. Lawyers call it 'valid consideration' (Seal, 2005), and have it as an underlying principle of their working contracts with clients. The concept implies that clients may be suspicious and feel undervalued if the 'involvers' reason seems too philanthropic. Using a previous example, sometimes it may be more empowering for clients to know an organisation is undertaking client involvement because *Supporting People*, or some other external force, is driving them to. I think this is sometimes better than the organisation feigning altruism, giving the message that it is happening because the worker is a nice person, or the organisation is benevolent. I think that for a client to know that the organisation will get into trouble if they do not do client involvement potentially places more power in the clients hands than if the worker or organisation is doing it because they choose to. In the latter case, it is the organisation that retains the power over how far client involvement goes or what is listened to, without comeback.

Value brings up the issue of incentives. In training, people are often obsessed with whether clients should get incentives or not. As Phillips says, it should be about giving them respect for the value of their contribution. If the client gets something back we are, at least symbolically, valuing what they say. I am in great favour of giving people money. This can worry some organisations as they argue that they may spend it on drugs, etc., and argue that we should give people vouchers. I think this is a patronising argument; if someone really wants to spend it on drugs they will just sell their voucher and get slightly less drugs. If the issue is handled badly, clients may also see it as some kind of bribery.

People often give incentives in the form of food for an event. I think this is fine but people often get caught in the trap of underestimating their client and thinking people 'just turn up for the food'. I can understand this, but I think it misunderstands the dynamics of the situation.

I would often pay people, say, £5–10 for a two-hour session, yet this is still only a token acknowledgement. It normally took up the best part of a day for a client, when one considers travelling time. Many clients I worked with could make a lot more money than this in a day! It was actually costing them to be there. Ultimately, I think people should be paid a decent amount for their contribution, and I am in favour of paying wages, but this is another story and brings up lots of questions about how we recruit etc.

Going back to our perceptions of clients' motivations, it is understandable that workers often think clients are only after the money, because this is often what clients told them. However, I think there is another dynamic at play here. I will give an example, but first I need to outline another debate about giving money for attendance, whether you give it out at the start or at the end of a session. Common wisdom was to give it at the end to stop people leaving once they got paid. This again seemed understandable as in similar sessions clients normally asked me if they could 'leave yet' throughout the session. I once paid people at the beginning, thinking this was more respectful, and I said to them that they could leave at anytime. I myself misunderstood the dynamics of the group as this was actually more threatening to them. In doing this they then had to admit, even just to themselves, that they were staying because they were interested, denying them the opportunity to say to their mates that they had only been there for the money! I had forgotten that many clients have an ethos of rejecting us and I was challenging this, opening up this to scrutiny too quickly and bluntly. Perhaps a useful thing to do at some point, but that was not my aim.

Conclusion: Recognising that involvement is an ongoing, ever evolving process

I want to finish this chapter on an overarching principle that I think encapsulates, and comes back to, my introductory comments. As such, it is normally the principle I start with on a course, combined with the principle that clients' knowledge is important. From these principles flow the fifth and sixth themes of the book; that client involvement takes time and resources and will evolve in ways we cannot always predict. I also think all the other principles flow from these two principles. It is only through recognising that client involvement is an evolving process that we recognise the other points; that access is as much about support and self-belief as practicalities; that people need to learn to articulate their needs (having been educated not to); that we should also consider the perspective of clients in everything we do and recognise that we will need a multiplicity of approaches to gain these views; that we will need to start where clients are at, rather than doing what is organisationally convenient or just relying on the obvious candidates (though we should not demean their contribution); that people need to feel free from retributions and we need to help them rebuild a trust that has been eroded in them; that we should acknowledge and build on what we do well rather than always going for the 'big event' but that there is the possibility for fundamental change; that we need champions, rather than relying on everyone to take responsibility or putting everything onto one person; and finally, that we should recognise that space and ownership is an issue, and that the balance of power is on our sides, necessitating a change in us, rather than the clients. I think Godfrey (2003) says it well in the quote I'd like to finish on, and it bodes well for *Supporting People*'s take on the matter.

> *. . . client involvement is not only about setting up structures and systems for consulting with people although that is part of it. It is a complex, fluid, dynamic and negotiated process . . . Involvement does not have a fixed end point. Rather, participation is 'both a journey and a destination: a way of doing things and an end result.*
>
> (Godfrey et al., 2003: 17)

6

Making Sense of Structures: Power, Influence and Managing Stakeholder Interests

There are issues of power and dependence in the relationship between service user and professional, or service user and carer that need to be understood.

(Cameron et al., 2005: 12)

Each profession assumes a language, a set of values and practices that privileges the practitioner. Hitherto, a clear division between the expert-provider and lay-client has reinforced their enhanced status.

(Barnes et al., 2003: 24)

Some people will want – or demand – more involvement than others. Others will wish not to be involved. Identifying these different interests – stakeholders – and negotiating the level of participation appropriate is the third dimension of the framework.

(Wilcox, 1995: 8)

This chapter will cover two related themes, how power and influence flow in organisations and how to manage different stakeholders' interests. Anticipating Cameron et al.'s thoughts above, we have already touched on the importance of considering matters of power in both Chapters 4 and 5. This chapter is predicated on the fifth theme of the book, that client involvement will entail fundamental changes as to how the agency functions and relates to its clients. This will mean a shift in the balance of power. As Linnett says: 'The purpose of client involvement should be to change the balance of power in an organisation' (Linnett, 1999). However, before we can do this we need to develop a model of power. This is the intent in the first half of this chapter, to expand on Marsh et al.'s thoughts and examine the various dimensions of power within organisations in relation to client involvement. .

I will develop a model of power that builds on the critical perspective on client involvement outlined in the introductory chapter. It will show how power, building on the work of Lukes (1974) and Thompson (1998), operates on three levels, overtly, covertly and institutionally or structurally. The Barnes quote above gives an example of how institutional and structural power manifests, perhaps in one of its most powerful forms, language. I also think it is important to challenge the construction of power that many workers have, that power is both finite and concentrated (Foucault, 1986; Giddens, 1996). Regarding the latter I will seek to make a distinction between power and influence and show how they can be viewed as a circuit that flows, and which can be influenced in unexpected and indirect ways. I will finish this first section by exploring a case study of how organisational power flowed in an organisation I worked with and then how we changed the direction of this flow.

The second section examines another dimension of power; managing the different priorities and interests of different stakeholders. As Wilcox states, some people will want, or demand, more involvement than others while some will wish not to be involved. It is what we do with this situation that is the question. In examining stakeholder interests I will define stakeholder as being beyond the client, the worker and the agency, and that it includes others like the community and other agencies. It will argue that identifying the different interests of stakeholders and negotiating the level of participation appropriate is an important dimension of the work, particularly if we are to go beyond tokenistic or symbolic client involvement and want clients to have real power and influence.

Section one: Overt, covert and structural uses of power

Luke (1974) sees power as having three dimensions. Overt power is where one party exercises control over another in a demonstrable way, such as when a worker and a client have an argument and the client ends up getting excluded by the worker for 'aggression'. Thompson calls this the 'personal' level of discrimination, as it normally involves individuals. An example in client involvement could be when an individual, who may be simply advocating a view, is accused of stirring things up. More subtly, returning to our first example, it could be where a manager, altercating after the argument, gives more weight to the worker's version of the event. Another manifestation is when a client starts to express challenging views, and the organisation starts questioning how 'representative' they are, when this had not concerned them previously (McGreggor, 1980), a phenomonen Campbell met with in survivor groups.

These later examples border on the second form of power, the covert or hidden dimension of power, where certain views or perspectives are excluded or marginalised from the decision making process. For Thompson (1998) this level is often expressed culturally in the conventions we have. In terms of client involvement it can be common worker projections about clients such as they are not motivated, not interested, would only do it if they get something out of it, etc.

The third structural dimension is where certain interests or views are institutionalised within society or an organisation. Power structures or views of 'common sense' are accepted and internalised without question or recognition. An obvious example of this is where workers determine the things that go on the agenda for discussion in client groups or will only consult on certain things. A more subtle example of this phenomenon discussed before is when a resident meeting only covers things like 'Sky' television, burying the fact that people do not feel able to put other things on the agenda, not that this is their only interest. A more institutional version of power is the culture that exists between clients and workers that goes unspoken, such as the idea that we should not tell clients anything about ourselves because they will use it against us. In terms of client involvement many of the power dynamics are institutionalised. They are encoded in the language we use and determine the structures we create for that involvement.

To develop an example, we noted in Chapter 4 that agencies often believe it is clients that need to change and learn how to respond to engage in strategic and managerial issues. I think Barnes earlier cast some light on the dynamics of this, it is a power issue linked to professional culture, where the emphasis is put on the client to learn this new language. The starting point for many managers is how to enable clients and clients to engage in their structures, rather than them asking themselves how they will need to change their structures and methods of planning to incorporate clients' culture and languages. Robson et al. (2005) distinguish between 'management-centred client involvement' – clients taking part in existing structures with the agenda defined by the organisation – and 'client-centred client involvement' – where clients' objectives and priorities became the organisation's objectives and priorities. They also found that clients only valued the latter.

As a trainer, I am often brought in to 'teach' clients skills such as how committees work, how to chair meetings or draw up agendas etc., the reason being that most client groups are structured like team and committee meetings, with chairs, agendas, a set format of contributing and minutes. However, who is this a familiar model to, managers or the clients? As a contrast, I remember working with a squatter movement some years ago and the way they conducted meetings was very different. The first ten minutes was spent discussing how people felt, whether it was a right time to discuss things and whether everyone who needed to be there, was. The next ten minutes were spent working out exactly what needed to be discussed, what actually were the issues, all this done without a chair or timekeeper. The meeting then went into discussing what needed to be done and it became a free-for-all, with people talking over each other, sub-conversations going on and people moving about and doing other things. Eventually this died down and people then checked out that they all knew what needed to be done and who was going to do things. No formal decision making had actually taken place and no action points were noted. I am not saying that this was a better method; just that it was a different one and, more importantly, it made sense to them. What looks like chaos to us can be other people's common sense and it is our clients' common sense we should be plugging into.

In training, I run a session exploring how we structure client involvement, and the effect this has on how clients respond. I set up three or four chairs in the centre of the room and hold a debate on a subject relevant to client involvement. I ask for volunteers to sit in the chairs, but leave one of the chairs free. If anyone else wants to make a point they can, but they have to come and sit on the chair, make their point and leave. During the conduct of the exercise I also change the rules a little. If someone sits down in their chair but does not make their point quickly, often because the others are in mid-flow, I tell them to sit down again as they have missed their chance. At some point, normally when someone is about to sit in the spare chair, I say that from now on if someone comes to sit in the chair they have to make their point and leave the room. I would also ask one of the people who have not sat in the chair yet to leave the room, as I do not think they are participating enough.

In feedback, we examine the processes of what happened. It often takes a long time for the first person to come up to the chair and as they have to walk all the way across the room, people feel they have to say something really good to sit down (conversely people often make extreme points to have an impact). People get frustrated when their point is not picked up after they have left and really frustrated when they have to leave the room and don't know then what happened. The people you say weren't quick enough to speak or weren't participating often get extremely frustrated, often towards you. Sometimes people start sabotaging the processes and start speaking from the floor and those who are outside the door hold their own conversation. The point is that there are parallels between how clients feel about how we constrict client involvement to certain structures.

I remember one client, who was allowed to come to the management committee of an organisation I worked for. He was given a five-minute slot towards the end to give client views.

We'd spent some time before hand talking about what he wanted to say, but when it came to it he said 'you're all a shower of bastards and you never listen to us'. When I discussed what happened with him afterwards, he talked about his frustration with the process. After being made to wait for hours outside, seeing us discussing things but not knowing what we were saying and then having to walk across the room with all eyes on him, ' you're all a shower of bastards and you never listen to us' was all that came out. His reactions were as much governed by the way we had chosen to structure things as his personality. Yet, back in the management committee, the conversation was about what training was needed to be able to engage properly, and even if there were other, more reasonable, clients we could ask along.

Brafield conducted research on strategic involvement and it is interesting as it reveals managers' intent towards how client involvement should be constructed. When she asked questions 'What barriers get in the way of having a service user consultation strategy for strategic decision making?' the responses were as shown below.

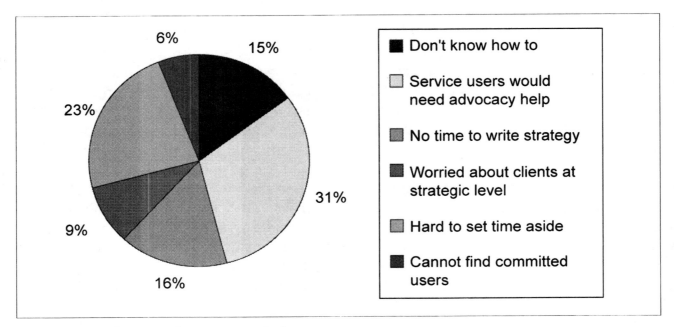

Figure 6.1 Barriers to service users consultation

I would classify 37 per cent of responses as expecting the client to change i.e. that clients need advocacy help or that the agency cannot find committed clients. In addition, 39 per cent of responses were about time constraints, which betray, to me, either a genuine lack of resources, a lack of will to change themselves, or that they do not see such as strategy as a priority. Worrying is the 15 per cent who are 'worried about clients being involved at a strategic level'. It is a shame that these views are not expanded upon, as they may be benign or they may not. Either way, when these factors are combined, 54 per cent either fear doing it, or do not see it as a priority, and a further 37 per cent see the challenge as being how to get the clients, and the right clients, to respond to us better. Only the 15 per cent who admit they do not know how to start involving people, seem to be looking at it in the right way for me. As Cameron et al. (2005) say 'Staff have to be able to step outside the world of the professional and deal with clients on terms and in language that they are comfortable with. To not do so will mean engaging in the forms of structural discrimination described. The final chapter will explore and point the reader towards other mechanisms for involvement that may break our common sense about the subject.

The fallacy of power being finite and concentrated

Many workers resist or constrict participation based on assumptions and fears that power is finite. They feel that if they then give some power to clients then they will loose influence.

(Wilcox, 1995: 34)

Power is commonly understood to be held within a small number of hands. This is simplistic, power flows, as in a circuit, rather than being concentrated; To affect participation we need to remove blockages and create links to allow power to flow in new ways.

(Clegg, 1989: 56)

Wilcox's comments are useful in understanding the phenomenon discussed in Chapter 4 where workers reacted to being disempowered by sabotaging client involvement, especially when they perceive that clients are being listened to more than they are. In doing this, they saw power as a finite commodity, embodied in the worker fear that if they empower clients they will give up what little power they have. I think this idea also explains the sometimes top-down approaches of managers in supported housing, where a climate of constant change means they feel they need to keep 'control' of the situation.

Clegg (1989) describes a second erroneous behaviour that comes from such a view of power which is that to influence things we should target the person who is meant to be in charge; the person who has the theoretical power in terms of the hierarchical structure of the organisation. As Clegg says, power actually is far more subtle than this. Influence and resistance have large parts to play in how organisations actually operate. As well as missing how power actually operates, such a view of power means that its holders, in our case workers, do not have to look at their own uses and abuses of power.

Many of the workers who take a finite view of power, that it is concentrated, also take the view, mentioned in Chapters 1 and 4 that examining power within the hostel is irrelevant, dependency-creating and that agencies should be concentrating on holding homeless people or rehabilitating them, until accommodation becomes available. If any power relationship needs to change, it is on a macro level – the client's relationship with the management, who are perceived to hold all the power, or society itself. The question of what effect experiencing homelessness services has had on them, and the power play at a micro level between workers and client, is ignored.

Foucault (1986), speaking at a societal level, rejects the idea of a single oppressive force and speaks instead of 'micro-powers'. He believes resistance can occur on a local level at the points where they emerge i.e. in the hostel, in the services that are provided to homeless people. Clients often do resist agencies. Snow and Anderson (1987) examined homeless people's construction of their identities and found a strong factor was 'institutional distancing' i.e. rejecting the services that they get. They put this distancing down to individuals trying to deal with the inconsistencies of their self-conceptions and their reality (Seal, 2007b). A different interpretation is that they are resisting the micro-power at the point where they can. Clients 'getting one over on workers' is part of this culture. The reason clients felt threatened when I gave them money before a focus groups, as we discussed in Chapter 5, is that I was taking away that opportunity to resist. Another example of this I remember from my own practice was when clients got loans or grants from the DSS on false pretences. It was not only for monetary reasons as clients often as not shared the money out. There was a definite idea of clients getting one over on the system, a system which workers are very much identified with.

Micro power and resistances also occur within organisations. The blame culture mentioned at the end of the last chapter is an example of this where managers say that workers are resistant to new ideas, whereas workers, conversely, say that managers are only doing it because they have to and clients are not interested. In reality, the ways in which decisions are made in organisations, and the blocks to successful implementation of those decisions are complex.

The flow of power and influence in one organisation

Explain your organisational systems, structures and policies and explain why and how these work. Help reps persuade other clients to follow in their footsteps.

(Novas-Ouvertures, 2001)

I am in agreement with the sentiment of the above statement. However, I have a problem with it in that it implies that it will be a simple process to explain an organisation's structures. I think the reality of decision making in organisations and where influence lies is more complex than any hierarchical flow chart. The important thing is to work out what an organisation's structure and systems are actually like rather than what we think they are in theory. To do this is no easy matter, as different stakeholders will probably have very various takes on it. Which of these stakeholder views are most relevant is a moot point. I always remember a colleague of mine who is an organisational consultant saying that if you wanted to know what was going on in any organisation, you should ask the clients or the cleaners.

He suggested the cleaners because they did not have any agendas, but had access to all corners of the building physically and had the ear of many of the other stakeholders in the organisation, who would talk more openly with them because they were seen as neutral and without vested interests. He suggested the clients for two reasons. Firstly, and particularly in supported housing, they had 24 hours a day to observe goings on, while workers only had 8 hours a day, five days a week. Perhaps more importantly, they often had a curiosity borne out of not being involved in official decision making processes, but also because they had an investment in finding out who they would need to talk to, to get leverage on a matter as it concerned them directly.

I remember one client, who was an undiagnosed schizophrenic, describing my organisation as a medieval court. There was a damsel in distress isolated in a tower (the manager). Below her were various knights battling it out, with associated knaves in support (the different departments and their workers). Below them, and outside, were the peasants (the clients) who were mere onlookers. He was not far wrong in his analysis, including his depiction of me as the joker, flitting between different parties but being largely ineffectual! The series of diagrams below illustrate how power and influence flowed in one supported housing organisation I worked in. To find this out we brought in some consultants to figure out how power and influence worked and they talked to all the stakeholders. Our original concern was that the client group, a weekly open event for all, was not working and we wanted to find ways of improving it. As you will see, this was not really the point.

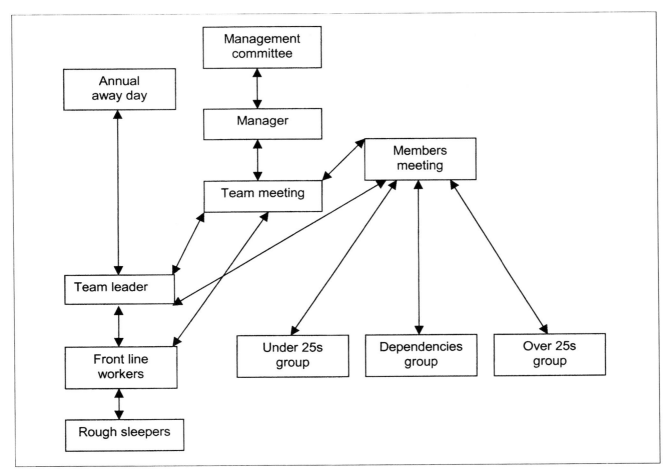

Figure 6.2   Organisational power and influence

This first diagram illustrates how power and influence was meant to flow in the organisation. In theory there was two way communication between all parties. Structures worth noting are the three specialist client groups, young people, people with dependencies and an over 25s group (set up because this group felt that they wanted their own group). We also felt that, as rough sleepers did not tend to go to the day centre they could be represented through the outreach workers, who were front line workers.

In reality this was not how power and influence worked at all. Most communication was one way from managers down through team leaders to front line workers. As a result, rough sleepers had no say at all, being represented through outreach workers who also had little influence. The annual review day, which was where all stakeholders came together, though notably not users, was tokenistic and not really linked into anything. Discussion revolved around things like mission statements and people did not feel able to be honest about their feelings.

Interestingly, the person who had most unofficial *influence* was the administrator, represented by the dotted line in Figure 6.3. She had been involved in the organisation for a long time and was a friend of the managers and hence had their 'ear'. She also ran the over 25s group and tended to feed the manager with this groups' view. The over 25s group was also the constituency that was most dominant in the day centre which served to re-enforce this power base. They also effectively controlled the open user group that was held weekly, which re-enforced their power base further. The young persons' group felt it was inadequate

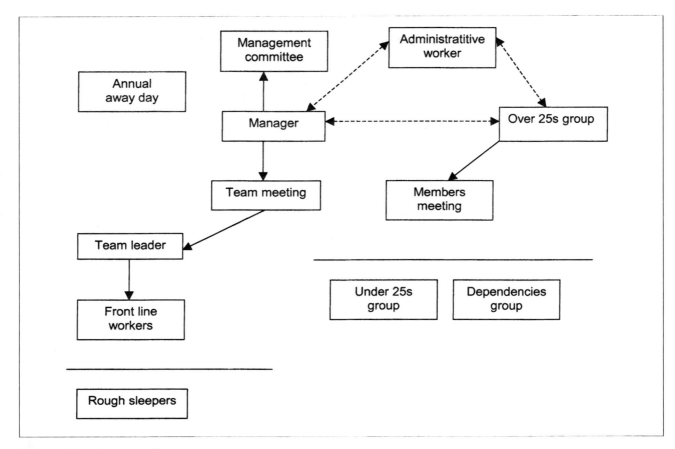

Figure 6.3 Power reality

compared to the over 25s group and was dwindling. More insidiously, the dependency group served to identify those who used drugs, who were then targeted by the dominant group who did not like them and sought to get rid of them.

This final diagram illustrates what we did about the situation. If it looks as if we got rid of the admin worker and that she was a Machiavellian figure, we did not and she was not. She did not realise the power she had and was mortified by it. She thought she was just having a word with her friend about what she thought they needed to know. We did, however get rid of the over 25s group and the user group. The former because it was a power base, and we reasoned that they had enough influence anyway, and the second because it had no credibility with other users and took the view that open meetings would always be dominated by a vocal minority.

We also got rid of the dependency group because it equally had little credibility. We did, however, try to re-vitalise the young persons' group and brought in a women's group and a black users' group as they had little representation in the day-centre. Rough sleepers were invited to the annual review day, which had a much more open agenda that was given over to control by the users and the front line workers. As a result, and through concerted effort on communication generally, people started talking more openly and the conversation genuinely became more open. I am not saying this structure was perfect and indeed it needed to change again a few years later. It just illustrates that the ways in which power and influence flow are not as simple as we think and the dictum that those at the bottom have the least power is not always true.

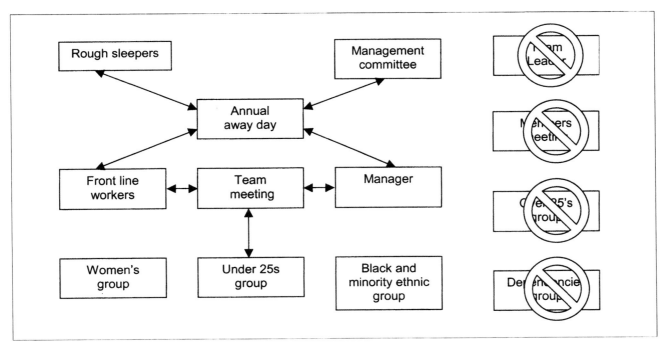

Figure 6.4   Revised power organisation

Section two: managing stakeholder interests

The term 'service user' can be much broader than simply those who are currently making use of the service. It can include both past and potential service users. It can include households who face barriers to accessing the service. It can include organisations who refer people to the service or whose work is directly or indirectly affected by the service.

(Cameron et al., 2005: 42)

Before starting a participation process it is important to reflect on the role you have – the hat you are wearing. The way you act may be influenced by how far you control resources, to whom you are answerable. People's attitudes to you will certainly be influenced by the role and power they think you have.

(Wilcox, 1995: 2)

The majority of people involved in council run tenant participation schemes tended to be ex-councillors, friends of councillors or 'professional clients.

(Smith, 1995: 76)

The Cameron et al. quote is important here. To take account of those who may influence the process, we should see stakeholders in client involvement more broadly. In the context of power, if we do not, we may be missing out a stakeholder who has an unacknowledged, and sometimes disproportionate, amount of power and/or influence. *Supporting People* acknowledge this, saying 'we should make explicit at the outset the kind of influence the different stakeholders will have on decision-making and the areas that are open to negotiation' (Godfrey et al., 2003: 78). Two stakeholders that are consistently missed out are funders and the local community (Godfrey et al., 2003; Wilcox, 1995). I think we are often nervous about involving the former because we don't like washing our dirty laundry in public and are very quick to accuse the later of NIMBYism (Not In My Back Yard).

Positively, and to allay fears, I have seen very successful speak-outs with clients and funders, that have ultimately been for the benefit of the agency. This was particularly so for one agency where the funders were thinking of cutting the service the clients themselves valued. I think positive engagement is often the case, but agencies fear it will not if, following my sixth theme, they have received some initial negativity. Following the Groundswell (2006) research for *Supporting People* to ascertain what they thought were effective services for homeless people, their findings bolstered the good practice of many agencies. Some agencies were challenged by it, no doubt, but they were the ones who I thought needed to be challenged. A friend of mine who works for the Government Office West Midlands in regeneration looks at funding bids, or listens to presentations for funding, all day. It is his role. He says that when there has been obvious client involvement, through examples of client stories, or that a client is on the presenting panel, it makes a big impression on him. This is not just because it hits all the right markers, remembering comments in Chapter 3 about participation being a common benchmark, but also on a human level they appreciate it because it is unusual and interesting. It brings the bid alive.

Seeing that the client involvement initiative fosters engagement with the community is also a benchmark for *Supporting People*. 'Client involvement has to encompass approaches and methods that enable people to gain greater access to, and integration within, the wider community' (Godfrey et al., 2003: 56). They go on to explain that they value such developments not only because it is a fulfilment of their overall aims, but also because it is effective. One of the examples from the section of working with the community in Godfrey's report tells of how clients and community engagement were able to break down some of the stereotypes that elements of the community had of them. These fears of homeless people are understandable given the way that the media and society constructs people who are in supported housing (Boydell et al., 2000; Liddiard,1999; Seal, 2007b). Positively, the project was able to break down fear on all sides.

I think we sometimes forget that many in the local community have had issues with housing themselves, especially when they are council residents, given who has access to public housing these days (Balchin, 1998). I think that if the community does have elements of NIMBYism it is often because we have made few attempts at all to involve them in the life of our projects. As a community worker, I remember one member of the community describing how the first thing he knew about a new supported housing project for clients in his local area was when they were putting up the sign for it outside the project. When work with the community has been done properly I have seen ex-homeless clubs in local community centres or projects that use the local community as a source of volunteers, or advocates in client involvement events.

Wilcox (1995) notes an additional angle in considering who our stakeholders are. He says we should reflect on who we are for, we are not neutral in the process and will certainly not be seen as such by the clients. We need to be clear of our role; is it as an advocate, a conduit, a facilitator or, occasionally, an agitator. We can be sure that they are labels that the other stakeholders will place on us, depending on what we are saying. As an ex-lead on client involvement in an agency, sometimes I would be asked for the 'client perspective'. Sometimes when I gave it, instead of asking the more pertinent question about how we could go about getting it, I would be accused of being an agitator or asked how I had come to that conclusion. A worker leading on client involvement must be clear about their role at any one point; if they are not who will be?

A wider aspect of this debate is who of these stakeholders is best to lead on client involvement. Interestingly, Godfrey et al. (2003) say that, if we are to involve the community more, for best practice, we should support workers in the process of giving up power. I found my own role, as lead on client involvement in the agency, moving through from being an agitator to advocate to organiser, to facilitator to occasional advisor. I could have done with that support. To suddenly not be as essential as I thought I was, took some working through. If funders or the community take a lead then many of the institutionalised barriers we talked about in Chapter 4 will not apply. I have seen an alliance develop between clients and the local community in the arena of public policy. This was the example I mentioned in Chapter 2 where initially the community and people in supported housing were set up against each other by the local authority. However, in the process, the two sides came together to pressure that local authority to build more social housing via planning gain with private builders, instead of taking the cash equivalent. The lead worker in the agency may only be a catalyst in this, but it is none the less an important role.

I do not want to paint too rosy a picture of collaborative working and the Smith quote illustrates that the community is not a neutral or homogenous grouping. Given this, to balance the different demands of different stakeholders will take some doing. Smith's quote reminds us that those who get involved, be that in the community or amongst clients, will be partial.

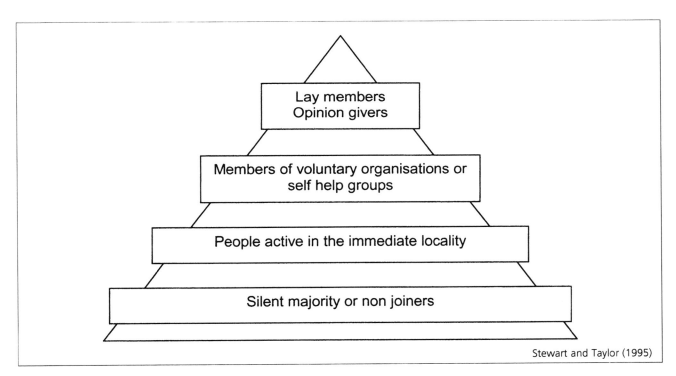

Stewart and Taylor (1995)

Figure 6.5 Tenant participation

The diagram above by Stewart and Taylor (1995) develops this point further and illustrates who tends to be involved in tenant participation initiatives in local authority properties. My issue with such schemas is that they can be used as an excuse for inaction. They can give the messages that we should not do anything at all until we have reached the real clients or the real tenants, which you may never do. I think we should start with whom you can work with, which is likely to be those at the top of the diagram and then start working down. It is important that we remember those we have not reached yet and only work with the obvious, something discussed in the principles chapter about not relying on and burning out your activists. However, it is equally important that we are not too critical about ourselves for not reaching the silent majority quickly, or at all. We should also not allow others to beat us up about it either. We have mentioned before McGreggor's (1990) notion that people in power do not question whom clients represent until they start asking awkward questions. They then start asking questions like 'are these just the vocal clients' or 'how about the quiet ones who are not here'. Going back to the issue of structural power, we need to recognise that legitimate questions may be asked by legitimate stakeholders but at inappropriate times and for inappropriate reasons. Learning to discern this is where we learn to detect the true nature of institutional power.

Conclusion

Thus far I have been quite benevolent in my interpretations of power. As with the administrator in the earlier example, I have portrayed abuses of power as an unconscious thing, where the individual or the organisation does not realise the nature of the power they have and the consequences of their influences. Foucault (1986) identifies a more insidious undercurrent. He holds that these micro-powers often serve, on a conscious level, to maintain power configurations and inequalities and allow those with power to sustain their own 'regimes of truth'. Paul Daly, looking at the American, Canadian and European contexts, saw shades of this in the supported housing sector:

> *There is a self perpetuating network characterised by common interests, mutual dependencies and self interest based on a charity model and naïve assumptions, motivated by the desire to exercise power and a need for control.*

(Daly, 1996: 194)

Other authors such as Brandon (1980) have portrayed the sector as rooted in and mired by patriarchal attitudes, where workers are recruited for commitment and idealism rather than skill. Clients were people 'to be pitied or even reviled, not empowered' (Brandon, 1980: 34). On a subtler level, Hoch and Slayton (1989) have noted how professionals have assumed that the needs of people in supported housing can only be met with the aid, and through the guidance, of professionals. They also note that, in response to the more reactionary trends Daly and Brandon mention, liberals shifted their culture to one whereby clients were seen as not being responsible for their condition. However, this was 'at the cost of portraying clients as dependant, isolated, and different from the rest of the population'. I have seen many instances of clients being constructed as incapable of thinking strategically or that they will be abusive of power if they get it. I fear that some of the 15 per cent cited in the Brafield (2003) example earlier in this chapter as being 'worried about the involvement of client at a strategic level' may be coming from this perspective.

These constructions may even have an impact on how we shape our services. Hoch and Slayton (1989) trace how researchers have tended to conduct their research through services, which in turn tend to serve those in crisis. I friend of mine, a drug service ex-client, spoke at a conference lately criticising how agencies mainly respond to crisis. He thought that this was for a multitude of reasons, from its being people's point of interest to it simply being one of the more exciting aspects of a worker's role. My friend noted that this responding to crisis in turn meant that clients responded by presenting in crisis, for that was what would get them a service. In the end this dynamic just perpetuated the situation. Clients had not been credited by agencies with having the insight to see the dynamics of the situation and felt that their response was therefore a learnt one. Agencies continued to think they were responding to need. It is no wonder then that research conducted through these services found clients to be vulnerable and in crisis. Finally, and on a positive note, Hoch and Slayton (1989) note that few longitudinal studies have been conducted on people in supported housing. Where they have been done, they tend towards the view that clients find their own solutions. This seems to give us a further justification for client involvement. If clients are ultimately capable of finding their own solutions, they are capable of being involved in shaping the part agencies play in this.

Van Doorn and Kain (2006) talking about the homeless sector, are perhaps less critical, seeing the lack of reflection of the sector as being the root problem. The third theme of the book concurs with this, saying the supported housing sector does not examine the paradigms that inform it, instead taking a 'common sense' approach, forgetting that the notion of common sense is one of those 'regimes of truth', mentioned by Foucault. Indeed, it has not taken time to analyse and acknowledge how this sector's rationales for client involvement have changed. The sector therefore needs to challenge its constructions that do not allow this to happen. As Van Doorn and Kain (2006: 123) say:

> *The sector needs to explore, discuss and identify, through honest appraisal and reflection, its culture and how it both supports and frustrates its work and its ability to meet the changes it faces.*

Part Three

Processes of, Levels of and Methods for Client Involvement

7

The Process of Involvement: Organisational Change and Initiative Development

The process of client involvement is neither simple nor straightforward. There is no one model that can be offered to guarantee success.

(Godfrey et al., 2003: 3)

People put different emphasis on product and process. In general workers and administrators are keen on work that can be readily seen and counted. They are interested in concrete results from their efforts . . . Process results are far less tangible. They are to do with relationships, the strengthening of people's competence and feelings.

(Jeffs and Smith, 1982: 3)

The clear central premise of the literature on organisational learning is that the need to shift to a learning organisation cannot be achieved by tinkering at the margins, but must be affected through radical change.

(Cibulka et al., 2003: 2)

This chapter expands on the fifth theme of the book; that we need to see client involvement as much a process as a product. It is based on the argument that to see it as a one-off event and to view client involvement as an add-on rather than as something that is integral to the planning and delivery is erroneous. The chapter will take a lead from the Jeffs and Smith quote and build on comments made in the principles chapter, developing an argument about what this process should look like. The chapter will have two halves, that mirror the two aspects of the process that client involvement will need to undertake.

Firstly, then, the chapter will examine the processes an organisation will need to go through to be able to hear the message of clients. This is in keeping with the second half of the fifth theme of the book, that we should be prepared for fundamental change. All too often I have seen agencies undertake a client involvement initiative without considering whether they are ready and able to hear its messages. It will build on literature about reflective and learning organisations (Senge, 1990; Cibulka et al., 2003) and will develop criteria by which we can judge an agency.

Then the chapter will examine the process any client involvement initiative may go through. This section is based on, and will build upon, the work of Wilcox (1995), contrasted with the *Supporting People* model as outlined by Godfrey et al. (2003). Wilcox's model identifies four stages in processes of involvement: initiation, preparation, participation and continuation. Following the *Supporting People* comment, I think the important thing to consider at each of these stages is less what you should be doing, and more the questions you should be asking yourself. With this in mind, I will finish the chapter by talking through examples of good practice at each of these stages, and develop a checklist for workers seeking to provide a client involvement initiative.

The learning organisation

Organisations where people continually expand their capacity to create the results they truly desire, where new and expansive patterns of thinking are nurtured, where collective aspiration is set free, and where people are continually learning to see the whole together.

(Senge, 1990: 3)

My issue with the above statement by Senge is that it is the kind of statement, in common with the universal claim to value client involvement, that all organisations would say applies to them. We therefore need to find other criteria by which to judge the genuineness of an organisation's stated aspirations. Cibulka et al. (2003), conducting a literature review of learning organisations, found certain characteristics that help us distinguish between those who say they learn and those who actually do. They think that these discerning characteristics are at a cultural level of the whole organisation.

- Closed, insular and autonomous systems are seen as impediments to environmental responsiveness.
- Permanence and stability are no longer seen as assets.
- Employees are seen as resources whose development is key to organisational performance, regardless of their specific role or status.
- Information (how to acquire, distribute, interpret and retain it) is seen as central to the organisation, whose design must now reflect that.

However, these characteristics still seem nebulous. It is unclear how we assess an organisation's views on these matters, beyond examining their aspirational mission statements. As the last chapter showed, there is a big difference between the system of power that organisations say they operate, and the one that they actually do. Furthermore, even if organisations display some of these characteristics, it does not necessarily mean that they are listening organisations. As Van Doorn and Kain (2004, 2007) note, the supported housing sector, particularly since the advent of *Supporting People*, has had to respond to an unstable and ever changing environment and has become quite adept at it. Many supported housing organisations therefore display Cibulka et al.'s second characteristic. However, this proves that they have become good at survival, and not necessarily that they are adept at learning from experience (Argyris and Schon, 1974).

Argyris (1980) may be able to help us in developing criteria for a learning organisation. He makes a useful distinction between theories in action and espoused theory, the nub of our current dilemma. Espoused theory is the framework or values, cultures, policies, etc., that we say we work within and theories in action are the models and values we actually work to. Sometimes they are the same, but often they are not. What is more, few people are aware of the maps or theories they do use in action, only the ones they espouse.

Developing this further, Argyris and Schön (1974) observed two models of theories-in-action that either inhibit or enhance organisational learning. I have adapted the characteristics they identified for each model, incorporating refinements developed by other authors (Smith,

Table 7.1 Attitudes to organisational learning

Inhibiting Model	Enhancing model
The agency has many 'holy cows', both overt and covert. These can be ideas i.e. *that clients just want a service,* to parts of the project e.g., *the day centre must stay open.* There are often histories associated with them. Workers and clients often only find out about them when they question them.	*The organisation regularly questions its fundamentals* both in terms of its ideas and what services it delivers. The organisation develops both formal and informal mechanisms for doing this. Social events and annual away days (not just when there are crises) are features of the organisation.
The organisation controls the environment and task of involvement unilaterally. The staff and management groups spend a long time defining involvement and foreseeing barriers without talking to the clients first.	*The organisation is open to involvement and the form it could take* – even to the point of people admitting that they do not know where to start – people experiment with venues and ideas from the outset and talk to and involve clients from the outset.
The organisation 'protects' itself and others unilaterally. Many ideas are squashed for reasons of risk or health and safety, without consulting those who for whom these policies are being invoked.	*The organisation takes risks or at least entertains them.* Ideas from clients are entertained unreservedly and then risk and health and safety factors are considered. The excuse that this is setting people up to fail is not used.
Un-illustrated and covert attributions and evaluations are made e.g. claims that clients are unmotivated or will not engage unless they get something out of the situation, without evidence beyond 'I know my clients'. This equally applies to managers e.g., the managers are only doing this for X reason, or 'workers will not change'.	*Attributions are only made with evidence.* Generally, claims are made, but where they are, they are evidenced and are checked out with the people that they concern. Similarly this applies to workers and managers' perceptions about each other.
Advocating courses of action which discourage inquiry e.g. lets not talk about the past, that's over – we want clients to concentrate on the positive. Where history is invoked it is as a reason for why ideas will not work.	*People are keen to learn from the past and see history as important.* Initially, people concentrate on the past, but in a positive sense; people want to learn from it. Rather than just raking over old coals, it is something to learn from.
There is an emphasis on the need for unity. Managers place great emphasis on loyalty and discourage dissent. Workers aren't 'burdened' with (and don't seek) decision making, but are expected to respect decisions and concentrate on their implementation.	*There is a great emphasis on the need to build unity.* Loyalty is seen as something to be earned. Dissent and contribution is encouraged. Views are sought at all stages of decision making, formally and informally. Many decisions are devolved to workers.
Stakeholders treat their views as obviously correct and defend them vigorously. Managers, workers and clients make claims to know client's thoughts, emotions and views on an almost instinctive level.	*Stakeholders question their views and those of others.* Claims of hierarchical authority are abandoned. Other claims of authority, like how long a person has worked in the sector, do not figure. Those with power adopt facilitative views of others.
There are defensive relationships between staff i.e. staff report feeling demoralised or powerless within the organisation. Conversely, managers deride staff as sabotaging efforts or being unionised etc. Resentments about this are played out in private.	*Staff may argue, but have respect for each other.* Conflicts are played out in the open, without maintenance of a 'united front'. Clients are open to criticise all parties. Formal structures exist to bring people together.
Choices are presented as free when they are actually hobsons choice. Choices for clients normally come down to 'you do it the organisations way or you can leave', or choice is given on mundane day-to-day issues.	*The degree of choice in a project is acknowledged.* People are honest about the scope for change or not. The starting point for discussions is that clients should be given a choice in this, and then people will backtrack if necessary.
Reduced production of valid information. The information that clients are given is minimal, with	

Table 7.1 *Continued*

Inhibiting Model	Enhancing model
rationales for not giving more, like 'they are not interested' or 'they would be burdened with such information' or 'they would take it the wrong way'. There is a lot of worry and procrastination when info is requested e.g. budgets, addresses of *Supporting People*. *Little public testing of ideas.* Initiatives are very much tried out in private, with people not wanting the findings, even if they are generalised and may be of use to others, to be made public, or conducted in public.	*Open production of information.* Clients have access to all information, aside from confidential matters. People are given this information and encouraged to challenge it. The spaces where this information is produced are open, such as the minutes of staff meetings. *Ideas and findings are open to all.* Agencies are keen for others to learn from their experiences and take the view that the difficulties will be outweighed by the positives that will come out about them.
Adapted from Argyris, Putnam and McLain in Smith (1985, p. 89)	Adapted from Anderson, 1997.

2001a; Anderson, 1997), set them in a supported housing context and applied them to client involvement. I present them in the form of a checklist. This is intended to aid someone developing an involvement initiative in discerning whether their organisation will actually listen to any arising perspectives from the clients.

In reality, it is unlikely that any organisation will display all the characteristics of one model. The lives of organisations are far more fluid and idiosyncratic than that (Smith, 2001b; Senge, 1994). I think it is therefore more useful to look at agencies' learning abilities as a continuum from inhibiting to enhancing learning. In terms of client participation, I would expand the two extremes, adding in client dead and client led. Organisations that are 'inhibited' at least have a stated intent of client involvement and to learn, whereas many organisations I have encountered do not even exhibit these characteristics, and they are indeed 'client dead'. I would also have 'client led' because this incorporates where the best learning comes from. It allows for organisations that privilege the perspective of the client. This is not to question Argyris and Schon, who were concerned with issues of power, but is rather to emphasise the role of clients in learning organisations and within the power dynamic. In reality, it will be more complex than this, as many agencies will display behaviour and attitudes that cross over these distinctions. Nevertheless, I hope the model will give the person trying to initiate client involvement a feel for where their agency is on the continuum, and highlight the challenges they may face in getting the agency to listen to the messages of clients.

Changing the model of an organisation is beyond the scope of this chapter, and indeed this book. However, I will outline some starting points. On a simple level, to develop awareness in the agency of the importance of being a learning organisation is a start. For the organisation to be honest about where it sits in this model is another step. This in itself may not be an easy thing to achieve as the agency will have to admit that they are not quite as open to learning as they consider themselves to be.

On a more strategic level, authors associated with the literature about learning organisations (Argyris, 1974; Argyris and Schon, 1976; Senge, 1990) advocate a systems approaches to management. For Senge, one of the key problems with most managerial approaches is that simplistic approaches are applied to complex systems. Agencies tend to focus on 'fixing' particular parts of the organisation that are seen as a problem, forgetting that any solutions will impact on the whole organisation. Senge contends that most agencies focus on flare ups, such as staff disputes, concentrating on 'solving' them, rather than seeing them as a symptom

Table 7.2 Agencies learning ability continuum

Characteristic	Client dead	Inhibiting	Token	Partial	Developing	Enhancing	Client led
Attitude to holy cows	Non negotiable	Most covert and fixed	Most overt but fixed	Some overt and debatable	Becoming overt and up for debate	Overt and negotiable	Overt, client created and negotiable
Control of involvement	Rationale for non existence	Unilateral control	Covert unilateral control	Consult within set structure	Consult about set structure	Open debate	Terms of debate set by clients
Protection of agency/clients	Rationale for non action	Unilateral application	Covert unilateral application	Risk one of many factors	Clients involved in risk assessments	All ideas up for grabs	Clients determine risk factors
Evidence for attributions	Non existent	Minimal and selective	Sought for clients views only	Sought inconsistently	Recognise need/ not sure how	Evidence seen as essential	Client views privileged
Attitude to enquiry	Not seen as necessary	Defensive	Defensive when challenged	Dissent sometimes sought	Dissent mostly sought	Dissent seen as positive	Dissent seen as essential
Rigidness of views	Absolute	Defensive	Defensive when challenged	Open on some issues	Open on most views	All views are open	Views are to be scrutinised
Inter staff relations	Non existent/one way	Defensive/overt attacks	Defensive/covert attacks	Mixed normally personal	Most good active promotion	Fostered, positive and open	Fostered, positive and open
Level and view of choice	No choice	Little choice	Hobsons choice	Some choice	Acknowledgement of limitations	Sought in all situations	Achieved in all situations
Dispersal of information	Closed	Guarded	Rationalised limited access	Inconsistent	Given if asked for	Given as a matter of course	Education seen as goal
Public or private	Private to management	Kept in house	Good side shown publicly	Some issues public	Guarded but public	All findings public	Public debate/ analysis

80

of a bigger picture, They fail to see the organisation as a dynamic process. 'We tend to think that cause and effect will be relatively near to one another. Thus when faced with a problem, it is the "solutions" that are close by that we focus upon' (Smith, 2001a).

Systems theory concentrates on creating 'systems maps', where we see the organisation as a dynamic system, rather than a static one. The analysis concentrates on phenomenon like feedback and delay. Feedback is where the effects of an action get amplified and impacts on unpredicted aspects of the organisation. We also need to take account of delays, which are 'interruptions in the flow of influence which make the consequences of an action occur gradually', i.e. the delays we referred to in Chapter 5. They will also have unanticipated consequences beyond the subjects of the delays. Systems theory propounds that feedback and delays create 'loops' that feed on themselves. It believes that while they may seem initially inconsequential, we ignore them at our peril. I think this has particular relevance to client involvement.

To give an example, I experienced the feedback loop vividly when undertaking the research on client involvement mentioned in Chapter 4 (Groundswell, 2005). In the course of the research the team noted a certain cynicism amongst staff about why the management were undertaking this initiative. We also picked up a general feeling of dissatisfaction and de-motivation amongst the staff. They felt they were systematically bypassed in decision-making in the organisation. During the course of the research, management made a decision that, while maybe necessary, had not been made in consultation with staff or clients. This event had a notable impact on the research. There was an increased cynicism from staff and clients about the sincerity of management in consulting them, with both parties seeking avenues to vent their frustrations, often at the researchers.

When we made the organisation aware of this effect, little was done. The decision was presented as something the staff and clients would have to accept. Management wondered 'what all the fuss was about'. Their view of learning I would place somewhere between inhibiting and tokenistic. Our recommendations included that staff motivation and inclusion needed to be addressed, otherwise, we felt that their cynicism would persist and even accelerate, leading to client involvement being undermined. Interestingly, it was this recommendation that was the most questioned of all the recommendations. Management cited that we did not 'know' the staff in the way they did; a criticism that they did not apply to other conclusions. In a subsequent review it was found that the recommendation had not been implemented, or even considered.

Argyris and Schön (1978: 220–1) outline a model for the formulation and implementation of an intervention strategy for an agency to become a learning organisation. It involves mapping out an organisations 'system' and developing a plan of action for change. In doing this the 'interventionist' will move through six phases, see Table 7.3.

By running through this sequence and seeing the 'enhancing' criteria as a model to work towards, it is argued that organisational development is possible. Argyris and Schon (1974) also highlighted key issues for the interventionist to concentrate on achieving *during* the process. These included: 'securing the maximum participation of stakeholders, minimising the risks of candid participation, starting where people want to begin (often with instrumental problems), and influencing stakeholders cultures to value rationality and honesty.'

I hope the above thoughts act as a starting point for those seeking to implement client involvement in their organisation. Considering whether an organisation is a learning one is vital and may mean further training needs to be undertaken and the process of involvement has to

Table 7.3 Organisational intervention strategy

Phase 1	**Mapping the problem as stakeholders see it.** This includes the factors and relationships that define the problem, and the relationship with the living systems of the organisation.
Phase 2	**The internalisation of the map by stakeholders.** Through inquiry and confrontation the interventionists work with stakeholders to develop a map for which they can accept responsibility. However, it also needs to be comprehensive.
Phase 3	**Test the model.** This involves looking at what 'testable predictions' can be derived from the map – and looking to practice and history to see if the predictions stand up. If they do not, the map has to be modified.
Phase 4	**Invent solutions to the problem and simulate them to explore their possible impact.**
Phase 5	**Produce the intervention.**
Phase 6	**Study the impact.** This allows for the correction of errors as well as generating knowledge for future designs. If things work well under the conditions specified by the model, then the map is not disconfirmed.

be preceded by organisational development. It is only when an organisation becomes, or starts on the journey to becoming, a learning organisation, that there is any point to undertaking a client involvement initiative that will have any potential impact. It is only when an agency is working to a developing or enhancing model, that we should look at the stages of developing a client involvement initiative.

The process of participation

Supporting People outlines a suggested process for planning and evaluating a client involvement initiative. I have combined this, and contrasted it with a similar view of the process as developed by Wilcox.

Initiation (reviewing objective, needs led services)

In the *Supporting People* version of the process the initiative for client involvement comes from the organisation. In contrast, Wilcox (1995) notes that the process of participation may be triggered by:

- A campaign of protest may be turned into collaborative programme of action.
- An authority may promote a project.
- Government may announce funding is available for client-based projects.

(Wilcox, 1995: 43)

Wilcox (1995) notes that the origins of the initiative will often be unclear and contested. I have been involved in participation initiatives that had all of the above triggers. As an example, 'speakouts' started out as a protest against sleepouts (see Chapter 5). They were then adopted by the local council in Camden as a method of consultation and are now permanent projects in, for example, Bradford where 'Bradford speakout' is promoted as an example of good practice by *Supporting People*. These developments could be seen as a natural evolution. The important thing being that the perspectives of the respective stakeholders were heard in how

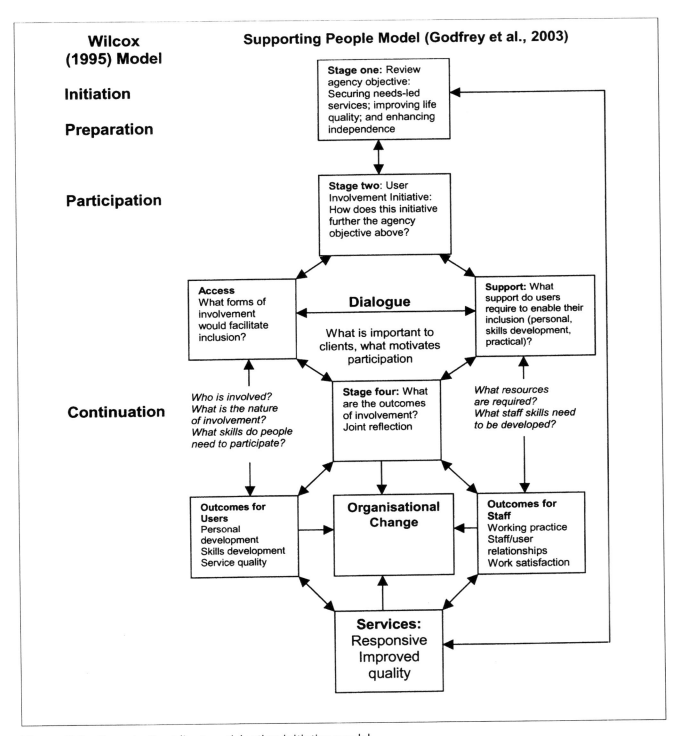

Figure 7.1 Organisation/client participation initiative model

the initiatives developed. Returning to systems thinking, the important thing is not to work out who is 'right' about the origins, but that people know and hear the different perspectives on the subject. It is from this understanding that 'systemic' thinking grows.

Wilcox (1995) identifies a series of related questions that stem from the question of where the initiative comes from. They include:

- Who is going to champion the process?
- Who pays?
- Who administers?
- Who convenes?
- What are you trying to achieve through participation?
- Who are the key interests within any organisation promoting participation, and what are their attitudes?
- What level of participation is likely to be appropriate and acceptable?
- How will you know when you have succeeded?

(Wilcox, 1995: 5)

For Wilcox, by developing a common(ish!) understanding of the multiple perspectives arising from these questions we should be able to find a way through them.

Preparation

Supporting People largely ignores this initiation stage, leaping straight to a consideration of the methods and techniques to be used in the participation initiative. Wilcox, by contrast, counsels us to take a step back at this point. Interestingly, what Wilcox calls the preparation stage has distinct parallels to the process I describe above of seeing whether an organisation is a learning organisation. He describes such tasks as establishing what the organisation wants to achieve from the participation process and whether it can respond to the outcomes of the process. In addition, he identifies human resource tasks such as establishing who is involved internally and whether they are committed to the process. He also looks at the practical side, emphasising the importance of establishing whether resources and time are available and researching the availability of additional resources, bringing potential funders into the process if necessary.

Wilcox saw the importance of looking at the interests of stakeholders beyond those internal to the organisation. The systemic approach also says we need to take account of this. Similarly, Wilcox feels we need to establish what level of participation we want and the techniques and methods we are to use, which is the subject of subsequent chapters. Until then I think it useful to share a checklist for those undertaking an initiative. We feel that we should, as far as possible, gain agreement of all parties as to:

- The aims of the process and how progress will be evaluated.
- The 'feel' of the process: the style and tone.
- The groupings, forums and decision cycles to be employed.
- Precisely what authority is being delegated to whom.
- The appropriate approaches and techniques, taking into account time scale, objectives, resources, openness of information sharing etc.
- The ground-rules: how are we going to deal with one another?
- The resources available and any conditions attached.
- The technical and administrative services available.
- The mechanisms for recording and disseminating information.
- The level of support and resources to be made available.

(Wilcox, 1995: 7)

Participation

We will come back to some of the methods and techniques of participation in the final chapter. At this point I just want to discuss criteria for their selection and structuring. *Supporting People* (Godfrey et al., 2003) poses the question at this stage what form of involvement would facilitate inclusion. There may well be things that most clients would get involved in, but does this mean that they are inclusive? Many hostels, or even supported housing units, may involve clients in cooking and cleaning, and cite that this is what they want to do. However, are these really about inclusion or simply the easy option?

Wilcox also provides some useful overall guidelines for a worker to choose between techniques and methods and then to devise a strategy that seeks to integrate them. I think these are worth examining in some detail:

- *Don't underestimate people. Give them tools to manage complexity, don't shield them from it.*

This principle fits in well with avoiding having an inhibiting model of learning in an organisation, whereby we 'protect' clients, normally without having consulted them about whether they need this protection.

- *Help people widen their perceptions of the choices available and to clarify the implications of each option.*

This stems from the principles of recognising the need for education for participation. Similar to the earlier discussion about systems thinking, clients will often think locally, going for easy solutions, without necessarily thinking of the whole or of alternatives. We need to undo this process and aid development.

- *Build in visible early successes to develop the confidence of participants. 'Staircase' skills, trust and commitment to the process: offer a progressive range of levels of involvement and help people to move up the ladder.*

This idea stems from, and ameliorates, the lack of trust that many clients will have as discussed in the barriers section. It sees trust as something we need to build in clients. We cannot expect them to believe us when we say we are trustworthy, even if we give guarantees.

- *Direct empowerment training for participants may not be appreciated – it may be better to develop skills more organically as part of the process.*

I think this is a particularly useful idea. Again returning to an earlier discussion in the chapter on barriers, agencies are often quick to identify the need for training for clients on involvement, such issues as confidence building, rather than looking at our hard-won training and development needs. Recently, in Ireland, we were brought in ostensibly to work with clients on 'confidence' building and assertiveness. The assumption that this was what was needed stemmed from a belief that clients were not becoming involved because they lacked confidence and assertiveness. This did not prove to be the case at all. In fact, clients did not get involved because they did not trust workers, were cynical about the agencies motives and questioned where the agency would actually listen to them. These skills were nevertheless important, and were learnt as people went along, together with developing trust.

- *If at all possible, avoid going for a comprehensive irreversible solution. Set up an iterative learning process, with small, quick, reversible pilots and experiments.*

Again, to have a pre-set agenda of what involvement looks like is part of an inhibiting organisational mentality. It means that the agency ends up concentrating on how to make their grand idea work, rather than looking at what method will have meaning for the client. The same may go for client's ideas and while we should privilege their perspective we should not descend into orientalism (Said, 1979). What will work is an organic thing that will take experimentation. As Godfrey et al. (2003: 45) note in their *Supporting People* guide to client participation, 'client involvement is a risky enterprise' and 'what will work is not always predictable'.

- *Continuously review and widen membership. As new interests groups are discovered how will they be integrated into the process?*

I wholeheartedly agree with this sentiment. However, as a corollary of this, and in keeping with the eighth theme of the book, agencies should see expanding membership and interests as an organic thing and not spend all their time worrying whether they are fully inclusive from the start. I ran a planning day in client involvement for an organisation. Many ideas were mooted. There was an arts group who were keen to get involved, some volunteers who had potential, some ex-clients who were keen to stay involved. However, all of these ideas were knocked back because they did not include everybody. At the end of the day the organisation had made no concrete plans. I do not think the notion of starting where you can is in conflict with the statement above, in fact they balance each other.

- *Help people to build their understanding of complex and remote decision processes which are outside the delegated powers of the participation process but which are affecting the outcomes.*

This again stems from the principle of learning for education. We need to enable clients to develop a wider perspective and to be able to think in a more systemic way. In the case of supported housing this may include considering the impact of funding regimes such as *Supporting People*, the impact of Housing Corporation regulations and even local authority politics. However, as a cautionary note, we must pitch such education at a level that clients can relate to and to develop their understandings at a pace dictated by them.

As an example of how *not* to do this, I was involved recently with running focus groups investigating client perceptions of *Supporting People* funded services. In keeping with the idea of promoting understanding, the ODPM, as it was then called, wanted to start with a presentation about *Supporting People* and the reasons behind the review they had commissioned. However, their initial idea was to have one of their officers, who the clients would have no relationship with, make a standard presentation of 30 minutes, too long for most clients, via power point, a medium they all found alienating. The content was to include sections on business planning, strategic developments and outcome management. All couched in language that went over the clients' heads. These perceptions are not projections but came from client feedback from the first few sessions, which were indeed conducted as above. The ODPM felt this format to be important for consistency's sake; they needed to be assured that everyone was given the same information. However, they missed the point that while clients had received the same message, few had heard it. To their credit they listened to constructive criticism, and started judging how to get the information across according to the needs of the audience.

- *Nurture new networks and alliances.*

In Chapter 6 I noted how 'bad' client involvement can involve the two most disenfranchised stakeholders in the organisation, the clients and front line workers, talking to each other. More positively, when an initiative starts working, I have seen these two groups forming alliances, both parties realising they have much to gain from doing so. As mentioned before, Groundswell organises an exchange programme, with clients of different organisations sharing ideas and experiences. As Putman (2004) notes, such coming together can be powerful, both politically and personally. We noted in the last chapter how groups that can be seen as mutually antagonistic, such as the local community and the homeless population, can come together to great effect.

- *Plans must be meaningful and lead to action.*

I think this is largely covered by the principle of starting from, and building upon, the point of interest of the client. I think it also links into demonstrating potency and qualifies my statement that we should not be quick to accuse a client of not being altruistic. While not all initiatives need to be of direct benefit to clients themselves, it is important to have some early quick wins; things that make something better for clients. Egan (1998) would say that without this we lose clients early on, as it is when they have built some trust with us and can see that we mean business and have integrity that they will see a point in being altruistic.

On a purely human level, I think action is important. Many of us do not enjoy committees for their own sake, particularly if attendance at them is voluntary. Workers themselves are often very action orientated (Seal, 2005). Yet many participation initiatives involve, and even have as a goal, clients sitting on committees. As we have discussed and shall see again in the final chapter, an orientation towards planning is not universal. Many clients would be more interested in other aspects of the organisation, particularly service delivery, yet our locus of concern is often to involve clients at the planning level.

- *Manage the link between the private ability of the various interest groups to deliver on their commitments, and public accountability and control of the implementation.*

On one level this comes back to how public the organisation wants to make the development of its participation initiative. The more private an affair they want to make it, the more likely they are to be an organisation working to an inhibiting learning model. On another level, involvement 'champions' may encounter dilemmas along the way. This is particularly so where they encounter resistance from the organisation that infringes on public accountability or individuals' rights. One way workers could become more empowered is through becoming unionised or going to an outside body, and the champion may know this. I worked with one supported housing organisation's client group on building their capacity. They encountered resistance from management on their opinions about the catering in the project and felt they had reached a dead end. I suggested contacting the organisations funders as a point of leverage. While doing this did not endear me to the organisation, I felt a moral obligation. A champion may also encounter such ethical dilemmas.

- *Build in opportunities for reflection and appraisal.*

This idea builds on an earlier principle on piloting, but extends it to a general approach. Argyris and Schon (1974) see reflection as essential to the process of becoming a learning organisation.

Given the complexity of situations and developments we can never rely upon predetermined ideas and models. Ideas will have to evolve. Positively this is something that *Supporting People* recognise:

> *Built into the process there should be opportunities for managers, staff and clients to reflect on, and evaluate the process and outcomes of involvement initiatives and to learn from these. Integrating involvement into the fabric and decision making structures of the organisation is not a once and for all process – it is an iterative and evolving one.*
>
> (Godfrey et al., 2003)

We therefore need a process of managing this evolution so that we do not make knee jerk or instinctive changes, but reflective ones. Models of reflective learning are numerous in learning theory; the most commonly used being those of Kolb (1984) or Lewin (1948, 1951) where learning is seen as a circle.

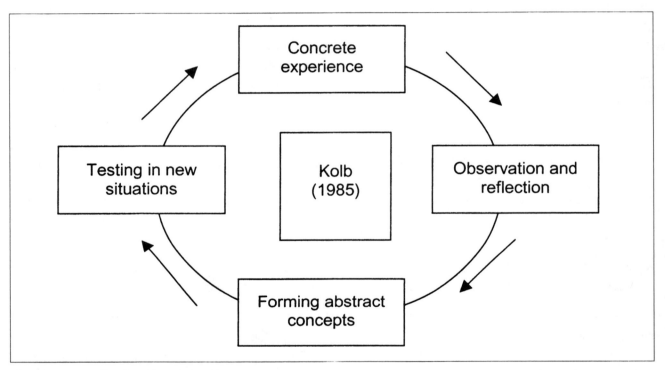

Figure 7.2 Kolb's learning cicle

Kolb and Fry (1975) thought we could enter this cycle at any point, the point being to abstract from our experiences and then keep testing and refining them. Later authors such as Jarvis (1994, 1995), develop Kolb's model, identifying different routes such as non-learning and non-reflective learning, as well as reflective learning, illuminating the knee jerk reactions we want to avoid. The skills of survival, that Van Doorn and Kain (2004, 2007) describe supported housing agencies as being adept at, is a form of non-reflective learning. To be reflective, reactions to clients not coming to, or valuing the organisation's 'residents group' should move from non-reflective responses such as thinking 'They are not motivated', to reflective ones such as considering 'Why would they turn up?' or 'What is it that makes them not value the group?' or 'What else motivates them and how do we capture this?'.

I think some expansion is needed on the process of abstraction and reflection, a criticism of Kolb being his lack of development of the process (Boud et al., 1985). Boud, Keogh and Walker (1985) identify three aspects to reflection: *Returning to experience* – that is to say, recalling or detailing significant events. *Attending to (or connecting with) feelings* – this has two aspects: using helpful feelings and removing or containing obstructive ones, and *Evaluating experience* – this involves re-examining experience in the light of one's conceptual framework, integrating this new knowledge into it. What seems important here is the attending to feelings and their impact on our rationalisations. The emotional dimension is something we have identified as particularly significant in client involvement, the biggest barriers to participation being fear, mistrust and resentment towards whomsoever is perceived to have power. Taking the previous example, reflections could be 'Do I feel resentment when clients do not turn up to meetings?' and 'How do I react towards people that I resent?'

- *Make sure people are having fun!*

This is one of my favourites. On a simple level, people will tend not to get involved in things that they do not enjoy. Given that some of the messages they might receive from clients may be difficult to hear at times, for staff and managers to receive these messages in an atmosphere of conviviality seems all the more important. Unless all sides see client involvement as ultimately liberating, they will not sustain their engagement and commitment to it.

Continuation

> *Feedback is absolutely essential to involving service clients. If service clients have no idea what impact their views have on subsequent developments then they have very little reason to remain involved.*
>
> (Cameron et al., 2005)

Wilcox (1995) identifies this as the final phase in an involvement process, although following the discussion of the last section, this stage may also represent the start of another process. Nevertheless, as Wilcox says, you should 'have worked through some prepared options with different interests and then agreed to take the results away for evaluation and implementation.' *Supporting People* (Godfrey et al., 2003) has a more robust approach. It makes a useful distinction between two levels of success. Firstly, it says we should judge success in terms of the experience of stakeholders of the process, and the changes in clients' lives and in terms of the services they receive as a result. Secondly, we should evaluate the initiative in terms of outcomes for staff, clients and, interestingly, its overall impact on organisational change. Positively, they recognise that good client involvement should enable a deeper and broader experience for all next time, although they miss out the stage of assessing whether the organisation is susceptible to that potential learning and change. Finally, both *Supporting People* (Godfrey et al., 2003) and Wilcox (1995) advocate a return to the original goals that were set for the initiative, although they accept that they have to be viewed in light of how these goals will have inevitably evolved. Both Wilcox (1995) and *Supporting People* (Godfrey et al., 2003) provide one last check list for evaluating the process and outcomes of the project. I have amalgamated them into one and I will finish on it. While it is not comprehensive, it should serve as something for the reader to reflect upon at the end of the process.

Checklist

- Did we achieve what we set out to do in the process, from staff, management and client perspectives?
- What were the outcomes for all parties, and how did they relate to what we expected them to be?
- Were these key interests happy with the level of involvement?
- Have we reported back to people on the outcomes?
- Are responsibilities clear for carrying projects forward?
- Are there major lessons we can learn for the next time?
- Has the initiative moved us toward broadening and deepening involvement?

8

Levels of Involvement: The Breadth and Depth

The presence of clients within a range of organisational activities had potential impacts on four levels: opportunities to influence formal decision-making; demonstrating clients' interest in getting involved; opportunities to become part of networks of clients and others; opportunities to learn about each other's experiences and priorities.

(Robson et al., 2005: 98))

Different levels of participation are appropriate at different times to meet the expectations of different interests.

(Wilcox, 1995: 5)

Service clients can have different levels of involvement in a service, from simply receiving information or involvement in a one-off consultation to taking the lead in managing the service.

(Cameron et al., 2005: 2)

This chapter will look at the levels of involvement for clients from two perspectives. Firstly, following on from the Robson quote, there is the breadth of activities that the client could be involved in, in the organisation, and beyond. Secondly, following Cameron, there is the depth of their involvement as in how far clients are allowed to influence these activities and their processes. I make this distinction between depth and breadth because there is conceptual confusion between them in the literature, both being referred to by different authors as the 'level' of involvement.

The first part of the chapter builds on the *Supporting People* guide to involvement (Godfrey et al., 2003) and develops a model identifying three levels of involvement in terms of breadth: developing voice, influencing policy and delivering services. The second part of the chapter builds on Arnstein's ladder of participation which outlines stages of involvement (which I would call depths) from manipulation to citizen control. I will, however, challenge some of this model's underlying assumptions and examine how it has been refined by other authors (Cameron et al., 2005; Wilcox, 1995). I will then present a unified model. I will finish the section by examining three common examples from practice, locating them within the model. They will highlight the kind of issues an agency will face when deciding the level of involvement that is appropriate. They are the recruitment of staff, the designing of a drugs policy and involving clients in the disciplining of other clients.

Breadth of involvement

Godfrey et al. (2003) identify three aspects of an organisation's activity that the client could be involved in, its day-to-day activities, planning policy and performance-management and service management. Other guides (FEANTSA, 2005; Cameron et al., 2005; Novas-Ouvertures, 2005) make similar distinctions. I have adapted this to developing voice, influencing policies, planning and monitoring and delivering services. The rationale behind these terms, particularly voice, is twofold. Firstly, there is the question of scope. As we explored in the chapter on balancing stakeholders' interests, some of the broad issues clients get involved in, while initially led by and within the framework of the organisation, may entail the clients going beyond the organisation, either into wider networks or in challenging that organisation and/or developing an alternative provision. While this book concentrates on what can be achieved within an organisation, our models should still acknowledge that there is a world outside of us. Otherwise, as noted by Robson above, and Velasco (2001), commenting on an earlier model of mine, we actually limit the potential scope of clients' involvement.

To illustrate, I worked with one group of ex-clients of a service which wanted to set up a group for people in a similar position. Much of their early debate was about whether the organisation would allow such a thing. I pointed out that they did not have that power, if ex-clients wanted to meet up, they could. The agency could deny good will, access to information and resources, but they could not stop them. Even current clients have the power for independent action. I worked with one agency where the client co-ordinator was being criticised for the actions of a residents' group. They had complained about the lack of repairs in a client's property. Despite following the agency's procedures, the clients felt that they had not responded legally, or within their own procedures, and reported the agency to environmental health. The agency wanted to know why the worker had allowed this to happen. He pointed out that he, or for that matter the agency, was not in a position to stop them, and furthermore they were within their rights.

The second reason to use the term voice is to recognise that clients do have agency. I think it is an important point because it recognises that all clients have a voice, and unless we nurture it, it may well become something else. Lowery, de Hoog and Lyons (cited in Somerville, 1998) theorised a model of empowerment, illustrated below, which I think is useful to explain what happens when clients do not have voice. Voice being where they can complain and have a say in how things are run. Without voice, people can be isloated, opt out or sabotage.

They discern four types of strategies clients have towards agencies: exit, voice, loyalty and alienation. They plot these strategies along two axes, from active to passive and from destructive to constructive. Exit is simply the power to opt out of the system: in our case, to leave the agency or not turn up to the residents' meeting we set up. Loyalty is where people passively accept what is on offer i.e. the passive person on the management committee. Alternatively, there is alienation which can explain some of the sabotages mentioned in earlier chapters. These strategies can be adopted individually or as a collective, from rioting to having an individual complaint. My main criticism is that I would not define loyalty as constructive or all alienation as destructive. I also think it is easier to move from alienation to voice than from loyalty to voice. Remembering the sixth theme of the book, alienation, anger and rejection is part of the path from loyalty to voice and we should not fear them or see their presence in our early stages as a sign of our having gone wrong somewhere.

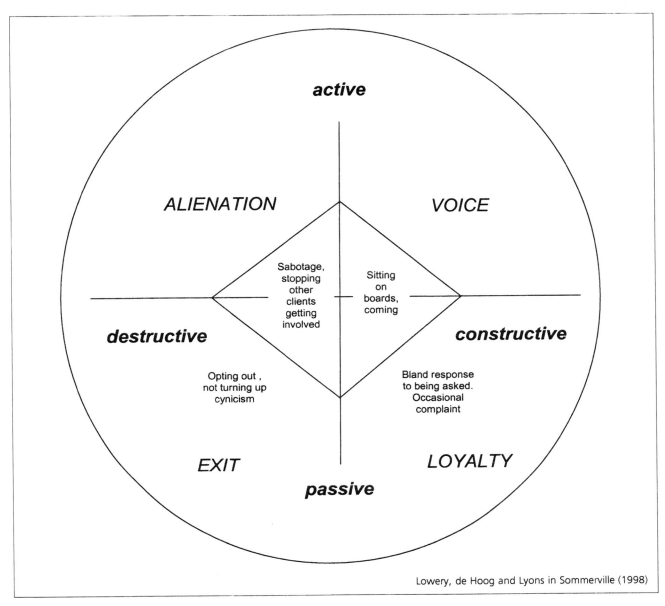

Lowery, de Hoog and Lyons in Sommerville (1998)

Figure 8.1   Strategic voices model

Despite these criticisms, I think the model explains some of the phenomena we encounter in clients' reaction to us. Its main value is that it makes clear that if we do not develop voice, something else will happen in its stead.

Developing voice

Within housing related support services, traditional approaches to client representation, with users on management committees, may not be the best way of achieving participation in running the service.

(Godfrey et al., 2003)

Godfrey et al. (2003) go on to note how in social housing the common model of 'client voice' is through certain representative systems whereby tenants are elected onto bodies, normally in some hierarchical structure, that then makes or influences decisions within the organisation or local authority. However, one should remember, particularly if we have been brought up in local authority traditions, that while this is the most obvious way of having representation, it is not the only way. Much supported housing provision is delivered by or in conjunction with the voluntary sector (Homeless Link, 2006). The voluntary sector often has different traditions and interpretations of democracy, stressing other factors such as equality of access and involvement (Osborne and McLaughlin, 2003; Wilson, 1998). Dahl (1989) makes the distinction between direct or participatory democracy, where all take part or are at least given the opportunity, and representative democracy, where smaller numbers take decisions for the majority, normally with some form of accountability to them.

Traditionally, the distinction between them is one of size, representative democracy being needed when the numbers become too unwieldy for effective decision making. However the divide is rarely that simple and is often ideological. To illustrate, I used to work for a Voluntary Action Council (Dahl, 1989), and I remember a meeting where the voluntary sector was asking some council officers how decisions were to be made regarding a restructuring of their planning processes. The officer, perhaps misjudging his audience, replied that it would be through the most democratic process they had, in that the councillors themselves would decide. I never heard what he said after that as it was drowned out by cries of derision about how unrepresentative councillors were. While we may have made a point, one could question how representative we were. I was there as an employee, representing the interest of clients who were not there and answerable to a forum of agency workers who had also been recruited to their jobs, normally by self-appointed management committees.

Yet many associate democracy with such mechanisms. I have worked with client groups who felt cheated without the 'opportunity' to vote, and felt that that alone would ensure democracy. I remember being asked by a small group of eight members to preside over their election of the four officers who ran the group. The rivalries were tearing the group apart, with bullying and intimidation on various sides, yet they insisted on having the election, feeling it would bring them together. The election was held just before the group collapsed.

In their guide to client involvement for *Supporting People* funded agencies Godfrey et al. (2003) give examples of many different forms of representation from traditional models with elected clients on management committees, clients being on the board only to represent their own views, annual forums being held with clients, to parallel structures where people can develop their own understanding of their needs, yet still feed into decision making processes. I do not think it of benefit to go over their examples, as they do this well enough and the document can be downloaded from swww.spkweb.org.uk/Subjects/Service_client_involvement.htm. What I think is missing from their analysis is some way of determining which method would be best for any particular organisation. It is left to the reader to pick the agency example which seems closest to their own, which in my mind feels a little haphazard. Dahl (1989) sought to develop criteria for democracy that go across the participative/representative spectrum. He felt any democratic process should meet these criteria and I think the reader should apply them to whatever example they may be following. I have related them to the principles in Chapter 5, as I think they are related:

- *Equal opportunity to participate.* This is linked to the principle of having diversity: no model will work for everyone and it is important to work out whom a particular method will favour. Even if they choose exit, loyalty or alienation, voice was open to them, and will continue to be, in a real sense.

- *Equal opportunity to express a choice that will be counted as equal in weight to the choice expressed by any other citizen.* This is related to the principle of cultivating permission and protection. Clients need to feel that what they have to say has worth and they are free to say it, being confident there will not be any comeback if they do. As we have established, trust is the major barrier for people in supported housing, particularly those marginalised and hard to reach groups.
- *Enlightened understanding – each individual should have equal opportunities for discovering and validating the choice on the matter to be decided.* This is related to the principle of recognising people's need to be educated to examine their situation, to understand what has happened to them and why. Again, this is not because people are stupid, but because many institutions have actively undermined people's confidence and ability to look beyond their immediate needs.
- *Control of the agenda – clients must have the opportunity to decide how matters are placed on the agenda (and actively be seen to do so).* This is related to the principle of 'seek to involve people in all aspects of the work'. It is also related to demonstrating potency and commitment; we need to show that clients have some say in the matters that are important to them.
- *Inclusion – The demos (constituency) should include all adults subject to the binding collective decisions of the association* (Dahl, 1989: 109ff). This again relates to being holistic and having diversity – we should try to include everybody, at least in intent. We covered some of these issues in Chapter 6 where we considered whom our stakeholders are.

Finally, Frost (2004), in considering Dryzek (2000), comes up with a useful checklist of questions we should keep asking ourselves when developing voice amongst clients. I will not attempt to expand on them, or to consider how we can answer them as they are a debate in themselves. They are intended as food for thought, and represent the kind of issues that may well arise for a worker developing an involvement initiative, or indeed for a group of clients who are seeking to be 'democratic' in the way they work:

- *Should clients be listened to if they have strong feelings on an issue which they cannot substantiate with a reasoned argument?*
- *How do you work with dissident views in clients such as racism or sexism? Should such views be automatically excluded, or do they have a place in democratic deliberation?*
- *How do you encourage a 'closed' group of clients to consider the needs of others beyond their own friends?*
- *Is participation a means to an end or an open process? What are the strengths and weaknesses of forcing a group to make a decision?*
- *What effect does worker intervention have on the deliberations of clients? Are you encouraging clients to reach their own conclusions or forcing a professional agenda?*
- *How do you work democratically with a group of clients who have differing views or ideas from the organisation they are a part of?*
- *Do all clients want to be heard; are there such groupings as natural leaders and followers?*
- *Should clients who are not members of a group, whether the group has formal or informal boundaries, be allowed to have a say?* (Frost, 2004, adapted from Dryzek, 2000: 6ff)

Influencing planning, policy and monitoring

Whoever they are, members of managing committees find their role at times boring and at other times baffling.

(Voluntary Action Leicester, 2002: 1)

Involvement in broad-based service planning is most effective where it is born of an established, positive dialogue between clients and providers. For example, securing clients' participation in shaping and designing new schemes often arises directly out of the experience of involving individuals in contributing to the refurbishment of their own homes.

(Godfrey et al., 2003: 56)

Part of our history that is vital to our future . . . is woven into our decision-making process . . . – ex-service client.

(Chair of Bridge HA quoted in Novas-Ouvertures, 2001: 28)

Many organisations I have worked with obsess about certain, normally visible, aspects of client involvement. One of those is involvement in strategic planning, probably because it is something the government sees as important (Beresford and Croft, 2006), and the other is having clients on management committees. I recently sat in a conference session which was trying to develop an action plan for the implementation of a housing strategy for a certain regional area. The discussion initially centred on whether all the key stakeholders were present, an issue we discussed in a previous chapter. Clients, of course, were not included in this discussion. The item on the agenda was how the sub-regions of the strategic planning body were to be organised. The main debate seemed to be whether it should be along local authority boundaries, health authority boundaries or the (then) new housing supply boundaries.

A driver for this debate seemed to be which other strategic planning bodies it would be important to dovetail into. I was there to represent the 'client perspective'. I mentioned that these distinctions and priorities would mean nothing to clients. What is the important distinguishing feature of communities in supported housing may sometimes be geographical, but rarely within local authority boundaries, or may be of interests, but would rarely dovetail into strategic interests. The looks I got were sympathetic but also pained. The fact was that irrespective of the clients' points of interests; this was how their planning mechanisms were structured. They, despite how senior they were, were not in a position to change that.

This brings me to a second obsession organisations often have, which is to have client representation on the management committee/board of trustees. The relief I felt on leaving the aforementioned meeting was similar to the feeling I had when I stopped being a trustee for Groundswell. Bear in mind that this book is dedicated to that organisation, which I continue to respect for its innovation. The fact is that however dynamic and innovative we tried to make the management committee, it remained a fairly bound institution which had to receive the accounts, the business plan, the five year development plan and the rest. I just do not find that kind of stuff interesting. The point I am trying to make is that, in common with me, I think there are a lot of clients out there who do not, and maybe never will, find this level of involvement very appealing.

While, as the Novas-Ouvertures quote implies, a clients' voice is important in both these aspects, I would emphasise another sentiment of this quote. We need to have a sense of history of how things have been planned or, in our case, put history behind us.

Yet clients can have involvement in these areas in different ways, and while we have restrictions, these are restrictions to be overcome, rather than things that bind us to our traditional ways. Within Groundswell, while the management committee retained its necessary legal aspects, passing budgets, receiving business plan, etc., it took a decision that other forums would determine the direction, goals and milestones of the organisation. Voluntary Action Leicester (VAL) (2002), outlines many different types of boards an organisation can operate; from ones that rubber stamp the decisions of the manager to activist ones where management committees are involved in the day-to-day operation of the organisation. Similarly, there are many books that outline innovative ways in which we can strategically plan (Forster, 2007; Van der Haijden, 2004); we just need to be more imaginative. I suspect that some of those other workers in that strategic planning conference would also feel relief at being allowed to do things differently.

VAL sees such blending of planning and activism as potentially problematic and confusing. However two factors mean that these should again, be problems to overcome rather than reasons not to integrate these aspects, for two reasons. Firstly, such blending fulfils the principle of starting at the point of interest of clients. Secondly, we must take account of the fact that a characteristic of the most vulnerable in supported housing, such as homeless people, is loss of the ability to have a vision of the long term (Daly, 1996; Seal, 2007). For them, the short term, the issues clients can readily see, may well be the ones they also have some active involvement in. Positively, Godfrey et al. (2003) recognise that the best kind of client involvement at this strategic level is both organic and is still located within clients' areas of interest.

I also think that starting organically may eventually lead to some clients developing any interest in strategic issues. I worked with a group of hostel dwellers whose original interest had been in service delivery and research, an area of work I will expand on in the next section. However, once they were engaged, the organisation asked them if they wanted to be involved in the design of a new hostel and they were keen to be involved. They were involved in everything from the recruitment of staff to the layout of the building, to the induction of both staff and clients, to the policies of the hostel, and to the mechanisms for continued client involvement. In this way I would say that policy, at least as a starting point, has more potential for meaningful client involvement. Their interests and learning developed organically. I distinctly remember one client saying that he never thought that looking at a five year development plan was something he would find stimulating.

On a final note for this section, the issue of monitoring can bring up particular issues for clients such as fear of reprisals, with staff feeling threatened about being judged by clients. However, it can be an area of particular importance. It is only through monitoring that we can pick up on things like the aforementioned policy slippage (Thompson and Wilson, 2005), and develop an accurate picture of whether the organisation is actually open to learning (Argyris and Schon, 1976.) However, those organisations that do not want to learn are also likely to have a static model for the board (Voluntary Action Leicester, 2005), or where the client may be in real danger of reprisals for challenging staff sabotage of policy. A model that ameliorated these effects was operated in London, actually prior to the advent of *Supporting People*, called the Audit Partnership. It was an inter-agency partnership whereby workers, and clients, would be trained up in the good practice that was to be expected from an agency. The 'team' would then audit another agency apart from its own, thereby eliminating some of the aforementioned issues for clients (it was also recognised that similar issues existed for workers, if they judged their agency too harshly).

While the project did not concentrate on client involvement issues, it could easily be adapted to do so. Another large provider ran a similar project but concentrated on research methods rather than auditing, starting from scratch in terms of what is good practice, an issue we will return to in Chapter 9 on methods. They were also large enough to be able to have clients from one part of the service researching a different part where they had no agenda. However, what this model did not illuminate was how the organisational culture mitigates against client involvement, which was substantial in this case, because the clients are a part of that culture. We as independent facilitators could, and did, name this culture, outlining why this book values independent advocacy highly.

Delivering services

Are there opportunities available for people to be involved in shaping what is provided and how it is provided on a day-to-day basis, whether formally or informally?

(Godfrey et al., 2003: 55)

Homeless people are part of the solution, not the problem.

(Groundswell, 2005: 2)

Taking account of some of the comments made in the previous section, it seems that active involvement is one of the most effective ways to develop client involvement, and what better way to do this than to involve clients in the delivery of the services designed for them. Positively, *Supporting People* recognises this in Godfrey et al.'s statement above. This was from a checklist in their section entitled 'involving clients in day-to-day activities'. Neale (1997) sees development in this area as neglected, noting that in the absence of support in hostels, clients provide it to one another. Groundswell takes this analysis a stage further, recognising that we need to challenge a culture that sees the involvement of clients in their own solutions, through such things as the development of mutual support, as a negative thing. In a recent piece of work (2007b), I talked about how the supported housing sector tends to see the influence of peers as a wholly negative thing. *Supporting People* (Godfrey et al., 2003) also recognises the benefit of clients mutual support. 'Clients develop self-esteem and derive support from each other. They also learn how to deal with conflict and tackle problems.'

I emphasise this point because it is in this area of involvement that I have encountered the most resistance from both agencies and workers. It is where the anti-client bias of many working cultures (Seal, 2005, 2007b), are exposed, such as self-revelation and confidentiality. To involve clients in delivering services can also encounter some resistance from workers because clients may literally be seen as 'taking their jobs'. The point is that all the difficulties with boundaries, confidentiality, appropriate remuneration for clients, etc., should be seen as barriers to be overcome, rather than reasons not to involve clients at this level. We should also not allow these barriers to mean involvement in delivery becomes purely domestic, often in the form of performing tasks such as tidying, cleaning or cooking the occasional meal for others in the house. This is not to say these activities are wrong, I think they are a good stepping stone and for some clients is the most appropriate level of involvement and the one that they want. We should just not limit involvement to these kind of activities. Taking on board Neale's comments, we should take as a starting point that clients are already supporting each other and build on this.

As an example, I was working with an agency recently who felt that the nature of their agencies mitigated against client involvement. They were a floating support agency which worked with individuals and families who were already in or about to go into, local authority accommodation and were deemed to need support for whatever reason. Work was conducted in people's own homes. The workers were struggling to get clients to come to meetings, citing travelling, isolation and lack of motivation as reasons why people did not want to come to meetings about the project. It seemed to me that the agency was not hitting people's point of interest. I asked whether people were often on the same estates (which they were) and why not see if clients wanted to meet up with each other to offer mutual support. Nowadays many people in social housing have got there through their vulnerability and may now want to offer support and empathy for others (I have said before that we are too quick to accuse the local community of nimbyism). The whole estate could act as a support mechanism. Furthermore, the council may well have a community centre that could broker and support such a scheme. This is not to say that there may not need to be training, vetting and all kinds of other things to overcome, but the initiative just seemed like a better starting point.

The hostel where clients were actively involved in its design built in many opportunities for client involvement in service delivery. A simple one being that the induction was done by a client rather than a worker (or at least part of it). Clients were also actively involved in staff induction, designing a days' training which involved them knowing what it felt like to be processed and spend a day in a hostel environment. Even experienced workers said it was one of the most illuminating training experiences they had ever had. On other levels, clients were to be involved in setting menus, within budgets, for the hostel, to be given cooking opportunities and (controversially for the organisation) in periodically reviewing the catering companies contract. Client involvement was to be embedded within key working (i.e. a session would be built in for feedback on the organisation periodically) and clients would, again controversially, be involved in staff appraisal and recruitment. Clients were to be given a small decorating allowance for their rooms (it was a long stay hostel) to use as they wished, with a team of volunteer clients to help them decorate. Finally, there was to be a buddying system whereby all clients would be given the opportunity to have recourse to a client who had been there for some time for support and advice.

Godfrey et al. (2003) detail similar projects where clients are actively involved in supporting one another. In each case they are taking the point of interest of the client and building on it. This point may well change as people move through projects. As mentioned before, in St Mungo's we found that clients in emergency accommodation were more interested in having complaints answered and the quality of services. People in the second stage wanted to be involved in the running and policies of the hostel, and those in the semi-supported projects became volunteer researchers. Very few wanted to be involved in strategic planning, but there were some, and they were given this opportunity.

Depth of involvement

As well as considering what people should be involved in, we need to consider how far they should be involved. Do we just tell them what is going on, involve them in decisions or let them

Table 8.1 Client depth of involvement

Arnstein (1969)	**Wilcox** (1995)	**Cameron et al.** (2005)
1. Manipulation.	1. Information.	1. Staff inform about available services planned changes.
2. Therapy.	2. Consultation.	2. Service clients occasionally asked views via surveys or meetings.
3. Informing.	3. Deciding together.	3. Service clients having a voice on the management committee.
4. Consultation.	4. Acting together.	4. Service clients forming a majority of any partnership managing the service.
5. Placation.	5. Supporting independent community interests.	5. Total control of the service by its clients.
6. Partnership.		
7. Delegated power.		
8. Citizen control.		

make the decisions themselves? There are several models for explaining the depth of involvement (Arnstein, 1969; Cameron et al., 2005; Wilcox, 1995). I will examine the three most common and try to come up with a synthesis of the best elements of them:

The first model outlined is the oldest, and perhaps most famous. It was developed by Arnstein in the late 1960s. It sees client involvement as a ladder to be climbed. Of particular interest in this model are the negative stages of manipulation, therapy and placation. The context of this model was within mental health, with the first two types of involvement being associated with a medical model. Manipulation is worse than therapy because it was without due care for the persons' welfare. The placation stage is interesting, particularly as it comes after consultation. For Arnstein, this is where there is an illusion that the clients are involved in decision-making, when in fact there is simply a 'co-option of hand-picked 'worthies' onto committees. It allows citizens to advise or plan ad infinitum but retains for power holders the right to judge the legitimacy or feasibility of the advice' (Wilcox, 1995: 12). My criticism of this stage is where it is placed; I would judge that to placate people in this way can be worse, and less about true involvement, than to simply inform them. Cameron et al.'s model is a simplified version of Arnstein and is set in the context of supported housing. It eliminates the more insidious elements of Arnstein's model, seeing the earlier stages are something of a base to start improving from.

The main difficulty with these two models is that they are a little simplistic in their linearity, assuming that (ignoring the first two stages which I would not argue with), that information giving is poor, while citizen control is the best and ultimate goal. For me, only giving information to people is not inherently bad, while setting up client-led projects can be tokenistic and damaging to participants. For instance, when there is an issue where there is no possibility of change, such as a new law, there is little more one can do than to inform people about the situation. To pretend there is more we can do is deceptive, but tempting. I am reminded of an incident during one of the aforementioned speakouts with local councillors. They were fine when clients brought up the subject of the homeless laws and how unfair they were as it let them off the hook, because councillors had no power over these laws. It was also deceptive because they could come up with ideas about what it could be like and write off to MPs, get petitions, etc., knowing that it would make little difference. Conversely, I remember the councillors getting nervous when two young women wanted to bring up the council's own leaving care policies as they were accountable for them.

I have also seen client groups set up as supposedly autonomous groups that are actually set up to fail. One group of clients I knew were brought together to produce a manifesto for homeless people. While a good idea, it did not come from them, one of the group describing themselves as a boy band in this respect. The group was high profile and the members enjoyed the interviews and publicity they received, created by the organisation's PR department, for the short time that it lasted. Understandably after the manifesto's launch the group wanted to keep the group going. However, they had no clear direction, people were unsure why they were there, they had no idea how to sustain themselves, the support from the organisation had gone and they ended up tearing themselves, and one another, apart.

For these reasons, Wilcox (1995) simplified the model to five stances, seeing them all as legitimate depending upon the issue under scrutiny. This is in contrast to Arnstein and Cameron's model that tries, erroneously in my opinion, to look at the level of involvement across the whole organisation. This becomes impossible if we accept that all stances have contingent legitimacy. This contingency means we can only look at particular issues, rather than across the agency as a whole. As we saw above, sometimes information is the best ploy, sometimes making decisions together. I have several criticisms of Wilcox's model. Firstly, in its distinction between deciding and acting together, it conflates decision making and involvement in delivery. For me, they are different considerations that could come together at any point, but are discreet. Acting together could be at the information stage in the form of peer education. Similarly, clients could make an autonomous decision about the confidentiality policy of staff that staff are responsible for enacting, not the clients. In fact, one could have two different models, one for decision making and one for degree of involvement in delivery. For the purposes of this chapter I will confine myself to looking at decision making.

My second criticism of Wilcox is that he misses out autonomous, or even majority decisions, within an organisation. Beyond partnership he only deposits an agency's supporting of independent initiatives, while I think there are other options. I would also criticise taking out the more negative stages. I think they need keeping in to remind staff of the dangers of having levels of involvement which look good but are actually tokenistic at best. I would finally agree with Velasco's (2000) criticism of Wilcox's model that it is too agency-centric. However, I would challenge Velasco's critique that a model that is agency-focused precludes independent action on behalf of clients. I think this is a separate issue. Clients are, of course, capable of independent action, and Groundswell is active in supporting such initiatives, but they are, as stated, independent. There may be alliances to be built, but the issue of autonomous action should be distinguished from client involvement within agencies. However, as I said before, a good model should acknowledge these possibilities.

Below is my synthesis model of the depth of client involvement. I have portrayed it as a sunrise with a series of stances we could make about the depth of client involvement on any particular issue. All the top spokes are legitimate stances an agency could make, depending on the circumstances. However, there are forces that may push us towards an illegitimate stance. In helping determine the appropriate depth of involvement there are also environmental factors which we will need to consider.

To illustrate how decisions can be made about which stance is appropriate, I will consider three common examples, the recruitment of staff, the designing of a drugs policy and, perhaps most controversially, the involvement of clients in making decisions about the consequences for other clients where they have broken the house rules (e.g. conditions of tenancy or a licence agreement). They are the examples that cause most debate in training.

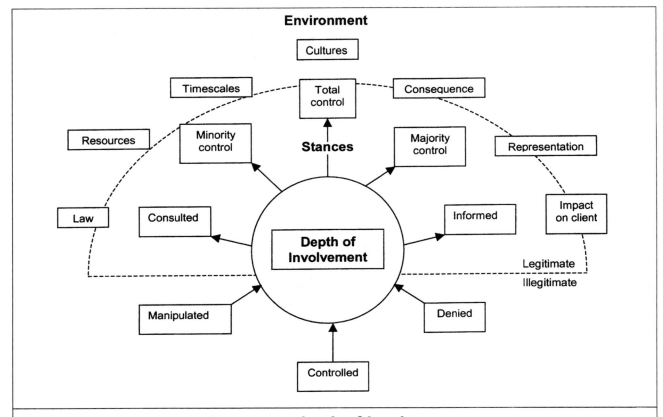

Stances on depth of involvement

1. **Total control:** Total control of the matter lies with clients.
2. **Majority control:** Clients form a majority of any decision making body on the matter.
3. **Minority control:** Clients have minority but a representative voice on what happens on the matter.
4. **Consulted:** Clients are asked for their views on the matter.
5. **Informed:** Clients are informed about what will happen to the matter because there in no point in further involvement.
6. **Manipulated:** Some clients have an unrepresentative voice on what happens with the matter.
7. **Denied:** It is deemed that it would be in the best interests of the client not to involve them in decisions on the matter.
8. **Controlled:** The question of client involvement in decisions on the matter is not even entertained.

Figure 8.2 Client depth of involvement

In training, I ask people to imagine giving total control to clients, and then to backtrack to the stance they think is appropriate. Hopefully, this avoids retreating into some of the negative stances.

Environmental considerations

Law – what are the limiting factors legally. What aspects have you some negotiation on?

Resources – have you the money and skills base to support greater involvement.

Representativeness – is this an issue where you want greater representation or depth or analysis. Remember the more depth you want the less people are likely to be involved and the less representative they will become.

Timescales – the more depth needed the longer it will take both to decide and to build the capacity to decide.

Cultures – do you have a shared language and culture about decision making and what are the parameters of the decision to be made. Have you built up trust and is the agency prepared to share the power in a meaningful way.

Consequences – Plan not just for your stance but how you will handle reactions to it. In the earlier stages you can really do no more. In later stages what if the options clients want go outside of your scope. Can you handle the unforeseen outcomes of your stance.

Impact on clients – applicable to all stages. As we shall see below, involving clients in decisions may mean that they are then judged or held to account, by other clients, for these decisions. While there is some accountability in this there may also be consequences.

Recruitment

To give a couple of examples of how not to do it, I have observed clients sitting on a recruitment panel simply reading out a predetermined question. Conversely, I have been on the receiving end of a panel of 15 clients who asked seemingly random questions (when I conferred with other candidates later), two of the panel left halfway through and two fell asleep – I was not present for the decision making, obviously, but I was not confident of its rigor. While the client will have insight into what makes for a good worker, the person must be able to fulfil the aspects of the job that are not to do with clients. The question for me is where clients can be most effective in the process, and this is not necessarily being on the panel. To sit on the panel may need training, support and especially time from the client. Even then, the questions are normally fairly standard and with a good matrix it should be relatively immaterial who is on the panel. When combined with the fact that clients, even if there is more than one or even a majority, are not the only decision makers, it is not that powerful a position.

However, to sit on the panel may well have consequences for the client. If the worker they recruited is not what other clients expected, they may well take it out on the client who was involved in the recruitment process. If clients do sit on the panel, workers often worry about the confidentiality of candidates' personal information, but I think this rather a red herring. Clients can be bound by confidentiality and we have no reason to believe they are going to be any less discrete with the information than anyone else. Identifying details, such as addresses, can be removed and for clients to be privy to other information such as work history, does not seem to me to be a bad thing. How much information do workers have on clients? I have seen alternatives to having a client on the panel such as alternate or parallel panels. They throw up similar debates about how they are constituted, what they are assessing and how much weight they will have. Positively, I think they have potential, particularly where an agency wants clients to assess particular aspects of a worker's skill.

Consultation, which can look like a step back from minority or majority control, can be very powerful in recruitment, depending on what is consulted upon. If the clients have input into the person specification, detailing the skills they think workers should have, it could be more powerful, and meaningful, than being on the panel. Clients could design the kind of questions they think will draw out these skills. I remember one client question, related to the skill of relationship building with clients was 'when was the last time you were intimidated by a client and why'. I think the answers were probably more revealing than standard questions about people's ability to work in a team, but also being able to work under their own initiative. In a piece of recent consultancy on inter-agency partnership working with young people I recommended the initiative they had client involvement at this level. Interestingly, they rejected this, saying that having clients on the panel 'looked' better and was easier to organise as they had a couple of clients who were interested. Arnstein's level of placation and my level of manipulation come to mind.

Drugs policies

Involving clients in designing a drug policy for a project has legal implications (HMSO, 1971, 2004). We cannot allow use of many drugs on the premises and need to be seen to take steps if we become aware of its usage. For this reason many workers in training say we cannot involve clients in the drawing up of policies. However, within this legal framework, we can. For instance, what counts as reasonable steps is open for interpretation and we could involve clients in determining them. Also, when it comes to drugs such as alcohol these restrictions do not apply. The nature of the approach may depend on the ethos of that hostel, but again that can be the framework to operate within. I knew one hostel in Southampton which ran a cognitive behavioural therapy project for chaotic clients, many of whom had issues with alcohol. The overall philosophy of the project was that the rules around alcohol had to help people in their therapy. How this was interpreted was determined by the clients in a weekly group. Sometimes they would decide there should be no drinking in communal areas, sometimes only in communal areas, sometimes anywhere and sometimes none at all; depending on the needs of the residents at the time.

While this would be difficult to implement in a larger, more transient hostel, it goes to show some involvement is possible. In such a hostel it may mean the rules are less about individuals, and the review periods may be further apart. Nevertheless, involvement is possible, and within the restrictions of the legal framework clients could have relative autonomy in what happens or at least a majority or minority role in decision making. To involve people also has an educative role, about the pressure and contradictions that agencies face. For instance, agencies may accept, from a harm reduction, and a realistic point of view, that people will use drugs on the premises and seek to make this usage as safe as possible. However, the law says we have to take steps to prevent people using on the premises. There is a contradiction here that we have to manage and because of this we often give out mixed messages. Clients may think we are anti-drugs, when actually it is a law that constricts us.

I will give an example of the consequences of this from my own practice. In one project I worked in we had an official no drug use policy, because we felt we had to. On the other hand we operated a harm minimisation policy towards drugs and gave out sharps boxes (a box to deposit used injecting needles safely). Therein lay the mixed message. I caught one client who instead of putting his sharps into the sharps box was putting them under his bed. When

I asked him why he did this instead of putting them into his box, he replied that he had assumed the box was there to entrap people. Looking back on the mixed messages we had given out I was not surprised. Involving clients may help them understand the different tensions we have to manage when coming up with a drugs policy. So clients could understand what we were trying to manage, whereas previously they just thought we were inconsistent.

Involving clients in the discipline of other clients

I want to conclude on this issue for it illustrates to me why we cannot advocate for no involvement on any issue, even on an issue such as this that, in training, probably causes the most controversy. When a course involves clients and workers, it also is the most polarising issue. Workers often at one end of the scale say that we should purely provide information to clients, as there are too many dangers to having more involvement. Clients normally advocate for at least minority control; saying that this is their home, so why shouldn't they have a say. Workers come up with concerns such as confidentiality, to which clients reply that they talk to each other anyway, and are often more honest to each other than they are to workers. Workers worry that clients may create kangaroo courts, to which clients reply 'what makes your kangaroo courts any better than ours?' Once, on this last point, a client replying to the statement that the worker thought they should not be involved in disciplining other clients stated that they already were, just not officially. He asked what the worker thought was discussed in the residents lounge and why people would just leave on occasion.

This statement brought home to me that we often cannot stop people being involved, we can simply try to influence how this happens and perhaps bring it above ground rather than underground, to use it as an issue to bring workers and client together rather than drive a wedge between them. If clients have no voice they will simply go for sabotage or exit and, only occasionally, loyalty. There are many obstacles to be overcome on this issue, we will need to protect all involved and ensure there is equity etc. The point being that they are obstacles to overcome and they should not be allowed to become reasons for not having involvement. Godfrey et al. (2003) catalogue examples where clients have been involved in disciplining other clients, detailing a successful example of clients sitting on eviction panels, and overcoming the difficult issues such as confidentiality. I worked with a mental health agency that successfully developed a peer advocacy scheme for those facing eviction. Even if clients are not involved in the direct mechanisms, they could be involved in developing and changing the policies that are used as guides to what disciplinary decisions are made. To finish, I would like to return to the principle of being holistic. The question is not how do we 'do' client involvement, with whatever we are developing, and whatever issue arises, the question is 'what is the best way to involve clients in this?'

9

Methods and Techniques for Involvement

Be prepared to reconsider your methods and respond to new or different ideas. They should be prepared to persevere when a client participation initiative fails to generate results and adapt their method or adopt a new approach.

(Novas-Ouvertures, 2004: 8)

Too often, the role for service client representatives involves attending committee meetings on a monthly (or less frequent) basis. At these meetings they are often a single client in a room full of people, usually experienced, senior professionals, who work with (or sometimes against) each other on a daily basis. The agenda, at least, will have been decided before they arrive and positional papers and proposals drafted and circulated.

(Bryant, 2001: 23)

There is a range of mechanisms by which service clients can be involved. The choice of method will be shaped by the purpose of involving clients, the size of the client group, the difficulty in accessing their views, and the resources available to do so.

(Cameron et al., 2005: 34)

This final chapter will examine the range of techniques of involvement. It is not intended to be comprehensive and will point the reader to other resources that investigate the methods in more detail. More to the point, taking a lead from the Bryant and Novas quotes, I take the stance that we should not be prescriptive about our methods, or, returning to an example from the previous chapter about having clients on interview panels, go for what looks good or is flavour of the month. Furthermore, noting Cameron el al.'s (2005) point, we should subject our ideas to challenge, reflecting upon whatever we come up with. We need to look at who it serves and what the objectives are. To these ends the chapter will identify methods on two axes, one about the numbers we involve, from individuals to group techniques, and the other about how incorporated the methods are, from being organic to being an adjunct or 'event'. I have a bias towards our techniques being organic but cannot deny the unifying power of a well-run event.

Group techniques

Group techniques without values and norms are dangerous. They may lead to control, domination and coercion without respect for human nature and members rights to determine their own processes and goals.

(Glassman and Kates, 1990: 22)

Hostels generally do try to run client groups, but motivation is low because it is hard, and often seen as ineffective, and again these groups have little actual power, tending to be led by the staff. Why is this?

(Wyner, 1999)

Residents asked for things which weren't on offer and therefore felt angry and aggrieved. This also made them feel bonded together against the staff, so instead of building bridges it divided people, and the staff felt very demoralised.

(Staff member, quoted in Wyner, 1999)

I will be concentrating on group work for three reasons: because it is associated with client involvement, because we are inexperienced at it and while it can be powerful, it can also be damaging, for worker and client alike. Taking the first point, when I talk about client involvement in training, workers tend to assume this is about getting groups of clients together. There are many positives to bringing groups together, as we shall discuss later, but I worry that we may be choosing group activities for the wrong reasons. We may choose groups because they are seemingly more efficient and cost effective – reaching more people. I think this a false economy, as the resources we need to invest, and the skills we need to develop to have good group work do not come cheap. We may choose to work with groups because they are visible, they 'show' we have involvement. This seems to be the wrong motive for me and betrays an organisation where client involvement is not integrated into working practices but is the aforementioned add-on. The quotes illustrate the third point that we should not undertake group work lightly. There may be unforeseen consequences for the group and facilitator alike. To effectively facilitate a group needs skills that workers often do not develop in their normal working. I have mentioned before (Seal: 2005), how the supported housing sector tends to operate to a social work model, where workers have individual caseloads, rather than running groups. It is therefore a skill that we will need to develop. In the college where I teach the group work course lasts a year for two hours a week, constituting 60hrs of training on the subject. I think this just about prepares people to run a group.

All too often I have heard workers in the supported housing field relay how they were thrown into a group with no training on group work and expected to make it work. I particularly worry where workers start randomly doing exercises they have heard about and like the sound of without, as Glassman and Kates warn, looking into their values and context. To use such exercises out of context can have unforeseen consequences. For instance, I have seen workers use trust games, a typical one being to have clients fall backwards and be caught by others. This was a technique developed within psycho-drama (Gale:1990), and I think is potentially very dangerous when used outside of a therapeutic setting. Given the levels of abuse in our client group, should we early on have them being physically held by strangers in a situation where they have to place trust in them.

Positively, there are good reasons to bring groups together. Brown (1993) lists groups as being useful for:

. . . expressing unexpressed point of views, developing conversational skills, exchanging information, sharing experiences, grasping abstractions, giving and getting feedback, learning about self, learning about others, changing attitudes, learning new behaviour, increasing self confidence, problem solving and decision making, discussing feelings, working with others and mutual aid and support.

(Brown, 1993)

While these claims can all be questioned, such a list is useful to give to those who are cynical about the benefits of bringing clients together. Godfrey et al. (2003) develop a similar list of the positives of bringing groups of clients together, which I think is worth summarising below as they come from a slightly different angle, seeing the benefits for workers and clients alike.

- *Personal development:* increased confidence, self-esteem, and problem-solving capacity and negotiating skills, including confidence that services are more responsive to client expressed needs and reducing social isolation.
- *Practical skills development:* that not only reduces dependence on other people, but has the potential to offer more adventurous activities and expand employment options.
- *Expanded knowledge and trust:* pooling skills and experience and knowledge, increasing trust and confidence between clients and staff.

Indeed, going back to the seventh theme of the book, many of these things are seen as being the role of a worker in their key working sessions, so why not achieve them this way instead. As noted by several authors, there are also limitations to groups (Brown, 1993; Douglas, 1991, 1995; Marsh et al., 1978). They cannot attend to the problems of an individual. In fact, they can exacerbate them as revelation in the group makes the rest of a group the audience. For effective working and to achieve a goal, often determined by the agency, individual needs and perspectives are put aside and co-operative working is needed. Often groups do not provide immediate benefit to their members, and while we don't want to fall back into the trap of saying clients will not do things for altruistic reasons, there can be frustrations for members at moving at the pace of a group. These needs may need to be met elsewhere, entailing another support mechanism, entailing more resources. We often assume that groups, in bringing people together who have a common aim and experience, will reduce isolation and provide mechanisms of support. In many cases they will, but as the worker in the Wyner (1999) quote experienced, groups can also heighten a sense of difference and separateness from those not sharing that experience, or indeed those who do. We should not, therefore, be complacent about what groups can achieve and see them as an easy option. To these ends Godfrey et al. (2003) develop a useful set of prerequisites for bringing clients together that I think is useful to reproduce:

- Ensure that the forms of involvement take into account the length of time clients are likely to remain in the service.
- Consider the resources that will be required (staff time and money), for example:
  o Dedicated staff time to provide continuity and support to the group.
  o Support, encouragement and training for staff to facilitate groups.
  o Skilled, independent advocacy support, separate from service providers.
- Secure financial backing to purchase equipment, organise publicity, and provide training opportunities and an accessible venue.
- Acknowledge that enhancing clients' capacity to organise themselves will not occur overnight. It will take time and investment in developing skills.
- Understand that not everyone will want to participate to the same extent and that opportunities for different levels of engagement should be provided.
- Ensure that too much pressure is not placed on individuals over an extended period of time and that it remains open to new participants and new ideas.

- Develop clear boundaries on the role and scope of decision-making power and the extent of involvement of clients and staff, so that both can sign up to, and accept responsibility.

(Godfrey et al., 2003: 78)

I would place particular emphasis on the need for training for those who will facilitate the groups and on the comment about clients not learning organisational skills overnight. In fact I think it will take some time. Not that I do not think they have the capacity, this is just to reiterate that I think group skills take a long time for anyone to develop, if we do not want the group to end up tearing itself apart. For more on group work, I will list some areas to consider and suggest further reading for the reader, going into even greater detail in the appendix to the book. The sources can all be found in the references section.

Ground rules

The purpose of ground rules is to agree on an understanding of how people are to behave in the group. Participants need to feel safe, comfortable and valued. However, as I mentioned in an earlier publication, '*Ground rules are not uncontested; it is legitimate to question whether a piece of paper actually makes people feel safe or valued*' (Seal, 2006: 12). For further discussion see Seal, 2006.

Group dynamics

The concept of group dynamics is the simple one that groups are more than the sum of the individuals in it and people are interconnected in the group. Homans (1951) book *The Human Group* still provides the best exposition of this idea. I will give a practical example of how group dynamics can operate and their consequences. In training on the principles of client involvement, I normally split the group into four groups of equal size. I then ask them to come up with three or four principles for client involvement, ones that would cover any initiative. When they have come up with some, I ask them to amalgamate with another/the other group and negotiate with them to come up with three or four principles between them. I would then ask people to either repeat this once more (if there are four groups) or to put up on the flipchart the principles they have come up with. As well as discussion about the content of their discussion I get them to look at the group processes. Certain tendencies often arise:

- The principles tend to end up being very wide and are often compromises.
- Radical, extreme and challenging views tend to get marginalised.
- Some people's ideas get lost and they feel umbrage.
- Negotiation between groups can get quite defensive and competitive.

These phenomena are not necessarily bad, it depends what we are trying to achieve. However, these tendencies will also engender emotional reactions in people. In training, I will sometimes ask people how they felt in the session. Some say they felt marginalised, especially when their point disappeared or was amalgamated. I ask the participant to imagine how this might feel if you were a client, who had come all this way to get an opinion across that ended up getting buried. Many of the ways we structure client involvement in supported housing have similar consequences.

Group roles

Group work authors often produce a list of roles that people play out in group situations. Belbin (1999) identifies the roles that are needed in a team and represents a good introduction to this approach. Personally, I find him over positive and have produced my own version of his roles (Seal, 2006). Some authors (Goffman,1971; Radley, 1991; Seal, 2006), warn of being simplistic with allocating roles, as the ones people play will shift and depend on the group they are in.

Group size

There are debates about the impact of the size of a group but it seems to be true that size will have an impact. Rogers (1986) looks at the impact that size has on how people speak together as a whole group. Boud et al. (1993) and Turkie (1995) have also written some interesting pieces on how larger groups, 25 plus, function and develop.

Groups over time

The most famous exposition of how groups develop over time is by Tuckman (1965) who sees a group as going through up to six stages, forming, norming, storming, performing, ending and sometimes mourning. Many variations of this have been developed and for an exploration of them see Johnson and Johnson (1998). However, there is a danger in seeing them as rigid stages, as in practice they are rarely as clear-cut as this (Seal, 2006). Tuckman designed them with a task orientated group with a distinct beginning and end in mind (Brown, 1988). This may not be the nature of the group of clients that are being brought together in client involvement. Nevertheless, the point that the nature of the group will develop over time is worth noting.

Types of exercises

Perhaps as many typologies of exercises used in group work exist as do exercises. It depends on what we see as the important features of exercises, something I will leave for the reader to discern for their context. My own preference is the distinction between analytical, creative and experiential exercises. The first type help you to analyse a situation, the second help us to be creative in how we think about, or come up with solutions for, that situation. Experiential exercises are where there is a 'direct encounter with the phenomena being studied rather than merely thinking about the encounter, or considering the possibility of doing something about it' (Borzak, 1981 quoted in Brookfield, 1986: 9), an example being the 'day in the life of a client' training mentioned in an earlier chapter.

Petty et al. (1995) in their excellent book, *Participatory Learning and Action: A Trainers Guide*, based on the ideas of Participatory Rapid Appraisal (based on anthropological research techniques used in the developing world) divide exercises into six categories. Getting started: exercises for introductions and icebreakers; Picking up the tempo: exercises for energising and forming groups; Keeping it together: exercises for enhancing group dynamics; Learning to listen: exercises to improve listening and observation; Learning to reflect: exercises for improving analysis; Summing it up: exercises for evaluation. Finally Ross and Thorpe (1988) produced a typology of exercises according to their style. The sources listed below are where I think the reader will find the best exposition of these ideas:

Name learning techniques, Petty et al. (1995)

Trust exercises, Brandes and Phillips (1990) Ernst and Goodison (1981)

Talking exercises, Brown (1988: 114)

Writing, Bolton et al. (2006)

Social skills training, Bond (1986) Priesteley (1978)

Psychodrama, Gale (1990)

Socio drama, Sternberg and Garcia (2000) Boal (2000)

Body sculpts, Jennings et al. (2004)

Arts and crafts, Liebermann (2004)

Indoor and outside physical activities, Barnes and Sharpe (2004)

Inter group and inter role activities, Houston (1993)

Before I move on, perhaps the question is more how we analyse and pick the group techniques. As Involve (2005) say in *People and Participation* (it can be downloaded from www.involving.org/mt/archives/blog_13/**People**%20and%20**Participation**%20final.pdf), there are hundreds of techniques and tools out there, the point is how we discern where and when each one may be useful. Involve analyse techniques according to the numbers they involve, the roles of clients, the budget needed, the time it will take, the expected outcomes and where it sits on Arnstein's ladder of participation (1968). I think this is useful from an organisational point of view but does not go deeply enough into the dynamics of the exercises, and the possible consequences the techniques may engender for clients. To these ends, I think Douglas (1993) does this better. He recommends six factors which we should consider in analysing the impact of the exercise:

- *Decisions:* what sort of decisions can people make: how much freedom to choose have they got? There is an assumption the few rules means freedom of decision but if we compare snap to chess, we see this is not necessarily the case.
- *Power:* how are participants controlled: who does the controlling and what authority is used? Are you the referee or the facilitator or simply the one who states things and learning.
- *Movement:* how much and what level of physical movement is required.
- *Competence:* what level of competence is required to participate? High skills based activities can put people off.
- *Interaction:* how much, and what types of, interaction occurs between participants.
- *Rewards:* what sort of rewards are there? Are they for the few or the many? How are they distributed? – are they built into the activity, dependant on the outcome or incidental?.

In later works (1995), he adds the idea of creativity as another factor linking it to the idea of diversity. This is something I would agree is a significant factor, as it allows for different perspectives to emerge and, if handled with skill, coalesce. I would use these typologies in combination and hope both serve as a guide for champions and agencies making decisions about what activities to use. I will leave this section with a warning from Douglas about the dangers of not doing so:

> *Workers often give highly subjective reasons for using certain activities in group . . . which seem to be aimed mainly at justifying what an organisation or worker needs and prefers to do for their own comfort and confidence and rather less at ensuring the selection of activities particularly appropriate to the group and its individual members.*
>
> (Douglas, 1995: 21)

Individualised techniques

While group work tends to be something new for workers, and may be an adjunct to what they do already, work with individuals is the mainstay of their roles in the supported housing sector (Seal, 2005). It is institutionalised through *Supporting People*'s emphasis on key working and support planning as the primary mechanism for the delivery of the support it funds. As we discussed before, client participation is embedded in the Quality Assessment Framework and is one of the determining factors in getting a 'C' or an 'A' grade. Simply put, this means that our paperwork and key working needs to become more client-friendly. I think this is a good starting point for individualised client involvement; if we have the key working right then other things will follow.

As an example, I have covered in a previous book how assessment is notoriously something thing we do to our clients rather than something we involve them in (Brandon, 1998; Seal, 2005). There are other, more imaginative ways of conducting assessment that involve clients (see Seal, 2005, 2006). Other books that I have found useful over the years are listed in the appendix.

Creative approaches also go beyond people's own care and can extend to asking for more generalised feedback on the agency. Dedicating an aspect of the key working session to this may be a breath of fresh air for both parties, as mentioned in Chapter 5. It can be quite intimidating, and even disheartening, for both parties, to spend all the time looking at a client's problems, or issues, all day (Frost and Seal, 2004). Clients may well want to give feedback, but in an individualised way, for all the reasons of the limitations of groups. The techniques can also be ones not to do with key working – I will discuss the merits of a few of the more common ones here:

Comments/complaints box

Instead of just having a complaints procedure, comments boxes are a way of getting opinions from clients. Similar things can be suggestion books etc. There is a presumption of writing but clients may well be able to find someone else to write things for them, or use another medium such as art or video. I knew one agency that set up its own permanent video booth, with an option to give opinions in shadow and they were also working on a way that people could disguise their voices. The reasons for this (discussed in Chapter 4), was that people had fears about repercussions if their complaints, or even a suggestion, could be identified with them. This brings up the issue of where we situate the suggestions/complaints box. I knew one agency who kept it in the staff office and clients had to ask to put a complaint in. The agency wondered why it was never used! I would keep it somewhere that is private to put things in. Remembering the old adage that if you want to know what workers really think of their bosses, read the toilet walls, why not put it in there, even in the form of a graffiti wall. The response you will receive may occasionally be crude, but they will certainly be more honest.

If we are to have complaints procedures then we should set a minimum. I remember asking one agency that had a minimal number of complaints per year, what their rationale was for this. Firstly, they thought that complaining was linked to people regaining their dignity and self-esteem. With reference to the Lowery, de Hoog and Lyons (1993) model of empowerment we encountered in the previous chapter, people were moving from loyalty to alienation, from something passive to something active, which is on the journey to voice. Linked to this, they saw having no complaints as a sign that people felt that there was no point complaining, that they were intimidated to do so, or that they had misplaced loyalty.

Questionnaires/surveys

As Godfrey et al. (2003) note, most agencies have some kind of annual survey of their clients' views, which often becomes a statistic of high satisfaction that is quoted in their annual report. However, they have three criticisms of such approaches. Firstly, clients may express high levels of satisfaction because their expectations are low, or they have little to do with it or they do not want to speak badly lest it reflects on the staff they do have good relations with. Secondly, peoples' experiences are likely to be considerably more complex than whether they are satisfied or not and thirdly, satisfaction questionnaires *tend to reflect providers' priorities, when these aspects may not necessarily be what are important to clients in terms of the quality of a service* (p65). This goes to show that an effective survey is a difficult thing to construct.

Interviews

> *Qualitative one-to-one and focus group interviews are more useful than structured (quantitative) methods in exploring the views and experiences that are most salient to clients . . . These approaches enable clients to talk about the things that are important to them in their own terms.*
>
> (Godfrey et al., 2003: 67)

As can be seen from the above quote, *Supporting People* favours one-to-one interviews to surveys, seeing them as more representative and qualitative. It should be noted that there are many types of interviews, typically classified as structured, semi-structured and unstructured (Cohen et al., 2000). I do not think it is my place to go into the relative merits and procedures of the different kinds of interviewing. Any research methodology text book would do more justice to it than I could here. However, the most common causes of bias in interviewing are caused by poor sampling, poor rapport between interviewer and interviewee, changing questions or prompt questions, a tendency for the interviewer to see the respondent in their own image, a tendency in the interviewer to seek answers that support their preconceived notions, and misinterpretations about what either party is saying (Cohen et al., 2000). I would also say that, to avoid bias of interpretation, interviews should be recorded and transcribed. However, an hour's interview takes on average 5–8 hrs to transcribe. This is a significant cost factor. Finally, attention should also be paid to how the interviews are analysed. It is not as simple as reading through them to get the gist. Again any decent research text book will lead the reader through the process of how to analyse ethically and with meaning.

Focus groups

I thought a word was needed about focus groups, as they are recommended by *Supporting People* and are commonly used (Groundswell, 1998). I think they are different from group work because they bring together people who are in a group for a very short time, typically an hour, and are therefore quite different in nature from an ongoing client group. However, my fears for the popularity of focus groups are in common with group work, as people think it is cheaper to bring people together rather than talk to them individually. Positively, they can be useful in discrete circumstances. Stewart and Shamdasani (1990: 15) have summarised the more common uses of focus groups to include:

1. Obtaining general background information about a topic of interest.
2. Generating research hypotheses that can be submitted to further research and testing using more quantitative approaches.
3. Stimulating new ideas and creative concepts.
4. Diagnosing the potential for problems with a new programme, service or product.
5. Generating impressions of products, programmes, services, institutions, or other objects of interest.
6. Learning how respondents talk about the phenomenon of interest which may facilitate quantitative research tools.
7. Interpreting previously obtained qualitative results.

However, similar restrictions apply to focus groups as to group work. You will tend to get in-depth discussion of a few issues rather than a breadth of opinion and outlying opinions will often not be expressed, or else they are expressed all too vociferously. For a more detailed consideration of focus groups, I would refer the reader to the books by Krueger (1994) and Stewart and Shamdasani (1990). Both are readily available and fairly easy to read.

Organic techniques or the main event

> Offer a choice between formal systems and informal systems of participation. Informal methods, such as social occasions or leisure activities, are more likely to appeal to people who are distrustful of authority or coping with extreme personal concerns.

> (Novas-Ouvertures, 2004: 24)

> Agencies seeking quick results may be tempted to focus on high profile activities that are visible rather than to engage in securing some deeper change that requires thorough groundwork.

> (Godfrey et al., 2003: 46)

> Significant client involvement requires genuine commitment on the part of services to consider and make fundamental changes in the way it approaches people, their problems and their aspirations.

> (Cameron et al., 2005: 5)

It would be very easy to follow the line of argument of Novas-Ouvertures and Godfrey et al. and say that all client involvement should develop organically, starting with the simple things and building up from there. Indeed, this is essentially my view and the standpoint of this book. However, I think it is worth remembering Cameron et als.' perspective and some of the radical oppositional stances taken by the survivor movements we encountered in the second chapter. Sometimes the big events and radical gestures make the smaller steps happen quicker. Also, if client involvement always stays rooted in what already exists, developing organically or in an evolutionary manner, they will not challenge an agency if it has got its fundamentals wrong (Friere, 1968). Indeed, sometimes client involvement would not take off without a showy beginning. Having said this, I have seen too many big events being done that do not have a radical effect, and in fact are not attended by clients. I do think there is some argument that even if we do not start with or concentrate on the simple things, we should not neglect them. In training, in an attempt to generate ideas, I often put up a graffiti wall (big piece of paper) and ask people to put down some simple ideas for client involvement they already do or could easily do. Below are a few of the ideas that have arisen from such sessions, and I think they make a good starting point for people. I am sure teams within organisations could come up with ones that are more specific and relevant to their agencies.

- Build it into your support planning sessions, or ask a colleague to do that session.
- Ask for feedback via text messaging.
- Have anonymous feedback space on your website.
- Set up a video booth in a spare space.
- Put a graffiti wall in a public space (or the cubicle of the loo).
- Build it into other sessions (e.g. art).
- Ask your managers/management committee to do surgeries once a week.
- Have a suggestions box as well as a complaints procedure.
- Give out minutes of the staff meeting (apart from confidential bits).
- Spend some time watching TV with people in the residents' lounge and talk to them.
- Ask the cleaners what they hear people talking about.
- Ask street teams for feedback on what people say about your project.

Wilcox (1995) came up with counters to what he calls 'easy but cheesy' solutions to participation, often including the larger events. I have adapted them to a supported housing context and truncated them somewhat. I think they are worth considering for when the reader encounters such proposals, which have not really been thought through:

- **What we need is a public meeting/speakout.** You will certainly need to meet the public and/or your clients, but remember all those previous comments I made about having a conventional set-up with a fixed agenda, platform and rows of chairs, etc. The event will undoubtedly be dominated by certain parties, not least of all workers.
- **A good leaflet, video and exhibition will get the message across.** As Wilcox says, these may well be useful tools, but it is all too easy to 'be beguiled by the products and forget what you are trying to achieve' (p32). We should also remember the dangers of purely giving out information and the resentment this can cause. As Wilcox says 'could you achieve more with lower-cost materials and more face-to-face contact?' (p32).
- **Appoint a liaison officer/worker.** While they undoubtedly may get things going, as I have discussed before, I have seen so many burnt out client involvement co-ordinators in my time. As we discussed in the principles chapter, the danger is that agencies often leave everything to them and do not give them the power to make the necessary changes. It is why we have the practice theme of having a system of champions throughout an agency to embed the practice and not leave everything to one person. In recruiting a worker, Wilcox suggests

asking oneself several questions: Do they have the necessary skills and resources for the job? Will they get the backing of other colleagues? Are they being expected to occupy conflicting roles? I think the last point is particularly important. It is difficult to present yourself as a neutral facilitator if you are also making recommendations on funding.

- **Set up a consultative committee.** As well as considering what has already been said about groups, Wilcox notes:
  - o Even if a committee is elected or drawn from key interest groups it will not be a channel for reaching most people.
  - o People invited to join a committee may feel uncomfortable about being seen as representatives.
  - o The committee can just reinforce 'them and us' attitudes if some members have more power than others.
- **Run a Planning for Real session (or some other trendy fad).** Wilcox admits that special 'packaged' techniques can be very powerful ways of getting people involved. However, as we have established, no one technique is applicable to all situations. It is quite tempting to look for the flashy quick fix. We should remember our principles and consider the aims of what we want the technique to achieve first, and then look for the methods that might achieve these things. All too often I have seen agencies do it the other way round.
- **It's technical – we require a professional solution.** Wilcox sees this in the context of underestimating the capacity of clients and not valuing clients' opinions, betraying our first principle of client involvement. I think it also applies to not valuing our own opinions and bringing in experts and consultants in participation too quickly – and this is speaking as one such consultant! It is an understandable anxiety but I think, with reading, reflection and support, an agency can work out its own way, and in a more organic and rooted form than many consultants will lead them into. As for anxieties, recognise them for what they are and move on. As I recently said to one agency, who said they did not know where to start, well just start!

Conclusion

This is not to say that we should not have grand gestures or large events. We should just not lose sight of the important questions of what it is we are trying to achieve. We need to ask if they are rooted in the clients' wants and perspectives and structured accordingly. We need to ask if the event is diverse enough so that everyone gets something out of it, but focussed enough that it is meaningful and brings people together. We need to have done our homework to know, not only if the client is able to come, but whether they want to, or feel there is a point in doing so. Importantly, we have to have some follow up to the event or it will leave a legacy of disquieting failure.

These are the fundamental questions, but they often get lost in the detail. It is all too easy to fall into what one of my colleagues calls the 'how many balloons mentality' i.e. they want to be told 'precisely' what incentives will 'make' people come. There are other considerations that are more fundamental, but we often get caught up in the obvious and then see it as important. Sometimes, the most unlikely events work for the less 'obvious', but more fundamental, reasons. One of the best events I have been to was large, slightly unwieldy, held on a Saturday in an unfamiliar venue, where people had to make their own way. However, come they did, because the organiser had done her homework on the other aspects I mentioned. It also had the one ingredient I have probably not emphasised enough – it was fun. People had a good time and enjoyed themselves. While it was serious, time was made for music, art and other forms of self-expression, as well as debate. Laughter was also a key ingredient and what is better to bring people together than laughter, especially when they are discussing what are sometimes difficult things.

Conclusion: Reflections on Training on Client Involvement

It is normal in a book to have a concluding chapter that sums up the themes and learning points from the preceding chapters. However, I think this function was served by the introduction, which outlined the themes and practice recommendations that thread through the chapters. If I were to go over them again I would only be repeating myself. Therefore, and in keeping with the theme of the book, I want the last words to go to a client, or rather an ex-client, and friend of mine, Jimmy Carlson. I have known Jimmy on and off for ten years and have worked with him closely for the last four. Jimmy has wisdom and insights that I think the reader will find illuminating, especially about how client involvement pans out in practice. I have presented his thoughts as an interview because this is the medium that Jimmy feels most comfortable with.

An Interview With Jimmy Carlson, Co-Trainer and Homeless Activist

So, tell me about how you first got involved in client involvement?
I volunteered to do a workshop at a Groundswell event. Up to that point my life had been about dependency, not just on the drink but actually on services, and I'd become institutionalised. At the actual workshop I was very nervous. I actually did it with XXXX who had been in recovery a bit longer than me . . . but he more or less left it to me! As I said I was very nervous, but when we got started it turned out to be a good workshop, people were asking questions and identifying the issues for them. We had about 20, no about 15, but by the time we finished there were people outside listening in. That was in 1999 and that were about the time I decided I wanted to start doing something . . . this parts important. We'd had a FOG day (Friends of Groundswell) earlier that year and I had actually let rip. I'd been sat there all day and they were just marking things on pieces of card. They had these little workshops and people were bringing their own agendas to them and I got really frustrated.

Towards the back end of the day I stood up, I was feeding back or something . . . I said that people had brought their own agendas and as for putting things on bits of paper that were no good to man nor beast . . . I said today we'd have a brilliant opportunity and I've been here all day and I haven't heard once anything about people living out on the street, people sleeping rough, people drinking on the streets. At that time that was what I was into, that being my life before . . . I really let go but afterwards people were coming up to me and saying that was brilliant jimmy, that's the sort of thing we want to be hearing. For me they were going about it all wrong. Putting pins on a map, what's all that about?

118

I said to them that I actually want to do something, I've got all this stuff inside of me wanting to get out and I don't know how to go about it . . . I need someone to show me or guide me and that's not guiding me. I've got a big heart and there's all this pent up frustration and anger inside of me and I need to let it out and be guided about what to do with it. Instead of just . . . most of my life I've been anti-authority and I've been bang, bang, bang . . . shouting and it's got me nowhere. I needed to be able to take that anger and channel it in the right way. I think that's what I started doing things at the forums (Groundswell used to run annual forums for clients and agencies, kind of an alternative conference). I remember sitting down and saying to my mate XXXX who came with me that this had been brilliant, I actually know now where I want to go . . . It really all started there . . .

That actually led onto the stuff I did with XXX around client involvement (a major alcohol agency). I think this tale is worth telling, cos it says a lot about client involvement and how it develops, sometimes in ways you can't predict at the start. I was sitting in the shop front and one of the workers came in and asked if anyone wanted to go to the client involvement meeting. This was a meeting every quarter, which were meant to be between management and clients. I sat in the meeting, but after a while I got fed up and started speaking up. I had a right go at the woman who was running the meeting. I said XXX agency isn't serious about client involvement. I've heard it all before. I told them that in 1999 they'd said the same thing, and had all these conferences about client involvement. So they'd had it but they'd forgotten to tell the clients about it! I said that, for instance, if this meeting had been the other side of the water (South London) the director would be at the meeting, and if not him, the deputy director but who've we got, you and this bloke (referring to the maintenance manager). She replied 'but I'm senior management', and I said, 'but we don't know you'. As I say, I gave her a real hard time. After the meeting she came up to me and said, 'Jimmy you know I agree with everything you said there, why not come on board and help me'. Well after all I'd said I couldn't really say no . . . she had me! So I agreed to come to the next meeting. Years later she told me that while I was going on she'd said to herself 'if I can get this guy involved, I can get anyone', I took it as a compliment.

So I went to the meeting, it was a steering group looking at how we should do client involvement. It consisted of two managers, two people from the board of trustees, a worker from each shop front and housing and two clients from each shop front and housing. It meant there was a majority of clients at the meeting, which was seen as important. We changed stuff from the outset. It was held in the posh room in a posh hotel and we said that we didn't want this, it put us off. We thought it better to move round the different projects, we had room so why not use it. Also to have simple food that everyone liked. Julie offered to pay us, but we said no, just our fares; fair enough, that wasn't why we were there. We said to donate the money to the xxx fund (set up to give out small amounts of money to clients in emergencies, or when they'd first moved into accommodation).

We set ourselves a year to meet every six weeks and come up with objectives on client involvement. There were ten of them that we broke down to seven as some of them crossed over. They were: For the organisation to communicate more effectively with clients; for there to be client representation on the Board of Trustees; for clients to be involved in representing the organisation; for clients to have involvement in recruitment of staff and considering staffing levels; for the organisation to recognise that clients have a range of skills and to support them in utilising these; for clients to be involved in review and development of organisational policies and procedures and to secure funding for a volunteering programme. What was interesting was that during this year something else happened. Everyone started speaking to each other, client to workers, workers to managers etc. Before this the only communication was between senior management and the board of trustees. It was managers on top, then workers and then clients. Now it was becoming clients, workers and managers coming together.

Towards the end of the year some of us then planned for a staff/client conference where there were four workshops, each one looking at two of these aims, with one dedicated to having clients on interview, cause it was the most controversial. Each one was run by two clients and the whole event was opened by two clients. We also had a video booth and a graffiti wall where those who did not want to speak in a group could talk or write something there. Afterwards all of this was written up and we took it to the board of trustees who agreed to everything, with the exception of having one person on the board. They thought it should be three so that clients could support each other, with one being reserved for a female. However, this was interesting. I was part of the group who presented the findings to the management committee. We were last on the agenda and it must have been about 9.30 at night by the time we came up. One of the board suggested putting it on the next agenda, or just agreeing it. Well, I put my hand up to speak. I said that if they did that they were just being tokenistic again. We had waited all night listening to this (holding up a thick wedge of board papers) and we wanted to have our say. The chair of the board said, fair enough, you can have your say and furthermore, at future meetings client issues will be first on the agenda, so we can give it proper attention.

At the very end of all this, Julie called a final meeting, mainly to say thank you for everyone for participating. But we said no, we wanted to keep the meeting going, but without the workers there. Julie asked why and we said, to make sure you do what you say you will and fair enough the group kept going. We decided to call it the Advisory to the Board group, originally it was to be the Board Advisory Group, but none of the women wanted to be known as a BAG lady, so it was known simply as the A to B group. What was interesting was after this everyone was talking to each other, clients, workers, managers, trustees, everyone, and it all went through the A to B group, 'cause we have the ear of the board of trustees, something I think is very important. Just to finish on this, after a few months I approached Julie and said that I wanted to take a step back. I had become too powerful, everyone was going through me 'oh Jimmy will do this' or 'oh ask Jimmy, he'll know'. I'd suddenly become a chief and it didn't sit right with me. That's when I started getting more involved with Groundswell.

And what happened next?

I think 2002 were a turning thing for me and also client involvement . . . from 1999–2001 a lot of my stuff with client involvement was around alcohol, street drinkers, rough sleepers, getting the wet centre set up in Camden. I got all this stuff inside me and thought people weren't listening and I thought I've got to start doing something about this . . . then governments started listening, so we could not keep bombarding them but it weren't getting to councils boroughs or agencies.

Then in 2001/2002 the government turned round and said OK we've heard what you've got to say and we agree. What we want to know now is how do we go about it. So Groundswell responded and Toby talked about getting involved in training. Going into services and training them on participation training. He asked me if I'd be interested . . . all this time I was changing . . . I wanted to have more of an impact. I thought well we can't just go on at government, councils are beginning to come round but services are still not catching up . . . We needed to show them how to do it. Then we trained up those other lads and lasses (Jimmy is referring to a Groundswell project where nine clients were trained up to be trainers and researchers on client involvement) and its gone on from there.

How have you changed since getting involved?

I don't think anyone can teach me about user involvement and I think that applies to many people – I've lived it and known it for years. But you can learn how to get it across. I think a few years ago no one would have listened to me, or want to have listened to me . . . As I said, I was all bang bang bang – it made sense to me, but not to anyone else. I'd be hammering at them and they'd just look confused or worried. It's like assertiveness, it's what we need to pick up. That first training course we did I was very nervous, but it was something a woman said to me at dinner time. It was a staff member and she said 'actually it's great to have you here (she didn't know me), it's great cos I can blabber on but they won't take any notice of me you can say the same thing and they'd listen to you, you've actually been through the experience and lived it. What you say they'll take in.' This made me feel I was right for doing the training. However, it didn't make me any less nervous! I got a lot out of that first one and the ones we did last year. I learnt a lot from them.

What barriers did you have to break down yourself?

For me doing the training gave me confidence, especially (about) doing things on my own. The first couple of months I was relying on you, but not now. It helped when I made a chart of my own (referring to a diagram of how power had flowed in his organisation). That said it for me, it was staring me back in the face, that's how I see user involvement. I can't portray my ideas to everyone 'cause everyone's different. It even took me a long time to know what I thought of the situation myself. Actually I think it helped me understand workers, but first of all it made me understand myself. A big thing for me, leading up to doing the training, was that I actually couldn't work with my peers, because they'd think I'm bragging or boasting. Who does he think he is, just because he's been a few years sober . . . That were a big thing for me, it was a big barrier to break down. A few years ago I had a chance to go on the street to interview people, some university wanted some peer research done with the liaison group and I knocked it back. I said it was about privacy but they were all excuses, what it were actually about was fear about working with my peers.

What it has given me, apart from a heck of a lot more confidence, although I were working on this when I was with ARP, is that it has helped me be open about myself. In the past, if people got close to me then that was the time to go. You can come so far but you can't go past that barrier. When they got there that was time to shoot off and start again. Even in recovery, I was very uncomfortable, people were prying and I worried that at a later time they would hold it against me. The training this year has gone a long way to breaking that barrier down. I don't know if it shows but I've actually opened up a bit more, I feel more confident. I've been nervous and butterflies on every one but now it's about doing a good job, not about doing it, but doing a good job. Before I was actually nervous about being there, now I know why I'm doing it and I want to do a good job. I think if I can walk away and feel I've done a good job then that's good, even if I don't get feedback you can tell. When I've got a quiet moment I can go, 'Yes', if you can get that into how you're doing training you'll soon have a bunch of experts.

What do you think are the biggest barriers for organisations developing client involvement?

Well, to be honest I think they need to stop worrying about what will happen if they involve people. I think they secretly worry about losing their jobs, or that clients might say their project is rubbish and then they might lose their funding or something. I don't think they mean to do this . . . well there are some but you'll always get that . . . its just that they're not used to listening to clients. It's like when there is some dispute in the hostel. The management will always come down on the workers side and that says something. It says that they think that clients can't be trusted. I remember one being in the residents' lounge; I'd had a few drinks like, and was watching a programme on the TV. A worker came in and turned the television over and sat down. So I thought, I'm not having that and got up and turned it back over. So we got into an argument. He said I should be in bed and I disagreed and it went from there. The point is that when the manager came in the morning it were me who got in trouble, he just took his side.

Another thing is that when they do hear from stuff from clients it's always the bad stuff, probably because those are the voices that get through, the loudmouths. Real client involvement should get to the quiet ones who sit at the back, who have something to say but are nervous. Especially when they see the same old people mouthing off who always do, they think 'what's the point?'. We've got to get to them, the quiet ones. Like at XXXX st hostel when we ran that action planning day. XXX had something to say, and even said it, but it got lost 'cause of others dominating, and she left at lunchtime. Something went wrong there, it's those people that we've got to get to.

And how about for clients?

Well, I think one of the biggest barriers, I'm talking about from my day, is clients themselves. We had this them and us thing. Don't trust the staff or those clients who do. Mind you, it doesn't come from nowhere . . . As I've said most of my adult life I've had people telling me what to do. In the army, by the police on the streets, in prison, in rehab, in hostels, I never had to make a decision. I was completely institutionalised. I didn't know I could be listened to, because no one ever had. I remember being at ARP, sitting in the shop front looking at the staff in the office. I was all right in the groups but afterwards I just sat in the shop front. I remember looking at them thinking – why aren't they over here talking to me, can't they see I'm suffering? – I thought 'I'm meant to be the con man but they are bigger con merchants than I'd ever be'. It was only when I went over there and talked to them that doors opened and I realised I had a voice.

For client involvement to work we, as clients, need to realise these things, but it isn't going to be easy. It's much easier us moaning on the sidelines, 'cause that's what we know. It's also easier for projects 'cause it's what they know. I think a lot of workers get into the field to help people, but that also means they think we can't do things for ourselves. Then when they meet someone who is institutionalised, we feed on each other. I mean, when I was in hostels they treated you like a number . . . I wasn't Jimmy, I was a number, the room number I was in. I knew one guy who when he moved out, or was moved out, he asked to take his door number with him, he was that institutionalised.

What are some of the problems you've seen in the way client involvement has developed?

The trouble is that it's too easy for it to become a tick boxing exercise. I also think it's become too professionalised. No offence, but I think it has. It's moved away from self help and people doing things for themselves to agencies having conferences on it and getting in professionals to do it for the clients . . . we're missing a trick somewhere. I think one of the problems, and we've talked about this before, is that agencies start off by working well with clients, building up their confidence and all that. But then they rely on those people to do everything. It's happened to me a few times, oh it's alright we can get Jimmy to do that, talk to Jimmy he knows who to speak to. Then those people end up burning out or getting professionalised. They lose touch with the clients. Even more important is that the project doesn't bother working with new clients, to build them up, they just keep going back to the same old people and it flatters them 'cause they're being asked. But that's when it becomes a real tick boxing exercise.

Say in five years, where would you like to see client involvement?

Ohh that's I hard one, I'll have to think about that one . . . I think practically, take say XXXX st hostel (a front line direct access centre for homeless people), I'd like to see people be greeted by a client when they come in, maybe not interviewed by them but shown around. So they can say what it's really like living there. And training the staff, showing them what it's like to live in their hostel for a day and how it feels to be greeted by one of them. As I said before, we need to lose this them and us mentality, it needs to be management, staff and clients coming together.

At the moment its staff up here (moves one hand in the air) and us down here (moves other hand below) or sometimes clients up here and staff down there (swaps hand positions over). It needs to be more like this (moves hands next to each other, but has them moving slightly, with one below and one going slightly above another and then the other going slightly above and the first hand going slightly below). It should never be this (moves hands together, equal but static) 'cause that means it's become a tick boxing exercise but moving a bit, 'cause that what communication's like.

How about the balance between supporting client led initiatives and working with organisations?

At the end of the day things should be user led and not just organisation led. You know, things coming from the clients. When Groundswell started out that's what we did, we worked with groups of homeless people and helped them come together. Things like the exchanges and the forums where people could come together to share ideas and talk. Then we'd give them the grants and whatever support they needed to set up initiatives and the like. It's what was needed, 'cause we'd never come together before and we needed to realise we had a voice. Then we did lobbying, setting up speakouts so the government and local councillors could talk directly to clients, to get things from the horse's mouth as it were, instead of going through agencies. That had never happened before and it was powerful. I talked earlier about how important I think training is. At the end of the day we need to do both of these things. Projects need to learn how to do client involvement properly, but we shouldn't let go of supporting clients doing their own projects. Things move on, but we have to remember where we came from, and not lose our principles.

Appendix: Resources on Client Involvement

Further reading

For reasons that I have outlined previously, the main body of the book has not outlined many techniques as I think that the context is all-important. However, there are a number of texts that are worth examining as they undertake this within specific client groups. I would recommend using them within the context of the principles.

A Guide to User Involvement for Organisations Providing Housing Related Support Services
Godfrey, M., Callaghan, G., Johnson, L. and Waddington, E. (2003) London: ODPM

This guide sets out how opportunities for client involvement can be developed for users of housing related support services. It is intended for use by staff and managers. The guide offers ideas for developing a strategy, drawing on examples illustrating good practice in the sector. It draws on theory as well, and is a good guide to knowing what *Supporting People* envisions in terms of client involvement.

Have We Got Views For You: Service User Involvement in Supported Housing
Novas-Ouvertures (2001) London: Novas Group

This report examines the role of tenant participation within the framework of supported housing from the perspective of a large provider. It includes an evaluation structure for measuring successful participation, and presents a range of good practice tips and recommendations. Good examples are provided although it is a little light on theory.

Community Participation and Empowerment: Putting Theory Into Practice
Wilcox, D. (1995) London: Partnership Press

This is an excellent resource both for practice and the theoretical background to participation. It is aimed at community workers, so some links and translation to a supported housing context will have to be made, but it is worth it. It has a good tips section and an a-z of participation. It is now out of print but the whole document can be downloaded from www.partnerships.org.uk/guide/index.htm

Tenant Participation in Supported Housing (Sitra workbook)
Keeble, M. (2001) London: Sitra

This was a workbook for staff working in supported housing aiming to help them develop imaginative ways to involve tenants in services. It is divided into study units which are in turn divided into learning outcomes/objectives with practical exercises to test understanding of the subject matter. It is a little simplistic at times, not taking into account some of the subtleties of client involvement, but is nevertheless worth getting if you can find a copy. Unfortunately it is now out of print.

Participatory Learning and Action: A Trainers Guide
Petty, J., Guijt, I., Scoones, I. and Whompson, J. (1995) London: IIED

Excellent resource if you are considering undertaking peer research or the training of clients to undertake participation. It has hundreds of exercises as well as some theoretical background to participatory research. It unusually comes from an anthropological viewpoint, and is based on PRA (Participatory Rural Appraisal), which are techniques used in the developing world. It has some interesting insights into the process of empowerment.

People and Participation: How to Put Citizens at The Heart of Participation
Involve (2005) London: Involve

This book is an excellent source of practical detail on a range of techniques from local planning to nanotechnology. It has a theoretical side and comes from a democratic renewal perspective, but its strength is the analysis of different approaches to public participation.

Participation Works: 21 Techniques of Community Participation For The 21st Century
UK Community Participation Network (1998) London: New Economics Foundation

Reviews a variety of participatory techniques used by members of the network. Includes such techniques as community appraisals and participatory appraisal. Has a basic introduction to principles of techniques and an interesting section on the responsibility of organisers. It pulls together a variety of ideas taken from development ideas in the South. It is more of a practical guide than an academic one.

From Paternalism to Participation: Involving People in Social Services
Beresford, P. and Croft, S. (1990) London: Open Service Project

Report from a Rowntree research project conducted with a series of social service departments. It has an interesting section on excuses made by departments why they do not have effective participation and gives counters to them. Develops principles for moving forward.

Deptford City Challenge: Housing Tenure and Tenant Participation
Centre for Urban and Community Research (1995) London: Goldsmiths

Reviews attempts by a regeneration project to involve tenants and the local community in the regeneration of an Inner London estate. Reviews the tenant's experience of transfer of local authority stock into the hands of housing associations and the development of a tenants and residents forum.

Empowerment and Estate Regeneration: A Critical Review
Stewart, M. and Taylor, M. (1995) Bristol: The Policy Press

Details residents' and community workers' experiences of estate regeneration including sections on housing, employment, social consumption, quality of life and estate-wide partnership strategies. Nicely unites community development themes with a practical review of developments so far.

Housing: Participation and Exclusion
Cowan, D. (1997) Collected Papers from the Socio-Legal Studies Annual Conference

Current themes in housing are explored in this collection of papers from the Socio-Legal Studies Association Annual Conference in 1997. The gamut of issues surrounding participation, such as tenant participation or decision-making participation, together with the forces leading to exclusion – such as in relation to ethnic minorities – are examined. The book should prove relevant to those in the housing movement together with those working in related disciplines.

General

Bailey, D. (2005) Using an Action Research Approach to Involving Service Users in the Assessment of Professional Competence. *European Journal of Social Work.* 8: 2, 165–79.

Begum, N. and Gillespie-Sells, K. (1994) *Managing User-Led Services.* London: Race Equality Unit.

Beresford, P. and Croft, S. (1997) *Citizen Involvement: A Practical Guide for Change.* London: Macmillan.

Beresford, P. (2000) Users' Knowledge and Social Work Theory. *British Journal of Social Work,* 30: 4, 489–503.

Beresford, P. (1997) New Movements, New Politics: Making Participation Possible. In Jordan, T. and Lent, A. (Eds.) *Storming The Millennium: The New Politics of Change.* London: Lawrence and Wishart.

Beresford, P. and Croft, (1997) Postmodernity and The Future of Welfare: Whose Critiques, Whose Social Policy? In Carter, J. (Ed.) *Postmodernity and The Fragmentation of Welfare: A Contemporary Social Policy?* London: Routledge.

Cairncross, L. et al. (1990) *Participation: A Tenants' Handbook.* London: Tenant Participation Advisory Service.

Herd, D. and Stalker, K. (1996) *Involving Disabled People in Services. A Document Describing Good Practice for Planners, Purchasers and Providers.* Edinburgh: The Social Work Services Inspectorate.

Lindow, W. (1996) *User Involvement: Community Service Users as Consultants and Trainers.* West Yorkshire: DoH.

Millward, J. (2003) *Encouraging Participation: A Toolkit for Tenants and Social Landlords.* London: CIH.

Morris, J. (1994) *The Shape of Things to Come? User Led Social Services.* London: NISW.

Morris, J. (1996) *Encouraging User Involvement in Commissioning: A Resource for Commissioners.* West Yorkshire: DoH.

Morris, J. and Lindow, V. (1993) *User Participation in Community Care Services.* Leeds: Community Care Support Force.

Smith, J. (1995) *Community Development and Tenant Action.* London: Community Development Foundation.

Stewart, A. and Taylor, B. (1995) *Empowerment and Estate Regeneration.* London: Policy Press.

Involving people with learning disabilities

Alexander, M. and Hegarty, J. (2001) Measuring Client Participation in Individual Programme Planning Meetings. *British Journal of Learning Disabilities,* 29: 1, 17–21.

Aspis, S. (1992) *Integration, Disability, Handicap and Society.* 7: 3, 281–3.

Downer, J. and Ferns, P. (1993) Self Advocacy by Black People With Learning Difficulties. In Beresford, P. and Harding, T. (Eds.) *A Challenge to Change: Practical Experiences of Building User–Led Services.* London: NISW.

Mansell, J. et al. (2003) Resident Involvement in Activity in Small Community Homes for People With Learning Disabilities. *Journal of Applied Research in Intellectual Disabilities*, 16: 1, 63–74.

People First (1993) *Self-Advocacy Starter Pack.* London: People First.

People First (1993) *Oi! It's My Assessment.* London: People First.

Schoulz, J. (1982) (Reissued in 1991) *We Can Speak for Ourselves: Self Advocacy and Mentally Handicapped People.* London: Souvenir Press.

Whittaker, A., Gardner, B. and Kershaw, J. (1991) *Service Evaluation by People With Learning Difficulties.* London: King's Fund Centre.

Disabled people

Barnes, D., Carpenter, J. and Bailey, D. (2000) Partnerships With Service Users in Interprofessional Education for Community Mental Health: A Case Study. *Journal of Interprofessional Care.* 14: 2, 189–200.

Barton, L (Ed.) (1996) *Disability and Society: Emerging Issues and Insights.* London: Longman.

Campbell, J. and Oliver, M. (1996) *Disability Politics: Understanding Our Past, Changing Our Future.* London: Routledge.

Cott, C. (2004) Client-Centred Rehabilitation: Client Perspectives. *Disability and Rehabilitation*, 26: 24, 1411–22.

Hampshire Coalition of Disabled People (1996) *Disability Rights: A Symposium of The European Regions.* Hampshire: Hampshire Coalition of Disabled People.

Plumb, A. (1993) The Challenge of Self–Advocacy. *Feminism and Psychology*, 2: 3, 22–32.

Mental health service users/psychiatric system survivor

Campbell, P. (1996) The History of The User Movement in The United Kingdom. In Heller, T. et al. (Eds.) *Mental Health Matters: A Reader.* Basingstoke: Macmillan.

Chamberlin, J. (1988) *On Our Own: User Controlled Alternatives to The Mental Health System?* London: MIND.

Coupland, K., Davis, E. and Gregory, K. (2001) Learning From Life. *Mental Health Care*, 4: 5, 166–9.

Crepaz-Keay, D., Binns, C. and Wilson, E. (1997) *Dancing With Angels: Involving Survivors in Mental Health Training.* London: CCETSW.

Crepaz-Keay, D., Binns, C. and Wilson, E. (1998) Survival Training: Misconceptions and Excuses Can Get in The Way of Involving Survivors in Training. *Open Mind.* 92, 11.

Leader, A. (1995) *Direct Power: A Resource Pack for People Who Want to Develop Their Own Care Plans and Support Networks.* Brighton: Pavilion and MIND.

Older people

Hackney Pensioners' Press (1998) *Speaking Our Minds: an Anthology.* Basingstoke: Macmillan.

Leaper, R.A. (1988) *Age Speaks for Itself: A Report of a Survey of Older People's Perceptions.* Exeter: Exeter Health Authority.

Lewisham Pensioners' Forum (1995) *Developing User Standards in Residential Care.* London: Lewisham Pensioners' Forum.

Robson, P. and Locke, M. (2002) *Changing Voices: Involving People with Dementia in The Alzheimer's Society. Learning to Live with Dementia Project Final Evaluation Report.* London: Alzheimer's Society.

Sarton, M. (1996) *At Eighty–Two: A Journal.* London: Women's Press.

People living with HIV and AIDS

Edward, M. et al. (2004) Developing Consumer Involvement in Rural HIV Primary Care Programmes. *Health Expectations,* 7: 2, 157–64.

Grabill, J.T. (2000) Shaping Local HIV/AIDS Services Policy Through Activist Research: The Problem of Client Involvement. *Technical Communication Quarterly,* 9: 1, 29–50.

People Living With HIV and AIDS (1996) *Living With HIV and AIDS.* London: National AIDS Manual Publications.

Walton, G. (1993) Working for Change as a Service User. In Beresford, P. and Harding, T. *A Challenge to Change: Practical Experiences of Building User–Led Services.* London: NISW.

People with experience of poverty

ATD Fourth World (1996) *Talk With Us, Not at Us: How to Develop Partnerships Between Families in Poverty and Professiona*ls. London: ATD Fourth World.

Beresford, P. and Croft, S. (1995) Its Our Problem Too! Challenging The Exclusion of Poor People From Poverty Discourse.*Critical Social Policy,* Issue 44/45.

Russell, H. (Ed.) (1996) *Speaking From Experience: Voices.* at The National Poverty Hearing, Manchester: Church Action on Poverty.

UK Coalition Against Poverty (1997) *Poverty and Participation: Learnings From A September 1996 Workshop Bringing Together People Living in Poverty Throughout The UK.* London: UK Coalition Against Poverty.

Children and young people

Fletcher, B. (Undated) *Not Just A Name: The Views of Young People in Foster and Residential Care.* London: Who Cares Trust and National Consumers' Council.

Freeman, F. et al. (1996) Consulting Service Users: The Views of Young People. In Hill, M. and Aldgate, J. (Eds.) *Child Welfare Services.* London: Jessica Kingsley.

Mcneish, D. and Parish, A. (1993) *Look Who's Talking: The Words of Children and Young People With Additional Material.* London: Barnardo's.

Whiting, C. and Brown, D. (2005) *Involving Young Tenants in Decision Making: A Guide for Housing Associations.* London: Housing Corporation.

Lesbians and gay men

Carabine, J. (1992) Constructing Women: Women's Sexuality and Social Policy. *Critical Social Policy,* 34, 23–39.

Journal of Gay and Lesbian Social Services, Haworth Press, USA

Logan, J. et al. (1996) *Confronting Prejudice: Lesbian and Gay Issues in Social Work Education*. Aldershot: Arena.

Black people and minority ethnic groups

Begum, N. (1995) *Care Management and Assessment From an Anti-Racist Perspective, Social Care Research Findings, 65*. York: Joseph Rowntree Foundation.

Butt, J. and Mirza, K. (1996) *Social Care and Black Communities*. London: HMSO.

Harrison, M. (2003) *Housing and Black and Minority Ethnic Communities: Review of The Evidence Base*. London: Communities and Local Government.

Macdonald, S. (1990) *All Equal Under The Act*. London: Race Equality Unit.

Patel, N. (Ed.) (1991) *Setting The Context for Change: The Report of The Community Development Project*. London: CCETSW.

Homelessness

Darlington, I. (2006) *Placing Service Users at The Heart of Service Development*. Http://Www.Homeless.Org.Uk/Developyourservice/Serviceusers

Davey, N. (2006) *Jumping Hurdles*, Connect No 23. London: Homeless Link.

Scottish Youth Housing Network (2000) *Young Homeless People: Speaking for Themselves*. Edinburgh: Scottish Council for Single Homeless.

References

Alinsky, S. (1968) *Rules for Radicals*. Washington, DC: Arrow Press.

Ames, J. (2007) Contesting and Working with Challenging Behaviour. In Seal, M. (Ed.) *Understanding and Responding to Homeless Experiences, Cultures and Identities*. Lyme Regis: Russell House Publishing.

Anderson, B. (1991) *Imagined Communities. Reflections on the Origin and Spread of Nationalism*. London: Verso.

Anderson, I. and Thompson, S. (2005) *More Priority Needed: the Impact of Legislative Changes on Young People's Access to Housing and Support*. London: Shelter.

Anderson, L. (1997) *Argyris and Schön's Theory on Congruence and Learning*. Available at http://www.scu.edu.au/schools/sawd/arr/argyris.html

Argyris, C. (1990) *Overcoming Organisational Defensiveness: Facilitating Organisational Learning*. MA: Allyn and Bacon.

Argyris, C. (1980) *Inner Contradictions of Rigorous Research*. New York: Academic Press.

Argyris, C., Putnam, R. and McLain Smith, D. (1985) *Action Science: Concepts, Methods, and Skills For Research and Intervention*. San Francisco: Jossey-Bass.

Argyris, C. and Schön, D. (1974) *Theory in Practice: Increasing Professional Effectiveness*. San Francisco: Jossey-Bass.

Arnstein, R. (1969) A Ladder of Citizen Participation. *Journal of the American Institute of Planners*, 35: 4, 216–24.

Audit Commission (2005) *Housing National Report: Supporting People*. London: HMSO.

Avruch, K. and Black, P. (1991) The Culture Question and Conflict Resolution. *Peace and Change*, 16: 1, 22–45.

Bauman, Z. (2001) *Seeking Safety in an Insecure World*. Cambridge: Polity Press.

Balchin, (1998) *Housing: The Essential Foundations*. London: Routledge.

Barker, M. and Wistow, G. (1987) *Power in Strange Places*. London: Good Practices in Mental Health.

Barnes, C., Mercer, G. and Din, I. (2003) *Research Review on User Involvement in Promoting Change and Enhancing the Quality of Social 'Care' Services for Disabled People*. Centre for Disability Studies, University of Leeds.

Barnes, C., Mercer, G. and Shakespeare, T. (1999) *Exploring Disability*. Cambridge: Polity Press.

Barnes, M. and Wistow, G. (1994) Learning to Hear Voices: Listening to Users of Mental Health Services. *Journal of Mental Health* 3, 525–40.

Barnes, P. and Sharpe, B. (2004) *The RHP Companion to Outdoor Education*. Lyme Regis: Russell House Publishing.

Barton, L. (Ed.) (1996) *Disability and Society*. London: Longman.

Belbin, R.M. (1999) *Management Teams: Why They Succeed or Fail*. Oxford: Butterworth Heinemann.

Beresford, P. and Croft, S. (1993) *Citizen Involvement: A Practical Guide for Change.* London: Macmillan.

Beresford, P. and Branfield, F. (2006) *Making User Involvement Work: Supporting Service User Networking and Knowledge.* York: Joseph Rowntree Foundation.

Bertram, M. (2005) *User Involvement and Mental Health: Critical Reflections on Critical Issues.* London: Psychminded.

Big Issue (2000) 2000 Vendor Survey. *Big Issue.*

Biggs, S. (1997) User Voice, Interprofessionalism and Postmodernity. *Journal of Interprofessional Care*, 11: 2, 195–203.

Boal, A. (2000) *Theatre of the Oppressed.* London: Pluto Press.

Boggs, C. (1976) *Gramski's Marxism.* London: Photo Press.

Bolton, G., Field, V. and Thompson, K. (2006) *Writing Works: A Resource Handbook for Therapeutic Writing Workshops and Activities.* London: Jessica Kingsley.

Bond, A. (1986) *Games for Social and Life Skills.* London: HST.

Bostock, L. et al. (2005) *Managing Risks and Minimising Mistakes in Services to Children and Families.* London: Social Care Institute for Excellence.

Boud, D., Keogh, A. and Walker, B. (Eds.) (1985) *Reflection; Turning Experience Into Learning.* London: Kogan Page.

Boud, D. et al. (Eds.) (1993) *Using Experience for Learning.* Milton Keynes: Open University Press.

Bowl, R. (1996) Involving Service Users in Mental Health Services. *Journal of Mental Health*, 5: 3, 287–303.

Boydell, K., Goering, P. and Morrell-Bellai, T. (2000) Narratives of Identity: Representation of Self in People who are Homeless. *Qualitative Health Research.* 10: 1, 26–38.

Brafield, H. (2003) *Consulting With Hard to Reach Users of Housing Related Support Services at the Strategic Level for 'Supporting People.* Southampton: ROCC.

Brandes, D. and Phillips, H. (1990) *Gamesters' Handbook.* Cheltenham: Stanley Thornes.

Brandon, D. (1998) Care Planning. In Bevan, P. *The Resettlement Handbook.* London: National Homeless Alliance.

Brandon, D. et al. (1980) *The Survivors: A Study of Homeless Young Newcomers to London and The Responses Made to Them.* London: Routledge and Kegan Paul.

Braye, S. (2000) Participation and Involvement in Social Care. In Kemshall, H. and Littlechild, R. *User Involvement and Participation in Social Care: Research Informing Practice.* London: Jessica Kingsley.

Braye, S. and Preston-Shoot, M. (1995) *Empowering Practice in Social Care.* Buckingham: Open University Press.

Brookfield, S.D. (1986) *Developing Critical Thinkers: Challenging Adults to Explore Alternative Ways of Thinking and Acting.* Milton Keynes: Open University Press.

Brown, A. (1993) *Groupwork.* 3rd Ed. Aldershot: Arena.

Bryant, M. (2001) *Introduction to User Involvement.* London: The Sainsbury Centre for Mental Health.

Burns, D., Hoggett, R. and Hambleton, P. (1994) *The Politics of Decentralisation: Revitalising Local Government (Public Policy and Politics).* London: Macmillan.

Burton, J. (1987) *Resolving Deep-Rooted Conflict: A Handbook.* Lanham, MD: University Press of America.

Burton, P. (2003) *Community Involvement In Neighbourhood Regeneration: Stairway to Heaven or Road to Nowhere?* London: CRA.

Butchinsky, C. (2007) Identities of Rough Sleepers in Oxford. In Seal, M. *Understanding and Responding to Homeless Experiences, Cultures and Identities.* Lyme Regis: Russell House Publishing.

Cameron, A. et al. (2005) *Crossing the Housing and Care Divide.* Bristol: Policy Press.

Campbell, J. and Oliver, M. (1996) *Disability Politics: Understanding Our Past, Changing Our Future.* London: Routledge.

Campbell, J. and Wilson, D. (2005) *A Study of Mental Health Legal Advice and Information Services in Northern Ireland.* Belfast: Law Society.

Campbell, P. (1996) The History of The User Movement in The United Kingdom. In Heller, T. (Ed.) *Mental Health Matters: A Reader.* London: Macmillan.

Campbell, P. (1999) The Service User/Survivor Movement. In Newnes, C., Holmes, G. and Dunn, C. *This is Madness: A Critical Look at Psychiatry and the Future of Mental Health Services.* Ross-on-Wye: PCCS Books.

Campbell, P. (2002) *The Service User/Survivor Movement.* London: Mind.

Carpenter, J. and Sbarani, S. (1997) *Choice, Information and Dignity: Involving Users and Carers in Care Management in Mental Health.* Bristol: Policy Press.

Cibulka, J. et al. (2003) *Schools as Learning Organisations: A Review of the Literature.* National College for School Leadership: National Partnership for Excellence and Accountability in Teaching.

Clegg, S.R. (1989) *Frameworks of Power.* London: Sage.

Cohen, A.P. (1985) *The Symbolic Construction of Community.* London: Tavistock Institute.

Cohen, L., Manion, L. and Morrison, K. (2000) *Research Methods in Education.* London: Routledge.

Coleman, R. (2004) *Recovery: An Alien Concept.* 2nd edn. Fife: PandP Publishing.

Cooper, C. and Hawtin, M. (1999) *Housing Community and Conflict: Understanding Resident Involvement.* London: Arena.

Council of Europe (1961, revised 1996) *European Social Charter.* Brussels: Council of Europe.

Craig, R.T. (1989) Communication as a Practical Discipline. In Dervin, B. et al. (Eds.) *Rethinking Communication: Vol One: Paradigm Issues.* Newbury Park: Sage.

Critical Mental Health Forum (2002) *Response to the Mental Health Bill.* London: CMHF.

Cross, M. (2004) The Development of Identity of Black Adolescents and the Failures of Western Technologies. In Roshe, J. et al. (2004) *Youth in Society.* London: Sage.

Cummings, B. et al. (2000) *Young Homeless People Speaking for Themselves.* Edinburgh: Scottish Youth Housing Network.

Curtice, J. (1999) *The Crisis of Local Democracy in Britain.* Oxford: CREST.

Dahl, R.A. (1989) *Democracy and its Critics.* New Haven and London: Yale University.

Daly, G. (1996) *Homelessness Policies, Strategies and Lives on The Street.* London: Routledge.

Daly, M. (1998) *Quintessence: Realising the Outrageous Contagious Courage of Women. A Radical Elemental Feminist Manifesto.* Boston: Beacon.

Dargan, L. (2004) *A New Approach to Regeneration? Reflections on The New Deal For Communities in Newcastle.* CURDS, Newcastle University.

Darton, K. (2004) *Notes on the History of Mental Health Care: Mind Fact Sheet.* London: Mind.

Davison, G.C. and Neale, J.M. (1997) *Abnormal Psychology.* 7th edn. New York: John Wiley and Sons.

DCLG (2001) *Best Value in Housing Care and Support: Guidance and Good Practice.* London: HMSO.

Dearlove, J. (1974) The Control of Change and The Regulation of Community Action. In Jones, D. and Mayo, M. (Eds.) *Community Work One*. London: RKP.

DETR (1997) *Involving Communities in Urban and Rural Regeneration*. London: HMSO.

DETR (1998) *Community Based Regeneration Initiatives: A Working Paper*. London: HMSO.

DETR (1999) *National Framework for Tenant Participation Compacts*. London: HMSO.

Dodson, T. (2007) Love on the Streets. In Seal, M. (2007b) *Constructing and Contesting Homelessness: Perspectives on Homeless Identities and The Homeless Sector*. Lyme Regis: Russell House Publishing.

Douglas, T. (1995) *Survival in Groups. The Basics of Group Membership*. Buckingham: Open University Press.

Douglas, T. (1993) *A Theory of Groupwork Practice*. London: Macmillan.

Douglas, T. (1991) *A Handbook of Common Groupwork Problems*. London: Routledge.

Driver, S. and Martell, I. (1998) *New Labour: Politics after Thatcherism*. Cambridge: Polity Press.

Dryzek, J.S. (2000) *Deliberative Democracy and Beyond: Liberals, Critics, Contestation*. Oxford: Oxford University Press.

Du Guy, J. and Salaman, K. (1992) The Cult(ure) of The Customer. *Journal of Management Studies*, 29, 615–33.

Edgar, B., Doherty, J. and Mina-Coull, A. (1999) *Services for Homeless People: Innovation and Change in the European Union*. Bristol: Policy Press.

Egan, G. (1998) *The Skilled Helper. Model, Skills and Methods for Effective Helping*. 6th Edn. Monterey, CA: Brooks/Cole.

Ernst, S. and Goodison, L. (1981) *In Our Own Hands, A Book of Self Help Therapy*. London: The Women's Press.

Everitt, E. (1995) *Evaluation in the Voluntary Sector; A Culture of Lying*. Department of Public Policy, Bristol University.

Evans, C. et al. (2002) *Applied Research for Better Practice*. London: Macmillan.

Exworthy, M. and Halford, S. (1999) Professionals and Managers in a Changing Public Sector: Conflict or Compromise? In Exworthy, M. and Halford, S. (Eds.) *Professionals and New Management in the Public Sector*. Buckingham: Open University Press.

FEANTSA (2005) *Involving Homeless People in Decision-making Affecting The Services That They Use: An Overview of Participation Practices Among Service Providers in Europe*. Brussels: FEANTSA.

Fletcher, S. (1995) *Evaluating Community Care: A Guide to Evaluations Led by Disabled People*. London: The King's Fund.

Foot, P. (2005) *The Vote: How it Was Won and How it Was Undermined*. London: Penguin.

Forbes, J. and Sashidharan, S.P. (1997) User Involvement in Services – Incorporation or Challenge? *British Journal of Social Work*, 27: 4, 481–98.

Forster, A. (2007) *Different Thinking: Creative Strategies for Developing and Innovating Business*. London: Kogan Page.

Foucault, M. (1986) *Power/Knowledge: Selected Interviews and Other Writings, 1972–77*. London: Longman.

Fraser, N. (1990) *Rethinking the Public Sphere: A Contribution to The Critique of Actually Existing Democracy*. New York: JSTOR.

Frost, S. (2004) *The Concept of Democracy*. London: YMCA George Williams College.

Freire, P. (1968) *Pedagogy of the Oppressed*. London: Penguin Books.

Fry, C. and Dwyer, R. (2001) For Love or Money? An Exploratory Study of Why Injecting Drug Users Participate in Research. *Addiction*, 96: 9, 1319–25.

Gale, D. (1990) *What is Psychodrama*. London Gale Centre Publications.

Garvey, M. (2005) *Selected Writings and Speeches of Marcus Garvey*. London: Dover Publications.

Geddes, J. (2007) Understanding The Refugee Experience. In Seal, M. (Ed.) *Constructing and Contesting Homelessness: Perspectives on Homeless Identities and The Homeless Sector*. Lyme Regis: Russell House Publishing.

Giddens, A. (1996) *Modernity and Self-Identity: Self and Society in the Late Modern Age*. Stanford: Stanford University Press.

Glassman, U. and Kates, L. (1990) *Group Work. A Humanistic Approach*. London: Sage.

Glenester, H. (1992) *Paying for Welfare in the Nineties*. London: Harvester Wheatsheaf.

Godfrey, M. et al. (2003) *Supporting People: A Guide to User Involvement for Organisations Providing Housing Related Support Services*. London: ODPM.

Goetschius, G.W. (1968) *Working with Community Groups*. London: Routledge.

Goffman, E. (1971) *The Presentation of Self in Everyday Life*. Harmondsworth: Pelican.

Goss, S. and Miller, C. (1995) *From Margin to Mainstream: Developing User and Carer-Centred Community Care*. London: Joseph Rowntree Foundation.

Grayson, K. (1998) *Opening the Window: Revealing The Hidden History of Tenants Organisations*. London: TPAS.

Groundswell (2005) *Taking Me Seriously: A Participation Strategy for St Mungo's*. London: Groundswell.

Groundswell (2007) Groundswell aims – www.groundswell.org.uk

Gyford, J. (1976) *Local Politics in Britain*. London: Croom Helm.

Hanseth, O., Monteiro, E. and Hatling, M. (1996) Developing Information Infrastructure: The Tension Between Standardization and Flexibility. *Science, Technology, and Human Values*, 21: 4, 407–26.

Hanson, J. et al. (2006) *Inspecting for Improvement Report: Portsmouth LIT Community*. London: Healthcare Commission.

Harrington, M. (1962) *The Other America: Poverty in the United States*. New York: Macmillan.

Hawkins, P. and Shohet, R. (2006) *Supervision in the Helping Professions*. Buckingham: Open University Press.

Henderson, P. (2005) *Including the Excluded: from Practice to Policy in European Community Development*. London: Policy Press.

Hennesby, S. and Seal, M. (2007) *A History of User Involvement in the UK*. Conference paper delivered at the FEANTSA Conference, 2007, Portugal.

Hoch, C. and Slayton, R. (1989) *New Homeless and Old*. Philadelphia: Temple University Press.

Hoggett, P. (Ed.) (1997) *Contested Communities: Experiences, Struggles, Policies*. Bristol: Policy Press.

Hoggett, P. (2006) *Supporting People: A Story of Success*. London: Homeless Link.

Homans, G.C. (1951) *The Human Group*. Routledge and Kegan Paul. New edn. (1992) Transaction.

Homeless Link (2000) Human Rights: Are You in on The Act? *Connect Magazine*, 8: 2, 20–2.

Houston, G. (1993) *Being and Belonging: Group, Intergroup and Gestalt*. London: John Wiley.

Illich, I. (1977) *Disabling Professions*. London: Marion Boyars.

Involve (2005) *People and Participation: How to Put Citizens at The Heart of Participation*. London: Involve.

Jarvis, P. (1994) *Learning*. London: YMCA George Williams College.

Jarvis, P. (1995) *Adult and Continuing Education: Theory and Practice.* 2nd edn. London: Routledge.

Jennings, S. et al. (2004) *The Handbook of Dramatherapy.* London: Routledge.

Johnson, D.W. and Johnson, F.P. (1998) *Joining Together: Group Theory and Group Skills.* Boston: Allyn and Bacon.

Kaminsky, A., Roberts L.J. and Brody, J.L. (2003) Influences Upon Willingness to Participate in Schizophrenia Research: An Analysis of Narrative Data. *Ethics and Behavior*, 13: 3, 279–302.

Kaur, A. and Seal, M. (2006) *Being Supported: Homeless Peoples' Views of Supporting People Services.* Groundswell: London.

Kemp, J. (2001) *Raising the Roof: Supported Housing Client Consultation.* London: Housing Corporation.

Kemshall, H. and Littlechild, R. (2000) (Eds.) *User Involvement and Participation in Social Care: Research Informing Practice.* London: Jessica Kingsley.

Keyssar, A. (2001) *The Right to Vote: The Contested History of Democracy in America.* Basic Books.

Kolb, D.A. (1984) *Experiential Learning. Experience as the Source of Learning and Development.* Englewood Cliffs, NJ: Prentice Hall.

Kolb, D.A. and Fry, R. (1975) Toward an Applied Theory of Experimental Learning. In Cooper, C. (Ed.) *Theories of Group Process.* London: John Wiley.

Krueger, R.A. (1994) *Focus Groups: A Practical Guide for Applied Research.* London: Sage.

Laing, R.D. (1960) *The Divided Self: An Existential Study in Sanity and Madness.* New York: Penguin Books.

Laing, R.D. (1967) *The Politics of Experience.* Harmondsworth: Penguin.

Lederach, J.P. (1995) *Preparing for Peace: Conflict Transformation Across Cultures.* New York: Syracuse University Press.

Lemos, G. (2006) *Steadying the Ladder: Social and Emotional Aspirations of Homeless People.* London: LemosCrane.

Lewin, K. (1948) *Resolving Social Conflicts. Selected Papers on Group Dynamics.* New York: Harper and Row.

Lewin, K. (1951) *Field Theory in Social Science.* New York: Harper and Row.

Liddiard, M. (1999) Homelessness: The Media, Public Attitudes and Policy Making. In Hutson, S. and Clapham, D. (Eds.) *Homelessness: Public Policies and Private Troubles.* London: Cassell.

Liebermann, M. (2004) *Art Therapy for Groups: A Handbook of Themes, Games and Exercises.* London: Brunner Routledge.

Linnett, P. (1999) Which Way to Utopia: Thoughts on User Involvement. *Openmind*, 98.

Lister, R. (2003) *Citizenship: Feminist Perspectives.* New York: New York University Press.

London Housing Unit (1999) *National Framework for Participation Compacts.* London: HMSO.

Lukes, S. (1974) *Power: A Radical View.* London: Macmillan.

Marsden, A. (2006) *Ok so Who's Fault is it: An Examination of Blame Culture.* London: Rossmore Group.

Marsh, P., Rosser, E. and Harré, R. (1978) *Rules of Disorder.* London: Routledge and Kegan Paul.

Masson, J. (1989) *Against Therapy.* Monroe: Common Courage Press.

McGregor, A. and Sue, L. (1996) Policy Intent, Family Reality: Using Family Impact Statements to Influence Policy Implementation. *Canadian Home Economics Journal*, 47: 1, 5–10.

McGreggor, A. (1980) *Radical Community Work in Scotland*. London: Routledge.

McKenna, T. (1999) *Food for the Gods*. London: Macmillan.

Meekosha, H. (1993) *Body Battles: Disability, Representation and Participation*. London: Sage.

Meyersohn, K. and Walsh, J. (2001) Ending Clinical Relationships with People with Schizophrenia. *Health and Social Work*, 26: 3, 188–200.

Midgley, J. et al. (1986) *Community Participation, Social Development and the State*. London: Methuen.

Millward, I. (2005) 'We are announcing your target': Reflections on Performative Language in The Making of English Housing Policy. *Local Government Studies*, 31: 5, 597–614.

Mind (2003) *The User/Survivor Movement*. London: Mind.

Mind (2004) *Are You Listening: Patients in Secure Settings*. London: Mind.

Mora, G. (1985) History of Psychiatry. In Kaplan, H.I. and Sadock, B.J. (Eds.) *Comprehensive Text Book of Psychiatry*. London: Routledge.

Morgan, P. (2000) *Response to the Housing Green Paper 2000*. London: TPAS.

Neale, J. (1997) Hostels: A Useful Policy and Practice Response? In Burrows, Please and Quilgars (Eds.) *Homelessness and Social Policy*. New York, NY: Routledge.

Novas-Ouvertures (2001) *Have We Got Views For You: Service User Involvement in Supported Housing*, Novas Group: London.

Oakley, D. (2002) The Politics of Urban Land Use Housing Homeless People: Local Mobilisation of Federal Resources to Right NIMBYism. *Journal of Urban Affairs*, 24: 1, 97.

Oliver, M. (1996) *Understanding Disability*. Basingstoke: Macmillan.

OPDM (2002) *Monitoring and Review of Supporting People Services: Using the Quality Assessment Framework*. London: HMSO.

OPDM (2004a) *Quality Assessment Framework Core Standards*. London: HMSO.

OPDM (2004b) *Quality Assessment Framework Supplementary Standards*. London: HMSO.

OPDM (2005) *Sustainable Communities: People, Places and Prosperity*. London: HMSO.

Osborne, S.P. and McLaughlin, K. (2003) Modelling Government: Voluntary Sector Relationships: Emerging Trends and Issues. *European Business Organisation Law Review*, 4: 383–401.

Peck, E. and Barker, I. (1997) Users as Participants in Mental Health: Ten Years of Experience. *Journal of Interprofessional Care*, 11: 3, 269–77.

People Not Psychiatry (1971) *People need People*. Manchester: PNP.

Petty, J., et al. (1995) *Participatory Learning and Action: A Trainers Guide*. London: IIED.

Phillips, J. (2004) Service User Involvement in Homelessness. *Changing Homelessness in Practice*, Feb.

Priestely, P. (1978) *Social Skills and Personal Problem Solving*. London: Tavistock Institute.

Prescott, J. (2005) *Introduction to Sustainable Communities: People, Places and Prosperity*. London: HMSO.

Putnam, R.D. (2001) *Bowling Alone: The Collapse and Revival of American Community*. New York: Simon and Schuster.

Radley, A. (1991) *In Social Relationships*. Buckingham: Open University.

Randall, G. and Brown, S. (2002) *The Support Needs of Homeless Households*. London: HMSO.

Roberts, A. (2007) A Mental Health History Timeline. http://www.mdx.ac.uk/www/study/MHHT.htm

Roberts, A. (2006) Mental Health and Survivor Movements. http://www.mdx.ac.uk/www/study/MPU.htm

Robson, P., Begum, N. and Locke, M. (2003) *Developing User Involvement: Working Towards User-Centred Practice in Voluntary Organisations*. Bristol: The Policy Press.

Robson, P., Locke, J. and Dawson, D. (1997) *User Involvement in the Control of Voluntary Organisations*, Social Care Research 93. Bristol: Policy Press with Joseph Rowntree Foundation.

Rogers, A. (1986) *Teaching Adults*. Milton Keynes: Open University Press.

Ross, K. (1995) Speaking in Tongues: Involving Users in Day Care Services. *British Journal of Social Work*, 2, 791–804.

Rowe, M. (1999) *Crossing the Border: Encounters Between Homeless People and Outreach Workers*. London: University of California Press.

Sackett, B. (1996) Evidence Based Medicine: What it is and What it isn't. *British Medical Journal*, 312: 71–2.

Said, E. (1979) *Orientalism*. New York: Vintage Books.

Sanderson, I. (1999) Participation or Democratic Renewal: From Instrumental Rationality to Communicative Rationality. *Policy and Politics*, 27: 3, 325–2.

Schwartz, S. and Sagie, G. (2000) Value Consensus and Importance: A Cross National Study. *Journal of Cross Cultural Psychology*, 31: 4, 465–97.

Seal, M. (2005) *Resettling Homeless People: Theory and Practice*. Lyme Regis: Russell House Publishing.

Seal, M. (2006) (Ed.) *Working With Homeless People: A Training Manual*. Lyme Regis: Russell House Publishing.

Seal, M. (2007a) *Working in the Homeless Sector: Worker Perspectives*. Occasional paper. London: YMCA George Williams College.

Seal, M. (Ed.) (2007b) *Constructing and Contesting Homelessness: Perspectives on Homeless Identities and The Homeless Sector*. Lyme Regis: Russell House Publishing.

Sedgewick, A. (1982) *Psychopolitics*. London: Mind.

Senge, P. (1990) *The Fifth Discipline: The Art and Practice of the Learning Organisation*. London: Century Business.

Smith, J. (1992) *Community Development and Tenant Action*. London: Community Development Foundation.

Sinclair, J. (1999) *The Active Community*. London: London Housing Unit.

Smith, M.K. (2005) Robert Putnam. *the encyclopedia of informal education*, www.infed.org/thinkers/putnam.htm

Smith, M.K. (2001a) Chris Argyris: Theories of Action, Double-Loop Learning and Organisational Learning. *the encyclopedia of informal education*, www.infed.org/thinkers/argyris.htm. Last update: January 28, 2005

Smith, M.K. (2001b) Peter Senge and the Learning Organisation. *the encyclopedia of informal education*, www.infed.org/thinkers/senge.htm

Smith, M.K. and Jeffs, T. (2001) *Space, Place and Community*. In Deer Richardson, L. and Wolfe, M. (Eds.) *Principles and Practice of Informal Education: Learning Through Life*. London: RoutledgeFalmer.

Smith, N. and Wright, C. (1992) *Customer Perceptions of Resettlement Units*. London: HMSO.

Snow, D. and Anderson, L. (1987) Identity Work Amongst The Homeless: The Verbal Construction and Avowal of Personal Identities. *American Journal of Sociology*, 92: 1336–71.

Somerville, P. and Chan, C.K. (2001) *Human Dignity and the 'Third Way': The Case of Housing Policy*, University of Lincoln: Presented at Housing Studies Association conference: 'Housing Imaginations: New concepts, new theories, new researchers'.

Somerville, P. (2004) *Transforming Council Housing*. paper presented to the Housing Studies Association Conference 2004, Sheffield Hallam University: Sheffield.

Somerville, P. (1998) Empowerment Through Residence. *Housing Studies*, 13: 2, 233–7.

Stein, D. (1996) The Ethics of NIMBYism. *Journal of Housing and Community Development*, 12: 4, 234–45.

Sternberg, P. and Garcia, A. (2000) *Sociodrama: Who's in Your Shoes?* London: Greenwood Press.

Stewart, D.W. and Shamdasani, P.N. (1990) *Focus Groups: Theory and Practice.* London: Sage.

Stewart, M. and Taylor, M. (1995) *Empowerment and Estate Regeneration: A Critical Review.* Bristol: The Policy Press.

Stonewall (2006) *Diversity Champions Information Pack.* London: Stonewall.

Strauss, A. and Corbin, J. (1998) *Basics of Qualitative Research: Grounded Theory Procedures and Techniques.* 2nd edn. London: Sage.

Sue, D. and Sue, S. (1990) *Understanding Abnormal Behaviour.* 3rd edn. Houghton Mifflin: Boston.

Supporting Children and Young People Group (2001) *The little Book of Evaluation.* London: Connexions Service National Unit.

Szasz, T.S. (1960) The Myth of Mental Illness. *American Psychologist*, 15: 113–18.

Thomas, D.N. (1983) *The Making of Community Work.* London: George Allen and Unwin.

Thompson, N. (1998) *Anti-discriminatory Practice.* Lyme Regis: Russell House Publishing.

Thompson, G. and Wilson, N. (2005) Implementation Failures in the Use of Two New Zealand Laws to Control the Tobacco Industry: 1989–2005. *Australia and New Zealand Health Policy*, 2: 32.

Tredgold, A.F. (1947) *A Textbook of Mental Deficiency.* London: UCU.

Trinder, L. and Reynolds, S. (2000) *Evidence Based Practice: A Critical Appraisal.* London: Blackwell Science.

Tuckman, B.W. (1965) Developmental Sequence in Small Groups. *Psychological Bulletin*, 63, 384–99.

Turkie, A. (1995) Dialogue and Reparation in The Large Group. *Groupwork*, 8: 2, 152–65.

Twelvetrees, A. (2001) *Community Work.* London: Macmillan.

Van der Haijden, K. (2004) *Scenarios: the Art of Strategic Conversation.* London: John Wiley and Sons.

Van Doorn, A. and Kain, M. (2007) Homeless Sector Culture. In Seal, M. (Ed.) *Understanding and Responding to Homeless Experiences, Identities and Cultures.* Lyme Regis: Russell House Publishing.

Van Doorn, A. and Kain, M. (2003) *To Boldly Go . . . Where The Homelessness Sector Has Never Gone Before.* Housing Studies Association, on line www.york.ac.uk/inst/chp/hsa/

Velasco, I. (2001) *Service User Participation and Homelessness Services: Concepts, Trends, Practices.* Edinburgh: Scottish Council for Single Homeless.

Voluntary Action Leicester (2002) *Governance in Voluntary Organisations.* Leicester: VAL.

Welsh Assembly (2004) *Consulting with Homeless People: An Advice Note Issued by the Welsh Assembly Government.* Cardiff: Welsh Assembly.

Whalley, J. (2003) *Globalisation and Values.* New York: SSTR Working Paper.

White, J. (2004) From Herbert Morrison to Command and Control: The Decline of Local Democracy. *History and Policy*, April.

Wilcox, D. (1995) *Community Participation and Empowerment: Putting Theory Into Practice.* London: Partnership Press.

Wilson, R. (1998) *Making Democracy Work: Participation and Politics in Northern Ireland.* Belfast: Democratic Dialogue.

Wyner, R. (1999) *User Involvement in Homelessness Hostels: A Therapeutic Community-Informed Approach to Work With Homeless People.* Association of Therapeutic Communities; www.therapeuticcommunities.org/wyner

Index

Russell House Publishing Ltd

We publish a wide range of professional, reference and educational books including:

Working with Homeless People
A training manual
By Mike Seal   2006   ISBN 978-1-903855-71-3

Understanding and responding to homeless experiences,
identities and cultures
By Mike Seal   2007   ISBN 978-1-905541-06-5

Resettling homeless people
Theory and practice
By Mike Seal   2005   ISBN 978-1-903855-65-2

Power and empowerment
By Neil Thompson   2007   ISBN 978-1-903855-99-7

Respect in the neighbourhood
Why neighbourliness matters
Edited by Kevin Harris   2006   ISBN 978-1-905541-02-7

For more details on specific books, please visit our website:

www.russellhouse.co.uk

Or we can send you our catalogue if you contact us at:

Russell House Publishing Ltd,
4 St George's House,
Uplyme Road Business Park,
Lyme Regis DT7 3LS,
England.

Tel: (UK) 01297 443948
Fax: (UK) 01297 442722
Email: help@russellhouse.co.uk